The Reformation: A Rediscovery of Grace

The Reformation: A Rediscovery of Grace

by

Wm. Childs Robinson, M.A., Th.D., D.D.

Professor of Church History and Polity
Columbia Theological Seminary
Decatur, Georgia

William B. Eerdmans Publishing Company
Grand Rapids, Michigan

To

the Graduates and the Students of
Columbia Theological Seminary
these Alumni Lectures are
affectionately dedicated

PREFACE

The Testimony of the Reformation

Standing today in the midst of an ecumenical movement which envisages unifications with non-Reformed churches, the heirs of the Reformers must understand their legacy. Otherwise we may surrender the truth of God for which so many of them gave the last full measure of devotion. This need for a re-study of the testimony of the Reformation is the more imperative when lone voices in the Roman fold, for example, W. H. van der Pol in *The Christian Dilemma* and Hans Küng in a German work on justification declare that *sola gratia — sola fide* is authentically Catholic. Do these occasional voices mean that after all the papacy is about to hear the witness of the Reformers, or will it cling to Trent and reject these results of a restudy of the Bible as it rejected the Jansenists?

In any case, the Reformers were not concerned to claim for themselves any exclusive rights in the doctrines they proclaimed. Their aim was to glorify Christ and the Gospel of the grace of God in Him. Luther wrote to Harmuth von Cronberg:

> They believe not for any man's sake, but for the sake of the Word itself. There are many who believe on my account, but the only true believers are those who would continue to believe even if they heard (which God forbid!) that I had denied the faith or fallen away from it . . . for they do not believe on Luther, but on Christ Himself. The Word has them and they have the Word; as for Luther, they care not whether he is a knave or a saint . . . I do not preach him, but Christ.

Zwingli counted Luther a true hero of the faith but insisted, "I am not willing to bear the name of any other than that of my chief, Jesus Christ, whose soldier I am." And when some ex-monks said that they had formerly trusted in the old doctors but would now trust in the new ones, he replied to them: "You should believe not in us but in God's Word."[1]

---

1. Cited by J. Courvoisier, *Zwingli*, p. 62; Merle D'Aubigne, *History of the Reformation*, **XI**, iii.

Likewise, at the 1528 Disputation in Berne, Bucer recognizes as a brother whosoever preaches Jesus as the only Saviour. For neither Luther, Zwingli, nor Oecolampadius desires the faithful to bear his name. Rather, God teaches those who belong to Him to look not to men, but to the testimony of the Word, and to the assurance of the Holy Spirit in their hearts.

This same Word overshadowed even more the names of the British than of the Continental Reformers. Miles Coverdale cast anchor in the inspiration of the Bible. Thomas Cranmer so devoted himself to it that his fellow students dubbed him "a scripturist." William Tyndale and John Rogers put their lives in jeopardy that God's Word might be read in English.

At the first assembly of the English Church in Geneva when the Confession of Faith and Book of Common Order were approved, John Knox prayed:

> Of Thy goodness, O Lord, Thou hast called us into this City most Christianly reformed, to profess Thy name, and to suffer some cross among Thy people for Thy truth and Gospel's sake, and so to be Thy witnesses with Thy prophets and apostles.

The Confession of Faith used in this congregation of Marian exiles in Geneva and approved by the Church of Scotland at the beginning of the Reformation carries on the apostolic testimony to "my Lord God," to Jesus Christ the only Saviour and Messiah, to the Holy Ghost, and to the only Holy Church. As good witnesses they directed their testimony not to themselves but to their God and Saviour.

When National Socialism ruled Germany, the Gestapo advised Pastor Martin Niemöller to celebrate Reformation Sunday with a sermon on Luther the German. Convinced that such a course would be true neither to Luther's witness nor to his own Lord, Niemöller proclaimed as the message of the Reformation, "Glory be to the Man on the Cross to all eternity!"

He paid for his testimony by years in a concentration camp, but millions heard Martin Luther's witness to Christ through this fidelity of Martin Niemöller.

On Sunday, October 16, 1955, Cambridge University celebrated the four hundredth anniversary of the martyrdom of Ridley and Latimer by unveiling in St. Edwards' Church a tablet to Thomas Bilney, 1531, Robert Barnes, 1540, Hugh Latimer, 1555, and by dedicating a Bible to John Rogers, 1551.

This great English university was not satisfied, however, merely to record the heroism of her sons who through faith quenched the violence of fire. At the same time her scholars were recovering the Gospel for which they died, that the candle they lit might never go out. Professor Norman Sykes was showing the truly Reformed character and accomplishments of the church leadership during the reign of Queen Elizabeth. Professors Gordon Rupp and P. S. Watson were vindicating the truly Protestant character of the English tradition and its genuine connection with Luther's proclamation of the righteousness of God.[2] Among the alumni, Dr. Leon Morris was valiantly proclaiming the Gospel on which the Reformation rests.[3]

In the United States, where there were no heroes of the Reformation, the matter has taken a different turn. Frequently, the theme for Reformation Sunday is some subject that stands on the periphery rather than at the center of the movement. And in treating the theme the address too often deals with the fruit rather than with the root out of which the fruit has come. It is well to remind our land of boasted freedoms that it was a conviction of the will of God based on His Word, not a humanistic glorying in self-will, that nerved John Huss for the flames at Constance and enabled Luther to face the Diet of Worms. The lone, unarmed Luther stood against the might of the Holy Roman Empire and the ban on the Pope, declaring, "My conscience is thus led by the Word of God. I can do no other. God come to my help."

When totalitarianism took over in Nazi Germany, every zealot for freedom of speech and press who stood on a purely humanitarian basis raised the white flag of surrender. There is no reason to expect a different outcome if Americanism becomes a religion with a totalitarian regimentation. We have the four — and the forty — freedoms only as the fruit which grows from the root of faith in the living God, the God and Father of our Lord Jesus Christ.

It is quite in keeping with Reformation history to offer a series of theses. Accordingly, we present the Testimony of the Reformation in a series of affirmations concerning the central themes of the Christian faith thus:

2. G. Rupp, *The English Protestant Tradition, Luther's Progress to Diet of Worms, The Righteousness of God;* P. S. Watson, *Let God Be God!* and critical edition of *Luther on Galatians.*
3. L. Morris, *The Apostolic Preaching of the Cross.*

I. GRACE

The Reformation was a revival of Augustinianism. Its cutting edge is formulated in the slogans of grace thus, *sola gratia, solo Christo, sola fide, soli Deo gloria, sola scriptura.*

II. GOD

The Reformation was a rediscovery of God, as He revealed Himself in His majesty and His holiness, in His mercy and His love, in His power and His acts.

III. THE GOSPEL

"The Reformation was a deeper plunge into the meaning of the Gospel than even Augustine had made" (Schaff). It proclaimed Christ — not as insufficient — but as all-sufficient. For the Reformation is Jesus Christ clothed with His Gospel.

IV. JUSTIFICATION

The article of the Reformation was justification: "We have only one doctrine — *Christ is our righteousness"* (Bugenhagen).

V. THEOLOGY

The Reformation was a theological revival, and the Reformers witnessed to a biblical theology as the very life of the Church.

VI. THE WORD

"The genius of the Reformation is best described as the rediscovery of the Holy Spirit as the dynamic presence of God in Jesus Christ under the veil of the preached Word" (H. A. Oberman).

VII. THE CHURCH

The sociological principle of the Reformation was the priesthood of all believers. Luther transferred concern from the Church Triumphant in Heaven and the Church Patient in Purgatory to the Church Militant here on Earth, and made every Christian under God a king for himself, a priest for others.

Through the Testimony of the Reformation, the sixteenth century heard the Voice of God. These studies are presented with the prayer that as we hear the witness of the Reformers, the Voice they heard may call us anew into the obedience of Christian faith. Slavery to Christ alone is the true and only freedom of the human soul,[4] and this liberty of the sons of God is the root out of which every other freedom grows.

---

4. Thomas Peck, *Ecclesiology*, par. 6, p. 107.

In a number of cases the Scripture has been directly translated from the original. Where the citation is from *D. Martin Luthers Werke, Weimar Aufgabe,* the reference is *W.A.* The references to Calvin's *Institutes of the Christian Religion* are frequently made by giving only book, chapter and paragraph.

In an earlier form several of these lectures were delivered to the Conference of the Reformed Church in America at Camp Calvin, Holland, Michigan, to the Lutheran Theological Seminary in Columbia, South Carolina, to the Belhaven (Presbyterian) College in Jackson, Mississippi, and at the Candler School of Theology in Emory (Methodist) University.

The thanks of the author are hereby expressed to the Faculty of Columbia Theological Seminary for its kind invitation to deliver the alumni lectures, and to the professors, students, alumni, and friends who faithfully attended them. Appreciation is likewise expressed to Mrs. Calvin M. Cheney for her careful work in typing and retyping the material for publication.

—W. C. R.

CONTENTS

CHAPTER ONE

THE SLOGANS OF GRACE

The Heart of the Reformation

IN THE OLD DAYS OF SCOTLAND, the clans rushed into battle, each shouting its own *slagan* or slogan. In the struggle for justification, the Reformers used short crisp phrases to set forth the sheer graciousness of God with unmistakable clarity. As Latin was then the universal language of culture, and as the Reformation was a university movement, these slogans were coined in that tongue. God led His people to victory in the Reformation under these banners or slogans:

sola gratia, or salvation is by God's grace alone;

solo Christo, or our righteousness is not wrought by ourselves but by another, by Christ alone, in all that He did and bore for us, particularly on His Cross, *sola cruce*;

sola fide, or by faith alone we receive Christ and His all-sufficient righteousness;

soli Deo gloria, or this faith takes all merit from the believer and gives all the glory of saving the sinner to God alone, Father, Son, and Holy Spirit;

sola scriptura, or it is only by the faithful exposition of the written Word of God that the Holy Spirit brings this Gospel to us.

Perhaps as good an American illustration of these slogans as can be found is the account of the conversion of Archibald Alexander during the Second Awakening in 1789. A deeply concerned lad of seventeen, the young man went to the foot of a rock in a wooded area near Lexington, Virginia. There he read his Bible and knelt in prayer, read and prayed, only to find his heart growing harder, until he was tasting of the bitterness of despair. In desperation he uttered a single petition, a broken cry to God for help. He writes,

> In a moment I had such a view of a crucified Saviour as is without parallel in my experience. The whole plan of grace appeared as clear as day. I was persuaded that God was willing to accept me,

1

just as I was, and convinced that I had never before understood the freeness of salvation, but had always been striving to bring some price in my hand, or to prepare myself for receiving Christ. Now I discovered that I could receive him in all his offices at that very moment, which I was sure at the time I did. I felt truly a joy that was unspeakable and full of glory.

He opened his Bible to the eighteenth and nineteenth chapters of John and found the sacred page to be illuminated.[1]

Here it is: Jesus did it all, all to Him I owe. In my hand no price I bring, simply to His cross I cling. Here I hold because here I am held, *teneo quia teneor.* Faith is simply the hand which grasps Christ and His righteousness. It is by grace alone, through faith alone, on the ground of Christ's righteousness alone, that God and God alone saves us. We supply nothing but the sinners to be saved. All the merit and all the praise for our salvation belongs to God, our sole and only Saviour.[2] This is the Gospel freely offered in the Good Book, and brought to our hearts by the Holy Spirit through the preaching, teaching and reading of that Word.

As everyone of these slogans inhere in the salvation of every sinner, so each of them is implied in every other. In the light of the whole saving work of God and of the interrelation of the sundry parts we wish to trace out the ramifications of these several aspects of justification.

1. Sola Gratia

"It is God who justifies. Who is he that condemns?" (Rom. 8:33). "Being justified freely by His grace, through the redemption that is in Christ Jesus" (Rom. 3:24). "To the praise of the glory of His grace which He graciously bestowed upon us in the Beloved, in whom we have redemption through His blood, the forgiveness of our trespasses according to the riches of His grace" (Eph. 1:6-8). "For it is by grace that ye are saved through faith, and that not of yourselves, it is the gift of God" (Eph. 2:8).

The Reformation was a revival of the doctrines of grace which hitherto had been associated with the name of Augustine of Hippo. The cutting edge of this revival of Augustinianism is set forth in each of our slogans, but particularly in the first, or *sola gratia.* For the teachings of the Reformers are the doctrines of grace.

---

1. James W. Alexander, *The Life of Archibald Alexander,* p. 70, citing A. Alexander's *Narrative of His Own Conversion.*
2. Cf. B. B. Warfield, *Studies in Theology,* p. 461.

Grace is not something separable from God. It is God Himself in His merciful disposition toward sinful men, in His will to be for us, in His coming to save us in Jesus Christ, in His forgiving us for Christ's sake, in His faithfulness to His saving purpose by which He restores us when we fall and raises us up when we are bowed down, until He finally brings us into the gates of His glory.

God is the author of every good and perfect gift. The most gracious and wonderful of all His works is the gift of salvation. Salvation is of the Lord. Even when we were hateful and hating one another, in His mercy God saved us (Titus 3:3, 5). To accomplish this, God spared not His only Son, but gave Him, the unspeakable gift of His love, for us men and for our salvation. In Christ and His work for us, God established His righteousness among men. He shares this righteousness by making us alive with Christ and forgiving our sins for His Name's sake. By the might of His hand, He brings us into the fellowship of His Son in whom there is pardon and peace. In this section, then, we are concerned to point out that salvation in general, or justification in particular, is God's act, and to note God's graciousness in this work.

Righteousness is a *gift* which God bestows upon those who long for it (Matt. 5:21) As both righteousness and the Kingdom are gifts from God (Matt. 5:33), grace reigns through righteousness (Rom. 5:21). In the Apostolic Gospel (Rom. 1:17, 3:21f.), *dikaiosune* is a dynamic term that brings home to us that all salvation owes its origin to God, that we can be accounted righteous only because of His activity.[3]

It is God who justifies. This is His work, or in the phraseology of the Reformation, His office. "Justification is not the office of man but of God." It is the office of God unto man only, not also the office of man unto God. "It is not a thing which we render unto Him, but which we receive of Him: not which we give to Him, but which we take of Him, by His free mercy, and by the merits of His most dearly beloved Son, our only Redeemer, Saviour, and Justifier, Jesus Christ."[4]

Justification is an act, an event in which God's power is not less effective than manifestations of His wrath. One is a judgment to pardon, the other to punish.[5] Indeed, the Apostle places

---

3. L. Morris, *The Apostolic Preaching of the Cross*, p. 252.
4. *Homilies for the Churches of England*, 1562, "Of Salvation."
5. G. Schrenk, *dikaiosune* in *TWZNT*, II, 206; O. Michel, *Der Brief an die Römer*, p. 87.

the Gospel as the power of God unto salvation over against the wrath of God revealed upon all unrighteousness (Rom. 1:16-18; cf. II Cor. 3:9). Thus the Gospel is neither subjective fancy nor formal dogma. Far from being a concatenated set of human ideas, the Gospel is the power of God acting for men and in them so that our faith rests not in the wisdom of men but in the power of God (I Cor. 2:5). Thus faith is the sign that God, in the power of the new age, is at work in the believer. Through the proclamation of the Gospel, God personally calls me, and faith in Christ is my decisive personal response. God's act calling me to faith and forgiveness, and my response in trust and penitence establish me in His personal fellowship.

God's gracious act in justification is His forgiving our sins. Forgiveness is not man brushing the cobwebs of mistrust from his mind; neither is it a static concept of some fancied attribute of God. God has acted, reconciling us unto Himself through the death of His Son. God does act in forgiving our sins, quite as definitely as when Christ said to the sick of the palsy, "Son, be of good cheer, thy sins be forgiven thee." In the Lord's Prayer, the Saviour teaches us to ask for forgiveness as often as we ask for our daily bread. Moreover, the call to forgive my brother seventy times seven in connection with the parable of the unmerciful servant indicates how much and how often the Lord knew we would need God's forgiveness (Matt. 18:21-35). If we confess our sins, He is faithful and just to forgive, and whenever we sin we have an Advocate with the Father, Jesus Christ, the righteous, the propitiation for our sins (I John 1:9, 2:1-2). The primitive Church went forward on its missionary work, proclaiming the forgiveness of sins (Acts 2:28, 3:49, 5:31, 10:42, 13:39). In the primitive creed, as imbedded in the Epistles, Christ died for our sins according to the Scriptures (I Cor. 15:3; Rom. 3:24, 4:6; Eph. 1:7; 1 John 2:2; I Pet. 2:24, 3:18; Heb. 10:12, 17).

The Church of the living God is the place where God acts and man serves. Accordingly, in Luther's Small Catechism the children are taught, "In which Christian Church He daily forgives richly all my sins, and the sins of believers." For Calvin, God both brings us into covenant with Himself by the forgiveness of sins and keeps us in His Church by that same mercy. "From the divine liberality, by the intervention of the merit of Christ, through the sanctification of the Spirit, pardon of sins has been and is daily bestowed upon us" (*Inst.*, IV, i, 21; cf. 20). The churches of the Reformation continue to minister the forgiveness of sins by using a general confession and a prayer for forgiveness as a regular part of the weekly worship.

In His justifying work, God is both the just Judge who imputes to us the righteousness of Christ and so accepts us as righteous in His sight and the gracious Father whose mercy intervenes to bring us and keep us in His family. The Apostle Paul began with the Jewish doctrine of legal justification (Rom. 9:30, 10:15), only to find that the law could not give righteousness (Gal. 3:21, 2:21). What the law could not do, God in His mercy accomplished for us in Christ (Rom. 8:3, 3:22-26; Titus 3:5; Eph. 2:6-10). The act of God in raising Christ our representative from the dead for our justification (Rom. 4:25) brought the verdict of acquittal from the final judgment, where it still stands for Judaism, forward into the present as realized eschatology. Thus Paul took the holy word of Judaism, righteousness, and used it to describe not a verdict of acquittal on the basis of good works at the final judgment but God's forensic act which forgives a sinner today by the mercy of God on the ground of the righteousness of Christ.[6]

From Genesis through Revelation, the Bible presents God as the Judge, and in this thought the Apostle fully shares (Rom. 2:5f.; II Cor. 5:10; II Thess. 1:5f.; Acts 17:31, 24:45). In the classic passage in Romans 3 which has been called "the Acropolis of the Christian Faith" the purpose of God's justifying work in setting forth Christ as a propitiatory sacrifice is to show that God is just even in justifying sinners who believe in Jesus. In Romans 3:4 and Luke 7:29, *dikaioo* is used of God, where it cannot have the meaning of to make righteous, but must mean to declare righteous. Moreover, *logizesthai,* which is used of God's act in Romans 4 and II Corinthians 5:9 and Galatians 3:6 has the sense of reckon or impute.[7] Thus when God is said to justify we have not a moralistic accomplishment, but a judicial or forensic act. But this does not mean an "as if."

6. G. Schrenk, *TWNT,* II, 204, 207. As the language of the Old Testament is steeped in the imagery of the law court (Isa. 3:13, 5:16, 31:1, 33:22; Ps. 9:7f., 11:7, 50:6, 96:13; Job 9:3,32, 13:18, 23:3-4, 40:8; Jer. 12:1; Judg. 11:27; Ex. 7:4), and as for Judaism righteousness was a forensic term (*SBK,* IV, 3-19), so the primary conception of *dikaiosune* in the New Testament is undoubtedly forensic, L. Morris, *op. cit.,* p. 249. It describes men's legal standing before God, based not on our law-keeping but on what Christ did for us on Calvary (Gal. 2:21; Rom. 10:4; Phil. 3:3, 6-9).

7. H. W. Heidland, in *TWNT,* IV, 292-295.

The Judge is God, and what He declares He does. No word from God is void of power (Luke 1:37). Moreover, this mode of Divine action may be understood to an extent from our human analogies, but far transcends these imperfect parallels. The content overleaps the form and permits this act of grace to outgrow all customary juridical figures. God exercises a holy, normative, covenant grace which through the work accomplished for us by Christ stands in full accord with the highest right. In spite of the very imperfect human representatives (Luke 18:1-8; Romans 13), the concept of judge and the acts of a judge are applicable to God, as are those of father and king and shepherd, despite the imperfections of human fathers, kings and shepherds. In each case God is the great and gracious original (cf. Luke 11:13, 18:1-7; Eph. 3:14-15), man the pale and paltry copy.

Because it is God who justifies, His justifying act is not only forensic, it is effective. The Word of forgiveness is the Word of the Creator who calls the things that are not, and being called they come to be (I Cor. 1:28; Rom. 4:17). The remission of our sins is through the redemption in Christ's blood by which we who were dead in sins are made alive together with Christ (Eph. 1:7, 2:5). The Gospel is so emphatically the power of God unto salvation (Rom. 1:16; I Cor. 2:2-5) that pardon is sealed with power as truly as it was for the paralytic (Mark 2:10-12). "Nothing is so creative in our lives as forgiveness."[8] Accordingly, Paul continues the thought of the righteousness of God from Romans 3 and 4 through Romans 5, 6, 7, and 8. The justifying act of God is not quietistic, but teleological. It brings one into God's all-embracing eschatological salvation. It leads into the kingdom of grace, the reign of righteousness, the age of life everlasting. God places the believer in Christ (I Cor. 1:30), under His Lordship that enriches unto the day of glory (I Cor. 1:4-9). The Spirit is life on account of a man's being justified (Rom. 8:10; Gal. 3:14). Thus the juridical sentence of justification does not conclude the process of salvation, but places the justified into a new position of service. Trust in the righteousness of God issues in the obedience of faith (Rom. 1:5, 16:26). Since the believer enjoys the status of reconciliation accomplished in the death of Christ and sealed to him by baptism, therefore he is called to be the servant of righteousness and to yield his members as instruments of righteousness unto

8. J. W. Earp, in a lecture in Ridley Hall, Cambridge, 1955.

holiness (Rom. 6:16, 18, 13, 19). The gift of righteousness commits the believer to the power of righteousness, which overcomes sin and leads to sanctification. The *indicative* fact lays the basis for the *imperative* call. The Spirit who works justifying faith is present, however, only in His first-fruits. "He breaks the power of reigning sin," and relying on His presence the Apostle calls to sanctification. Whom God justifies, them He also glorifies (Rom. 8:30). Since it is God that justifies, the creative word of His righteousness is not fictional, but effective. For justification is "at the same time both a judicial sentence and a creative act of salvation."[9]

In his Argument of the Epistle to the Galatians, Luther first insists that the believer rests not on the active righteousness of His own works, but on a passive righteousness which we receive of God and suffer Him to work in us. "I rest upon that righteousness which is the righteousness of Christ and of the Holy Ghost." Yet he adds, "When I have this righteousness reigning in my heart, I descend from heaven as the rain makes fruitful the earth, that is to say, I come forth into another kingdom, and I do *good works,* how and whensoever occasion is offered." The believer comes to trust the grace Giver, the Father, who has given him righteousness on the ground of the obedience of another. Grateful trust becomes responsive love to God and to His will. Thus the believer gives more obedience to the will of God than does the legalist. Only the penitent believer is concerned for heart obedience, the kind the Saviour rendered the Father.[10] And thinking of that obedience the forgiven sinner never pats himself on the back as though he had perfectly accomplished it. Rather he glories in the free grace of God which receives him that believes in Jesus, who alone has perfectly pleased the Father in His life and death of obedience. Commenting on Galatians 5:6, Calvin says that "true faith cannot be separated from the Spirit of regeneration." According to the third book of the *Institutes,* this Spirit-wrought faith in Christ is effective at the same time for Christian living and for Christian standing, or justification.

"It is God who justifies. Who is he that condemns?" Apart from God's forgiving our sins, there is no peace; but rather there is turmoil like the troubled sea that casts up mire and dirt (Isa. 57:20). Those who have not the peace of God are continually excusing their sins by accusing others, or are seek-

---

9. O. Michel, *Der Brief an die Römer,* p. 223.
10. Luther, *Commentary on Galatians; Introduction to Romans.*

ing to vindicate themselves by sundry forms of worldly success
(cf. Jer. 9:23-24). Only when God justifies is there a peace
within which does not need to vindicate itself by harsh judgments upon others, nor by grasping a place in the sun. As
the Father of our Lord Jesus Christ forgives, He brings us into
His family where we seek the likeness of the forgiving parent
by forgiving. He translates us from the kingdom of darkness
into the reign of the Son of His love — the reign of graciousness.

God's justifying work is wholly gracious. In the covenant of
grace made with His beloved Son, the Father chose us for His
family before the foundation of the world; through the redemption in Christ's blood He set forth the riches of His
grace; in the power of the Spirit making alive with the Lord
Jesus those who were dead in sins, God exercised the energy of
His grace (Eph. 1:3, 7; 2:5). On account of its rediscovery of
the doctrines of grace, the Reformation has been hailed as a
revival of Augustinianism. The Milan rhetorician found himself formally free, but actually enslaved, by his own pride and
lust. God broke the shackles by calling him to put on the
Lord Jesus Christ and make no provision to fulfill the lusts of
the flesh (Rom. 13:13). Luther, Zwingli, Calvin, Knox — all
echo Augustine's conviction that grace does not find us willing;
it makes us willing.

While current semi-Pelagianism offers an *ordo salutis* in
which our repentance and faith are alleged to precede God's
regeneration, the Reformers held that

> repentance . . . is not a condition preliminary to salvation; it is
> part of the experience of being saved. It is not something which
> we produce out of our own resources, and bring to God, in the
> assurance that now of course He will forgive us; it is something
> which is only produced in us by the sense that there is already
> forgiveness with Him; it is a saving Grace begotten in our hearts
> by that Passion of love in which Jesus made our sins His own.
> It is not a substitute for the Atonement, or something which makes
> it unnecessary; it is the fruit of the Atonement, and of nothing
> else.[11]

Moreover, those who study the Reformers sympathetically
often come to an appreciation of their use of election in Christ
as a means of safeguarding the truth of *sola gratia*. For example,
Doumergue began his studies of the life of Calvin as a French
Arminian, but he ended by appraising predestination not at
all as an exclusively Calvinistic doctrine but as *par excellence*

11. James Denney, *The Christian Doctrine of Reconciliation*, p. 325.

the dogma of the Reformation.[12] Likewise, from English Methodism, Britain's great Luther scholar, even though he professes to be "allergic to Calvin," writes:

A doctrine of Predestination is in any case an integral part of both Protestant and Catholic divinity, as it must always be of any Gospel which gives God the glory, and which maintains the divine freedom and initiative in creation, and which acknowledges that the ultimate judgment is not our verdict upon God, but His upon us.[13]

To these testimonies may well be added a thoughtful word from the late Dean F. N. Parker of Emory University: "My father was the Methodist pastor in New Orleans. His closest friend was your [Presbyterian] Dr. Benjamin M. Palmer. My father preached prevenient grace. Your Dr. Palmer preached predestination, but they meant exactly the same thing."

A German-American philosophical theologian speaks of that "creative justice" which demands for every being its claim to the re-acceptance into the unity to which it belongs.[14] On the contrary, Luther bids us contemplate the gratuitous electing love that was set on us before the foundation of the world, that our love to God may be the more inflamed. On Ephesians 1, Calvin writes: "We were not then in existence, and therefore there was no merit of ours. The cause of our salvation did not proceed from us, but from God alone." On Titus 3:5 his comment is:

He has with propriety assigned the first rank to goodness, which prompts God to love us: for God will never find anything in us which He ought to love, but He loves because He is good and merciful. Besides, although He testifies His goodness and love to all, yet we know it by faith only, when He declares Himself to be our Father in Christ.

For Aristotle, in the *Nicomachaean Ethics,* Book VIII, it is an axiom that one can love only those who are worthy of love. For Cardinal Sadoleto, our love is the first and chief cause of our salvation.[15] But according to Luther, whereas man's love is aroused by what is lovable, the love of God finds nothing lovable in man, but creates in man what God loves; that is,

12. E. Doumergue, *Jean Calvin,* IV, 407.
13. G. Rupp, *The Righteousness of God,* p. 281; cf. P. S. Watson, *Let God Be God!,* R. Prenter, *Spiritus Creator.*
14. Paul Tillich, *Love, Power and Justice,* p. 86.
15. Cardinal Sadoleto, *Letter to the Senate and People of Geneva;* "Reply by John Calvin," *Tracts,* I, 10, 44.

God's love confers good not because we are lovable but because we are loved.[16] For Calvin, "in adopting us . . . God does not inquire what we are, and is not reconciled to us by any personal worth."[17] According to his *Catechism,* there is no worthiness in us why God should either show His power to help us or use His mercy to save us. God's gracious choice of us before we were in existence means that His electing love was bestowed upon us apart from any worth, either moral or ontological. He chose us to be holy and without blame before Him in love: we sinners are that only in Christ. In his *Sermons on the Canticles,* Bernard's theme is love for no other reason but itself, of love that loves because it loves, or loves only to be loved again, of grace that triumphs over the greatest of sins. Professor Norman Snaith rejects the view that there must be something in the loved one before the lover can love. Instead he sings the unmerited love of God in the words of Charles Wesley:

> He hath loved,
> He hath loved us,
> Because He would love.[18]

2. Solo Christo

"Being justified freely by His grace through the redemption that is in Christ Jesus whom God set forth to be a propitiation" (Rom. 3:24-25). ". . . Who is he that condemns? It is Christ Jesus that died, yea rather that was raised from the dead, who is at the right hand of God, who also makes intercession for us" (Rom. 8:1, 30). "Christ Jesus is made unto us righteousness from God" (I Cor. 1:30; Rom. 10:4; II Cor. 5:18).

God's free grace comes to us through the redemption that is in Christ Jesus. For the Apostle, as for the Reformation, faith is faith in Christ (Phil. 3:9), who is made unto us righteousness from God (I Cor. 1:30). Luther cannot speak of faith on the one hand, nor of the righteousness of God on the other, without the theme of Jesus Christ. "True faith lays hold of Christ and leans on Him alone." "So now Christ is our righteousness and our peace which God has given us."[19] God in Christ

16. Luther, *Opera Latini,* I, 403: *"Amor Dei non invenit, sed creat suum deligibile, amor hominis fit a suo deligibili,"* cited by A. Nygren, *Agape and Eros,* p. 233.

17. Calvin, *Commentary on Ephesians,* 1:5.

18. N. Snaith, *Distinctive Ideas of the Old Testament,* pp. 175-176.

19. Luther on Galatians 2:5; and *W. A.* 4, 16, 20.

is the perpetual object of saving faith.[20] In the *sola fide* which is the article of the Reformation, faith means faith in Jesus Christ.[21] The Augsburg Confession repeatedly asserts that we are justified *propter Christum* (Art. iv, Art. v, Art. xii, Art. xx). The third of the Theses of Berne declares: "Christ is our only wisdom, righteousness, redemption and satisfaction for the sins of all the world; therefore to confess any other ground (*Verdienst, meritum*) of salvation and satisfaction for sins is to deny Christ." The Heidelberg Catechism begins:

> My only comfort in life and death is that I with body and soul, both in life and death, am not my own, but belong to my faithful Saviour Jesus Christ, who with His precious blood has fully satisfied for all my sins, and delivered me from the power of the devil, and so preserves me that without the will of my heavenly Father, not a hair can fall from my head: yea, that all things must be subservient to my salvation.

The whole of God's saving work is founded on Christ. Before the foundation of the world, the Father of our Lord Jesus Christ chose His family in Him (Eph. 1:3-5), redeemed us in the Beloved (vv. 6-7), raised us up from the death of sin with Him (2:6), in the ages to come will show the riches of His grace toward us in Christ Jesus (v. 7), and finally accords to Christ the honor of presenting to Himself the glorious Church (5:27). Thus, from the making of the covenant of grace, through the events of saving-history to the eschatological consummation, God has been pleased to deal with His people in Christ Jesus. He is the author or the cause of eternal salvation to all those who obey Him (Heb. 5:9). As truly man, He is "the brightest example of gratuitous election"; as truly God, He is "the author of election"; as the Mediator, the electing love of God rests first on Him. For "the love which God had for us before the creation of the world was founded on Christ," and "the material cause of eternal election and of the love which is now revealed is Christ the Beloved . . . by whom the love of God is communicated to us."[22] The Reformers' way into the labyrinth of predestination is to find oneself in the wounds of Christ, and to refuse to contemplate one's election apart from Him. To a woman troubled about the matter,

20. Luther on Galatians 3:7; Calvin, *Instruction in Faith*, 14; *Homilies for the Churches of England*, "Of Salvation," 1562.

21. H. I. Iwand, *Rechtfertigungslehre und Christusglaube*; H. Thielecke, in *Kerygma und Mythos*, p. 159; K. Barth, *Kirchliche Dogmatik*, IV/1, 588.

22. Calvin, *Inst.*, III, xii, 1; III, xxii, 7; II, xvi, 4; *Commentary on Ephesians*, 1:5.

Luther replied, "Hear the Incarnate Son. He offers thee Himself as Predestination."[23] From John 1:17 and Ephesians 1:4-5, Tyndale understood that God loved us and chose us in Christ before the world began.[24] Calvin prays, "May we be led to Christ only as the fountain of Thy election."[25]

"No man is loved by God but in Christ" (*Inst.*, III, ii, 32, III, xxiv, 5), and this love of God focuses on Christ's laying down His life for the sheep and taking it again (John 10:17-18). God's rich mercy rests upon His great love wherewith He loved us in the Cross and made us alive together with Christ (Eph. 2:4-6; Rom. 5:8). Luther finds the Cross everywhere in the Scripture.[26] According to Calvin, from the Fall, sin has so disturbed all of man's knowledge of the Creator as Father that it is only by the preaching of the Cross that we return to God as our Father (*Inst.*, II, vi, 1). Christ was always revealed to the holy fathers as the object to which they should direct their faith, and it was only on the basis of the grace of the Mediator that God was propitious to ancient Israel and adopted them as His people (*Inst.*, II, vi, 2).

The riches of God's mercy fix upon the act of love in the Cross (Eph. 2:4; John 10:17), and the wrath of God revealed from heaven (Rom. 1:18) is turned away as we are reconciled to God by the death of His Son and justified in His blood (Rom. 5:9-10). "Punishment was laid on Him that we might have peace" (Isa. 53:5, Nygren transl.). In giving Himself "a sacrifice of reconciliation" (Rom. 3:25, Goodspeed transl.) Christ made propitiation and showed that God was righteous even in justifying believing sinners (Rom. 3:26, 4:5). Biblical righteousness is never blind vengeance which like the Greek fate governs gods and men. It concerns the acts of the Lord "righteous in all His ways and gracious in all His works" (Ps. 145:17). In the Cross of Christ, God's wrath is united with His love and love averts or overcomes wrath.[27] He satisfies who renders to an offended party that which he loves as much or more than he hates the offense.[28] Not in any quantitative measure, but in

23. G. Rupp, *The Righteousness of God,* p. 170.
24. Tyndale's *Doctrinal Treatises*, pp. 11, 14, 19.
25. Prayer in connection with commentary on Mal. 1:2.
26. *W. A.*, 3, 63, 1, "*Crux enim Christi ubique in Scripturis occurrit.*"
27. L. Pinomaa, *Der Zorn in der Theologia Luther*, p. 191; cf. Calvin, *Inst.* II, xvii, 2.
28. Thomas Aquinas: "*Respondeo dicendum quod ille proprie satisfacit pro offensa qui exhibet offenso id quod aeque vel magis deligit quam oderit offensam,*" *Summa Theologicae*, III, XLVIII, ii.

this personal sense God's righteousness was satisfied, His wrath was removed; for He loved Christ in His Cross and Resurrection more even than He hated the heinousness of our sins. As He is pleased with His Beloved, so does He graciously deal with us who are received in Him.

> *Look, Father, on His anointed face*
> *And look on us as found in Him.*
> *Look not on our misusings of Thy grace,*
> *Our prayer so languid and our faith so dim,*
> *For lo, between our sins and their reward*
> *We set the passion of Thy Son, our Lord.*

God acted to establish this righteousness for us not in some far-off beyond, not in some world of worths or ideals of philosophy, but here in our human life history where Christ was delivered up to death for our trespasses, and raised on the third day for our justification (Rom. 4:23-25; I Cor. 15:3-4). The Lamb of God who bore our sins as our substitute was also the Second Adam, our representative. As the age of sin and the kingdom of Satan came through the disobedience of Adam, so the reign of grace and the age of righteousness came through the obedience of Christ (Rom. 5:12-21). When as our substitute He had endured the whole curse, then as our representative He arose for our justification. When He had suffered, the Just for the unjust, then He was raised in the blessedness of pure righteousness. Thus He became the end of the requirements of the law as far as righteousness is concerned (Rom. 10:4). Christ Jesus is made unto us righteousness from God (I Cor. 1:30), that we may be found in Him, not having our own law-righteousness but the righteousness of God which becomes ours by faith in Christ (Phil. 3:9). Salvation is God making us alive together with Christ, and raising us up with Him and making us to sit with Him in the heavenly place at His own right hand (Eph. 2:5-6). Thus, justification means redemption in Him, even the forgiveness of our sins (Eph. 1:7), the adoption as sons through Jesus Christ (Eph. 1:5), sharing in His righteousness (I Cor. 1:30), and in His status of resurrection victory, of ascension reign (Eph. 2:5-6), and of advent hope (Phil. 3:20).

At the same time, as the Spirit makes us conscious of this saving Gospel, He ingrafts us into Christ and implants Christ in our hearts. Thus, after ringing the changes on our being *in Him* and *with Christ* for the first half of the Epistle to the Ephesians, the writer prays that by the Spirit Christ may dwell in our hearts through faith (Eph. 3:17). The whole work of saving the Corinthians from the first gift of grace through the final revelation of the Lord is in Christ Jesus (I Cor. 1:4-9). "In that I believe in CHRIST FOR ME, He becomes CHRIST IN ME who raises me from the dead, works in me, leads me to the field of battle against sin, and conquers. Therefore is He called THE LORD OF HOSTS."[29]

The Lord to whom Luther looked works in His people so that they love God and His law. Christ is not *otiosus,* but *activissimus.* Calvin feared nothing more than an absent Christ. Separated from Him we are only dead wood. Christian life is the life of Christ in us; all other life is in reality death. Only as Christ gives us to share in His life is our death overcome. "As the root sends its substance and strength into all the twigs, so we gain the substance and life of our Lord Jesus Christ. He wills to dwell in us, not merely in our thoughts and feelings, but in reality."[30]

The Reformers wove the Church's doctrine of the Person of Christ into the web of justification. Our righteousness comes not out of the infusion of Christ's divine nature, as Osiander taught, but by the gracious imputation of the obedience of His earthly life and of His suffering of death as the penalty of our sins. Luther understood the weeping in the Psalms and the cry of dereliction from the Cross primarily of Christ.[31] In distinction from Roman theologians who qualified Scriptural statements to fit their conception of the hypostatic union,[32] Calvin accepted the Gethsemane account of His fear and torments (*Inst.,* II, xvi, 5), and beheld Him putting His faith and hope in the Father by clinging to His Words, as Matthew 4:4, 27:43 and Hebrews 2:11 teach. "To draw Christ deeply into the flesh," we are suggesting that the full scope of Christ's work in His human nature may be safeguarded by expressly combining with the three offices of Christ their respective correlatives. Christ was expiatory sacrifice as well as High Priest; obedient servant as fully as Shepherd-King; believer who lived by the Word of God as truly as final Prophet. It is out of His gracious fulfillment of these several offices, by the obedience

---

29. Luther, as summarized by P. Althaus, "Die Gerechtheit des Menchen vor Gott" in *Das Menchenbilt im Lichte des Evangeliums,* p. 34.

30. Calvin as cited by W. Kolfhaus, *Vom christlichen Leben n. J. Calvin,* p. 97.

31. G. Rupp, *op. cit.,* pp. 145-146, with notes.

32. Cf. G. C. Berkouwer, *The Person of Christ,* pp. 221-227.

of this One, that the many of us sinners are made righteous (Rom. 5:19). The last words of the late J. Gresham Machen as given in a telegram to his fellow professor John Murray were: "I'm so thankful for active obedience of Christ. No hope without it. Jan. 1, 1937." Protestant justification rests upon the full human obedience of Christ, the Son of God who became the Servant of the Lord.

It is, however, the living Christ who calls us to Himself and who lives in us today, and He must needs be a divine Person. We believe in Him who became truly man for us men and for our salvation, who suffered under Pontius Pilate, was crucified, dead and buried, yea who for us descended into hell: but we also believe in Him who conquered death and hades, who arose from the dead and ascended in victory to the right hand of God, and who in the full plenitude of Divine power calls us from our death in sin to His life and standing with God. By His resurrection from the dead, the man Christ Jesus became our Lord, the head of the new humanity. As "Rabbi" Duncan said, "The dust of the earth is on the throne of the majesty on high."

The perversity of the human mind shows itself in its repeated efforts to divert the glory of saving sinners from the Saviour to some act, attitude, or action of the saved sinner. In the twelfth century, Bernard of Clairvaux charged Abelard with locating the glory of redemption not in the value of Christ's blood, but in its effects upon our walk and conversation. Against this ever recurring tendency, justification ravages the citadel of self and enthrones Christ. And conversely, because justification dethrones self, therefore the old man is ever finding ways of averting the full drive of gratuitous justification.

In his *Table Talk,* Luther tried to drive home, with his parable of the Prince and the Pauper, the message that the credit for saving sinners belongs exclusively to Christ. A beggar accosts his Prince Elector and asks for alms. The Prince replies that he has no money with him, but that if the Pauper will come to his castle the following day, he will give him a hundred florins. Now obviously the beggar must come in order to get the money, but surely the graciousness which makes the gift is the heart of the Prince, not that of the Pauper, and the basis on which the gift is expected is the promise of the Prince. Faith is the empty hand of the beggar lifted to Christ for justification. So little would Luther see saving faith concerned with a quality in the believer, so exclusively would he have it determined only by its object by the historical Christ *extra se,* that, in his exposition of Psalm 90, he described our subjective faith as a mathematical point.[33]

Calvin sought the same end when he described the righteousness of Christ as the material or the meritorious cause of salvation.[34] Thereby he meant that "the whole of our salvation and all the branches of it are comprehended in Christ" (*Inst.,* II, xvi, 19); "It is in Him that we are to seek the cause of our salvation" (*Inst.,* II, xvii, 2), for "the Name of Christ excludes all merit, and everything which men have of their own."[35]

Calvin also warned against treating Christ as only the formal or instrumental cause of justification, which place he reserved for faith.[36] In justification we are righteous only because the righteousness of Christ is imputed to us and not because faith receives the Spirit of God by whom man is made righteous, "which is too repugnant to the foregoing doctrine ever to be reconciled to it" (*Inst.,* III, xi, 23). Calvin maintained, and John Owen supported, the distinction between the obedience of Christ as the material cause and the illumination of the Spirit or faith as the instrumental cause of justification.

By means of sundry theological refinements, however, some theologians presented faith as a new law, or as a sincere obedience, or as a condition that fulfilled caused salvation. About 1670, Bishop Bull interpreted faith to mean "all inward and outward good works." So much in the way of resolution and effort and moral achievement was packed into "evangelical faith" that it came to approximate very closely Roman Catholic *fides formata caritate.* The Roman phrase rests salvation on the love we exercise toward God; the true Reformation doctrine rests it rather on the love we trust, the love of God which acted for us in Christ.

In his zeal against antinomians, Richard Baxter erected what he called a "full justification" on the ground of Christ's obedience and of our obedient life. Therein the heart's subjection to Christ as Lord is "just as much an essential part of justifying faith as is acceptance of Him as Saviour and affiance in Him." Later Baxter modified these *Aphorisms on Justification,* but a copy of the unmodified form fell into the hands of John

33. *W.A.,* 40, III, 572, 23; 40, II, 527, 9, cited by H. Thielicke in *Kerygma und Mythos,* p. 159 (178).
34. *Inst.* III, xiv, 17, and *Commentary on Romans,* 3:24.
35. *Commentary on Ephesians,* 1:4.
36. *Inst.,* II, xvii, 2; III, xiv, 17; *Commentary on Romans,* 3:24.

Wesley, with the result that England's great evangelist was at times Calvinistic on justification, at other times Baxterian.[37]

For example, in his letter of October 15, 1756, Wesley objected to the phrase "the imputed righteousness of Christ" in James Hervey's *Theron and Aspasio*. On the other hand, in his sermon on *The Lord Our Righteousness*, Wesley professed his agreement with Calvin on justification thus:

> The righteousness of Christ, both His active and passive righteousness, is the meritorious cause of our justification, and has procured for us at God's right hand, that upon our believing we should be accounted righteous . . .
>
> > *Jesu, Thy blood and righteousness*
> > *My beauty are, my glorious dress,*
> > *Midst flaming worlds in these arrayed,*
> > *With joy shall I lift up my head.*[38]

The process of deflection from the sole glory of Christ has also appeared in the history of covenant theology. There was a period in Scotland in which the covenant of redemption between the persons of the Trinity was distinguished from the covenant of grace with sinners. According to this scheme Christ satisfied the conditions of the covenant of redemption, but faith meets the conditions of the covenant of grace. Thus we were almost left with two Saviours: Christ and faith. The Gospel became a new law, the law of faith. To avoid these pitfalls the evangelicals of the days of Robert Traill and the Marrow Men preferred to think of one covenant for which Christ is the sole and whole surety, and to speak of faith as the instrument for apprehending Christ.[38a] Likewise, as the Auchterarder Creed shows, they regarded as unsound the teaching that a man must first abandon sin and cease to be a sinner before he is entitled to come to Christ and enter into a covenant with God. For them, the Table of the Lord is spread with the Gospel feast and no needy sinner is guilty of presumption when he heeds the gracious invitation and comes.

In New England, also, too much legalism was brought into the covenant. It was treated as an agreement between God and man on a level with business contracts between equals.

37. Fred. J. Powicke, *Richard Baxter*, pp. 240, 245.

38. Wesley, *Letters*, III, 371-388; sermon in *Works of J.W.*, I, 169f. Prof. John Deschner of Southern Methodist University has called attention to the Baxterian element; Dean Wm. Cannon of Emory University emphasizes the Calvinistic in his *Theology of John Wesley*.

38a. John Macleod, *Scottish Theology*, p. 134, *passim*.

Faith was even presented as fulfilling the condition and thus obligating God to grant salvation, or even as being the cause that actually produced the result.[39] Against this drift Jonathan Edwards proclaimed the sovereignty of God's saving grace and his sermons on justification led to the Great Awakening.

When our distinguished Southern theologian, Dr. Robert L. Dabney, was old and sick and blind he fell into great anxiety lest he have not enough faith for the hour of death. His friend, Dr. C. R. Vaughan, wrote that if a traveler would come to a bridge over a fearful chasm he would not turn his eye upon himself to scrutinize his own confidence, but would carefully examine the bridge. Do not lay stress on your faith but grasp the great ground of confidence, Christ. Faith is only an eye to see Him. Think of the Bridge! Think of the Master when you want your faith to grow.[40]

In an effort to present Luther's doctrine less as an intellectual abstraction and more as a dynamic for life, Karl Holl sought to construe it as an analytical more than as a synthetic judgment.[41] This means that God declares us righteous because of the good work He has begun in us and which He sees developing in fellowship with Himself, because we are righteous in germ or in process. This idea is reproduced in Dr. H. E. Fosdick's *The Meaning of Faith,* and it is to be feared in many fundamentalistic pietists as well. In the sixteenth century Osiander, as in a different way Cardinal Newman in the nineteenth and his disciple Dr. C. J. de Vogel in the twentieth,[42] likewise made justification to depend on sanctification. Thomas Adam, an old English evangelical, contrasts this with the Reformation position thus:

> Justification by sanctification is man's way to heaven, and it is odd but he will make a little serve the turn. Sanctification by justification is God's (way), and He fills the soul with His own goodness.[43]

The forgiveness of sins is our only way of access to God.[44] In Luther's mature thought justification is a synthetic judgment in which the predicate *righteous* adds something not contained in the subject *sinner.* We sinners are not righteous by any

39. Perry Miller, *Jonathan Edwards,* p. 78.

40. T. C. Johnson, *Robert Lewis Dabney,* pp. 479-480.

41. K. Holl, *Gesammelte Aufsaetze zum Kirchengeschichte,* I, iiif.; III, 525f.

42. C. J. de Vogel, *Newmans gedachten over de rechtvaardiging.*

43. Thomas Adam, *Private Thoughts on Religion,* p. 242.

44. J. Schniewind, in *Kerygma und Mythos,* 587 (96).

quality inherent in ourselves, but by the judgment of God imputing to us an alien righteousness. We are righteous not *in re* but *in spe*, not in fulfillment but in promise, not in ourselves but in Christ. In the measure in which our sanctification is conceived as the cause of justification the most profound and purely religious conception of Luther's interpretation of Christianity is lost.[45]

Justification is an unconditional juridical act of God, in which the believing sinner is declared righteous through the forgiveness of sins and by the imputation of Christ's righteousness.[46] But the new life is not a purely "forensic" judgment remaining outside us, but an "effective" power working in us. The God who declares us righteous is the Creator whose Word is never void of power (Luke 2:37, ARV); who gives life to the dead and calls into being that which was not (Rom. 4:17). And the reception of justification is just the reception of Christ in faith, that is, *of the Christ for us* and *of the Christ in us.*[47] For, "Christ never is where His Spirit is not." Where there is the gratuitous righteousness of faith, "there too is Christ, and where Christ is there too is the Spirit of holiness, who generates the soul to newness of life. On the contrary, where zeal for integrity and holiness is not in vigour, there neither is the Spirit of Christ, nor Christ Himself; and wherever Christ is not, there is no righteousness, nay, there is no faith; for faith cannot apprehend Christ for righteousness without the Spirit of sanctification."[48] Faith apprehends Christ who has been given to us for justification and for sanctification (I Cor. 1:30).

From our standpoint, "demythologization" is open to serious objections. Our faith accepts the miracles of the Creed neither as myths nor as parables, but as events in God's saving intervention to be proclaimed in the conviction that the Holy Spirit will use the whole testimony of Jesus to the glory of God. While we rejoice in the accents of Luther found in the leader of demythology, at a crucial point he seems to differ from the Reformer. To Professor R. Bultmann the proclamation of Christ and His Cross is the true offense of the Gospel and calls

45. G. Aulen, *The Faith of the Christian Church*, pp. 294-300.

46. P. Althaus, "Die Gerechtheit des Menchen vor Gott," in *Das Menschenbild im Lichte des Evangeliums.* W. Joest, "Paulus" und das Lutherische Simul Justus et Peccator," in *Kerygma und Dogma*, October, 1955, pp. 269-320.

47. J. Schniewind, in *Kerygma und Mythos*, p. 587 (96).

48. Calvin, "Reply to Sadolet," *Tracts*, I, 43; cf. *Inst.*, III.

men to existential decision. Moreover, the decision of faith goes back not to some inner-worldly motive, but the believer understands his faith as a work of God in him. The decision of faith understands itself as a gift.[49] And yet one is left with the impression that Bultmann locates the glory of salvation too much in the change wrought in the believer by the appeal of the Cross and not exclusively enough in the objective fact accomplished on the Cross of Christ.[50] The decision of the disciple to reject the world and live for God, the obedience in which the Christian must die to the world and to self, seems to take the place of faith in Jesus Christ who was delivered for our offenses and raised for our justification.[51] It is not my existential decision, but my Saviour who is made unto me wisdom from God and righteousness and sanctification and redemption. Therefore, he who glories, in the Lord let him glory (I Cor. 1:30).

Here we concur with Professor T. F. Torrance. Justification means justification by Christ alone — that is the reference of the expressions *sola fide, sola gratia, sola scriptura* used in Reformed theology. Justification means that we look exclusively to Christ, and therefore we look away from ourselves in order to live out of Him alone.[52]

3. Sola Fide

Faith in Jesus Christ, wrought in the heart by the Holy Spirit, is the way by which we receive the righteousness of God. That righteousness is obtained by faith is set forth in such passages as Romans 1:17, 3:25; 4:3-4, 9, 24; Gal. 2:16; that it is fixed upon Christ is taught in Romans 3:22, 26; 4:25; Philippians 3:9; Galatians 2:16-17; and that it is worked in us by the might of the Spirit is indicated in Ephesians 2:5-10; I Corinthians 1:30; 2:4-5, 10-16.

On the one hand, then, faith lays hold on Christ in the completeness of the work He has accomplished for us, on the other it is the work of God in us so that by the power of

---

49. R. Bultmann, *Theologie des Neuen Testaments,* pp. 326, 370, 423.

50. R. Bultmann, *Kerygma und Mythos,* p. 42 (45), cf. pp. 16, 20, treats the objective representations of the New Testament, namely, the death of Christ as a propitiation or a sacrifice, or a satisfaction for sins, as myths which factually mean that the believer is freed from the ruling power of sin through the Cross of Christ.

51. Cf. K. Barth, *Kirchliche Dogmatik,* IV/2, 570.

52. T. F. Torrance, "Justification in Doctrine and Life" in *Scottish Journal of Theology,* 13:3:237-8.

the Holy Spirit Christ is present in the one who believes in Him. While different passages of the Word generally stress only one of these two aspects, leaving the other implied, at times both become explicit. When Peter confessed his faith in Christ, our Lord replied that this faith was the revelation of the Father (Matt. 16:16-17). Jesus told Nicodemus that a man must be born of the Spirit and also invited him to believe in the Son of God (John 3:1-16). In the discourse on the bread of life, Jesus said, "No man can come unto Me except the Father draw him," and "him who comes to Me, I will in no wise cast out" (John 6:44, 37). According to the best reading of Philippians 3:9, the true Israel are those "who worship by the Spirit of God and glory in Christ Jesus, and have no confidence in the flesh."

As *sola gratia* describes God's action in attributing righteousness to the sinner, so *sola fide* describes man's way of getting this righteousness. In place of the Judaistic formula that a man is justified or accepted by God on the basis of works, Paul teaches that one obtains life by faith. "Faith takes the place of deeds." But this does not mean that my faith as a psychological phenomenon is an achievement for the sake of which God justifies me. There is an achievement for the sake of which God justifies, but it is not my own achievement; rather it is the achievement of Christ for me on the Cross.[53] *Sola fide* thus means *sola cruce*.[54]

"Faith is an orientation on Jesus Christ to the exclusion of everything else, including self." God saves us through the faith which relies entirely upon the faithfulness of Christ. "The exclusiveness of faith means the exclusiveness of Christ: *sola fide,* because *sola Christus.*"[55] Faith is the means by which we hold to the Redeemer. It is the receptive instrument, *organon lepticon,* "which seizes the redemptive work of Jesus with both hands and presents it to God and says: I believe that Christ gave Himself for me, Gal. 2:20." "Faith for Paul is faith in this act of atonement fulfilled by Another."[56]

---

53. So J. Jeremias, in *The Expository Times,* September, 1955.
54. So E. Stauffer, *Die Theologie des Neuen Testament,* pp. 22-23.
55. G. W. Bromiley, in *Scottish Journal of Theology,* 8:2:186, 184.
56. Even in the Habakkuk Commentary, "the just shall live by faith" means "he shall live by faith in the Teacher of Righteousness." This is not, however, as it is for Paul, faith in an act of atonement accomplished in the death of Christ for the forgiveness of sins. O. Cullman, in *Journal of Biblical Literature,* LXXIV:iv: 1955.

The primary concern is thus the object of faith, not the mere phenomenon of faith. This is true of Calvin and of the English homily *Of Salvation,* but it is, in the first place, true of Luther. In his early commentary on Psalm 31 (32) (*W.A.,* 3:169), in his commentary on Romans (*W. A.,* 56:255), and in his treatment of Galatians, faith is ever faith in Christ.[57] "God does accept or account us as righteous only for our faith in Christ." Faith is ever directed to Christ. "Faith takes hold of Christ and has Him present, and holds Him enclosed as the ring does the precious stone." Faith is necessary but faith is not meritorious.

Christ is the object of faith, but He is not only object. In the faith itself Christ is present even as God is in the midst of the darkness of Sinai and of the Temple. "Who although He be not seen at all, yet He is present."[58] Faith is as close to Christ as the ring to the precious stone it enfolds, as close as the form is to the matter in the Aristotelian analysis, or "this faith does couple Christ and me more nearly together than the husband and the wife."[59] Indeed, this faith joins me to Christ so entirely that He and I are made as it were one person. And the Christ to whom I am united is not another Moses, but the Saviour; not the law which condemns, but the Lord who forgives. Christ, who alone is my righteousness and life, lives in me (Gal. 2:20).[60] "Wherefore Christ apprehended by faith, and dwelling in the heart, is the true Christian righteousness for which God counts us righteous and gives us eternal life."[61] Faith means unity with the one believed in, which in this case is Jesus Christ.

God offers justification to us in the preaching of the Word of Christ (Rom. 10:17 (ASV), 1:3; Acts 10:43; Gal. 3:1-14; I Cor. 1:30), and He seals it upon us by baptizing us into Christ (Rom. 6:3; I Cor. 6:11; Gal. 3:24-27; Titus 3:5-7). It is the Holy Spirit who effectually uses the hearing of the Word, as well as the laver of baptism, to unite sinners to their Saviour. He employs the Word, confirmed by the sacraments, to arouse, to revive, and to sustain in our hearts faith in Christ.

The Reformers carried forward the teaching of the Word of God in its correlation with faith as the work of the Holy Spirit

---

57. *Luther on Galatians,* ed. by Watson, pp. 227-229, 232-233, 252, 137.
58. *Ibid.,* pp. 134-135.
59. *Ibid.,* p. 170.
60. *Ibid.,* p. 168.
61. *Ibid.,* p. 135.

in man.[62] Both Luther and Calvin keep the Spirit, the Word, and faith close together in this process. In *Spiritus Creator,* Regin Prenter finds almost a reciprocal relation in Luther's teaching concerning the Word and the Spirit. "Now the Word is seen as an instrument in the hand of the Spirit by which the merits of Christ are given or the church sanctified, and then the Word is seen as an instrument in the hand of the Triune God by which the Spirit is given." Moreover, it is only as the Spirit uses the Word both in God's *opus alienum* and in His *opus proprium* that faith is wrought in the sinner.[63]

In keeping the Spirit, the Word, and faith close together, Calvin followed the one whom he called "my revered father." In different places he denominates the instrumental cause of justification as "the illumination of the Spirit, that is, faith" (*Inst.*, III, xiv, 21) ; as "faith" (III, xiv, 7) ; and as "faith in the Word" (*Commentary on Rom.* 3:24). Faith proceeds from the Spirit (III, i, 4; III, ii, 7, 8, 33), and has such a perpetual relation to the Word that the Word may be used metonymically to denote faith (III, ii, 6, 30, 31; III, xx, 13, 28). In bringing salvation to men the Spirit and the Word are in "mutual connection" and in "inviolable union" (I, xi, 1, 3).

According to Luther, the Spirit "takes the crucified and risen Christ out of the remoteness of history and heavenly glory and places Him as a living reality in the midst of our life with its suffering, inner conflict and death."[64] The Spirit makes the difference between the distant Christ of imitation and history, and the present Christ of faith and the gospel. For Calvin, "the Holy Spirit is the bond by which Christ unites us to Himself." "Till our minds are fixed on the Spirit, Christ remains an object of cold speculation without us, and therefore at a great distance from us." The Spirit is the internal Teacher by whose agency the promise of salvation in Christ penetrates our minds. The light present in the Word only illumines our sin-blinded minds when they are opened by the Spirit. He is the key by whom the treasures of the Kingdom are unlocked to us. Complete salvation is in Christ. To make us partakers of it, the Holy Spirit enlightens us in the faith of the Gospel, purges us from profane impurities, and consecrates us as holy temples to God (*Inst.*, III, i). Christian faith is engraved on our hearts

---

62. K. Barth, *Die protestantische Theologie im 19. Jahrhundert,* p. 411.
63 R. Prenter, *Spiritus Creator,* pp. 256, 226.
64. *Ibid.,* p. 54.

by the finger of the living God, who by His Spirit seals and attests to us the things of Christ.[65]

The Spirit who so unites Christ with His righteousness to the believer is God, the Holy Spirit, and thus the Creator Spirit. The *imago Dei* is grounded in the grace of God by which it is made in the first place and remade in the second place.[66] God's acts of creation — both in the first place and in Christ, are *ex nihilo* (cf. Rom. 4:17; I Cor. 1:28; Eph. 2:1-10). "The Reformation doctrine not only entails but strenuously insists that there is nothing on which deliverance can 'take hold', and that he [the sinner] is therefore incapable of deliverance save by the recreation of his dead soul by the almighty power of the Holy Spirit."[67] Or, as Prenter has recently summarized Luther: "To a man dead in sin the Spirit descends and makes all God's reality present in the midst of death. The Spirit is the presence of the living God Himself in His all-embracing, eschatological act, with man in Christ Jesus as the new sphere of life in the midst of death." "In the hidden reality of faith He brings to us Christ as the master over death and hell that we may take refuge in His alien righteousness and be the tool through which His love comes to our neighbor." "The message about the creative Spirit shows us God on the way to distant man, who is lost in sin and death, in order constantly to create new life out of nothing, life out of death."[68]

Calvin is likewise sure that God is the author of our spiritual life from its commencement to its end. Man has not even the smallest particle in which he can glory, for all is of God. Our salvation is entirely gratuitous both because we who are unworthy in ourselves have been chosen in Christ "on account of His great love wherewith He loved us," and because the beginning of all good is from the second creation.[69]

In the power of the Holy Spirit the risen Christ confronts the sinner and brings him to faith and repentance. This encounter with the living Redeemer keeps faith from being only an abstract legal transaction, while the Spirit's bringing of the life of God into the soul of man delivers it from a merely deistic confrontation. The resulting faith and repentance, or knowing Christ in the power of His resurrection and the fellowship

---

65. Calvin, "Reply to Sadolet," *Tracts*, I, 53.
66. T. F. Torrance, *Calvin's Doctrine of Man,* pp. 114, 132.
67. B. B. Warfield, *Perfectionism*, I, 20, 30, 36.
68. R. Prenter, *op. cit.*, pp. 185-191.
69. *Inst.*, II, iii, 6; *Commentary on Ephesians*, chaps. 1 and 2.

of His sufferings, gives a content to conversion which keeps the word "confront" from becoming a mere magical or mystical formula. Accordingly, in the third book of Calvin's *Institutes,* the chapter on the illumination of the Spirit is followed by one on faith and then one on repentance. The Anglican Catechism of 1549 requires of those to be baptized: repentance, a death unto sin, and faith, a steadfast believing of the promises of God. Calvin's *Catechism* describes our part in the right use of baptism as standing in faith and repentance, "that is, in that we be sure that we have our conscience cleansed in the blood of Christ: and that we both feel in ourselves, and make known to others by our works, that His Spirit abides in us to mortify our affections and so make us ready to do the will of God." In his graphic account of his own conversion, Thomas Halyburton tells how the living Lord confronted him with His Word (II Cor. 4:6), shining into his heart to give the light of the knowledge of the glory of God in the face of Jesus Christ. But the same autobiographical account records the concrete effects of that conversion in his obedient thinking and living: confrontation and content came together.

As Christ entered into the veil of death and agony, sorrow and fear, so the Holy Spirit uses the law to bring the knowledge of sin into sharp focus and the experiences of life to manifest the death and impotence of the whole old man. Christ shares with us in our humiliations so that we enter into the fellowship of His sufferings and find our peace in Him who when He was reviled, reviled not again. "The Cross of Christ and the Cross of the Christian are inseparable." As we come in sight of His *via dolorosa,* we learn that if one died for all then were all dead, and we who live should no longer live unto ourselves but unto Him who for our sakes died and rose again. Blessed be His Name, the same Holy Spirit who sustains us in the depths of death and darkness brings us into the sunlight of God's love as faith receives Christ for our justification. What matter if man condemn, if I condemn myself? It is God who justifies.

For Luther there were continual temptations or struggles to win the fight of faith. *Anfechtung* was his word to describe the whole battle of the Christian's warfare. These battles were not chiefly of the flesh but of the spirit. They concerned faith and hope, salvation and predestination — a man's standing with God. The question was not, What do I think of God, but What does He think of me? How can I know that God is gracious to me, a sinner? Luther likened the battle to the story of the

Canaanite woman given in Matthew 15:21-28. Though repulsed by Jesus, she held to her confidence in His good will toward her. So faith clings to God's words and promises when He shows a frowning face. It turns away from the rebuff it feels, and grasps the deep Divine *Yes* beneath His *No*. It sees and feels the wrath of God, but it nevertheless breaks through to the goodness of the Most High. "Though He slay me yet will I trust Him." When in despair, anguish, and the agony of death, one begins to cry unto God, then hell becomes no more hell. Then is faith no more the sleeping thing as the monks thought: faith is the splendid active grasp on the goodness of God in Christ which leads to victory in the field of battle.[70]

This faith knowledge is a light in the midst of struggles that threaten to dash the torch from the Reformer's hand. Except Christ sit at the right hand of God and daily pour forth the Holy Spirit, Satan would allow none of us to abide by our Christian faith or the Easter message for a single hour. For Calvin also this kind of knowledge far exceeds our understanding and is marked by imperfection (*Inst.*, III, ii, 18). Indeed, "our knowledge of everything is very imperfect, in consequence of the clouds of error by which we are surrounded" (III, ii, 4). As the illumination of the Holy Spirit, faith is an acknowledgment of God's prior knowledge of us confirmed by a persuasion of His truthfulness. "Faith consists more in certainty than in comprehension" (III, ii, 14). As no authority can be higher than that of God Himself, so no certainty can be greater than that imparted by the Spirit shining on the Word, namely, the witness of God concerning His Son (I John 5:9). As long as Peter's eye was focussed on his Lord he walked the storm-tossed sea; but when he began to think of himself and the imperfections of his believing, he began to sink. May the hand of the Saviour that grasped Peter and brought him into the boat be close to us whenever we turn from the all-sufficiency of Christ to insufficiencies in our believing. In Him we stand, in ourselves we fall. There is also a hint in the story of the man born blind. When cross-examined by questions he could not answer; he replied: "Nevertheless one thing I know, whereas I was blind now I see." The secret of assurance is in not letting the things we do not know upset our confidence in the things we do know.

Standing in the Reformed tradition with its emphasis on the certainty of faith, Principal John Macleod nevertheless came to

---

70. So in substance Dr. Gordon Rupp's *Lectures on the Reformation*.

this valuable distinction: There is no doubt in faith, but there is doubt in believers.[71] At the foot of the Mount of Transfiguration our Lord accepted the imperfect faith of the distraught father who prayed: "I *believe,* Lord, help Thou mine *unbelief.*" Calvin recognizes that owing to the imperfection of faith in the present life we are never to be completely cured of the disease of distrust and entirely filled and possessed by faith (*Inst.,* III, ii, 18), and that "to speak of such a perfection, as unto which nothing can be added, it can not be found in men."[72] There may well have been much superstition behind the hand that reached for the decorations fringing the hem of the Saviour's garment, but in response to the timid touch of an imperfect believer there went healing. The Old Testament promise is that the bruised reed He will not break, the smoking flax or the dimly burning wick He will not quench. Our Lord said, If ye have faith as a grain of mustard seed . . . Luther commented that even weak faith does it. We boast not of the greatness of our faith, but of the graciousness of our God and the sufficiency of our Saviour.[72a]

At Campus in the Woods a bright college student came to talk about his spiritual condition: "I accepted Christ two years ago. At least I thought I did. But did I accept Him a thousand percent? Am I really saved?" "Son," the counselor advised, "if you are not sure you accepted Christ two years ago, accept Him here and now. I offer Him to you in all His fullness — our Saviour who died for our sins, our risen Lord and Friend. Will you accept Him here and now?" "Yes," was the glad response, sealed with a united prayer.

Two nights later the lad was back with the same problem. "I thought I accepted Christ two years ago. I thought I accepted Him with my whole heart two nights ago, but did I? Did I make a thousand-percent committal, was my faith whole and complete?" Then the light began to dawn for the advisor. "No, son," he replied, "you did not exercise a thousand-percent faith. You are not an angel. But you do not hate God as you did before that committal two years ago. The natural man is at enmity toward God. The fact that you no longer

71. John Macleod, *Scottish Theology in Connection with Church History.*
72. J. Calvin, *Catechism,* 360, cf. 320.
72a. The Church's faith is "the knowledge that it can expect nothing from itself, or even from the intensity of its faith, but everything from the freedom and faithfulness of its Lord." E. Schweizer, *Church Order in the New Testament,* p. 225.

hate God, that in your imperfect way you trust and love **Him**, is the evidence that God's love for you has been shed abroad in your heart by the Holy Ghost. Your faith is only a faint flicker, as mine is, as Luther's was. But that flicker is the work of the Holy Spirit. It is the gift of God and thus the sign that God is for you. And if God be for you who can be against you?"[73]

Our acceptance of Christ is the sign that He has accepted us and fitted us into His all-embracing work of salvation and into His program for the spread of His Gospel.

4. SOLI DEO GLORIA

"To the praise of the glory of His grace . . . to the praise of His glory . . . unto the praise of His glory" (Eph. 1:6, 12, 14) "To show His righteousness . . . for the showing of His righteousness . . . that He might be just and the justifier of him that has faith in Jesus" (Rom. 3:25-26). "Abraham wavered not through unbelief, but waxed strong through faith, giving glory to God, and being fully assured that what He had promised, He was able also to perform" (Rom. 4:20-21). "The Word of the Cross . . . unto us who are saved it is the power of God . . . Christ the power of God and the wisdom of God" (I Cor. 1:18, 24). "God commends His own love toward us, in that, while we were yet sinners, Christ died for us" (Rom. 5:8).

The final cause of our salvation is the glory of God our Saviour. He who glories, in the Lord let him glory (I Cor. 1:31; Jer. 9:23). Man's chief end is to glorify God and to enjoy Him forever. Recent studies in Luther have made it clear that *soli Deo gloria* is as true to Luther as it is to Calvin. Indeed, it was Calvin's merit to have prevented this theocentric note of the Father of the Reformation from being lost. The passages cited above show that this was the teaching of the Apostle as it was of our Lord (Matt. 5:16, 6:10).

In Romans 3, God's pure grace to us acts in this way, namely, through the redemption which is in Christ Jesus whom God set forth a *hilasterion* in His own blood to show that God is just in justifying the believer. The act of God in giving His

---

73. Cf. O. Michel, *Der Brief an die Römer*, pp. 47-48: "Faith is the fruit and effect of the Gospel and must be understood accordingly. One cannot look upon it as the presupposition and condition of an expected salvation. It is misunderstood when it is presented as the necessary mental act or accomplishment of man. On the contrary, it is the sign and the seal of the Gospel rightly understood." R. Bultmann, *Theologie des Neuen Testaments*, pp. 370, 423. "The believer can understand his faith only as a work of God on him." "The decision of faith understands itself as a gift."

own Son to die for sinners, in reconciling us to Himself by Christ's death and in justifying us by His blood (Rom. 5:8-10), in using His obedience to justify many (5:19), demonstrates that God is righteous both in passing over or postponing the reckoning for the sins done aforetime (3:25) [74] and in justifying those who now believe in Jesus (3:26). The repetition of this thought in these two verses, as well as the fundamental place that righteousness occupies in the Epistle to the Romans, shows that the main drive of the Apostle is to vindicate God's righteous dealings in this way of saving sinful creatures.

God's righteousness towers above every human analogy and expression, but it is not so disparate from our thinking as to have no meaning for us. A judge is the one who frees some, and condemns others, the one whose judgment all have to fear. But fundamentally, the judge is the man who cares for order and peace, who maintains the right and wards off the evil. Thus his coming and work must not be a thing of terror, but may signify a benefit, a bringer of help and salvation as the Judges in the early period of Israel's life in Canaan.[75] When the Apostle reasoned of righteousness, self-control, and judgment to come, a Roman governor understood him well enough to be terrified (Acts 25:25), and even certain of the Areopagites clave unto him (Acts 17:30-34). As the Apostle expounded God's righteousness, it included, at least as an element therein, distributive justice, thus: the manifestation of God's righteous judgment in rendering to every man according to his deeds (Rom. 2:5-6). Even Roman judgment is given provisional commendation as a minister of God for good to those who do good and of wrath to those who do evil (Rom. 13:1-7; cf. I Pet. 2:14). Yet Paul rises from this relative justice of the Roman governors to the higher plane of the judgment administered by Christians (I Cor. 6:1-7), and thence to the judgment of God, immensely higher than the believer's judgment of his brother (Rom. 14:10f.), or even of himself (I Cor. 4:4). Calvin speaks of the divine justice as too high to be measured by a human standard (*Inst.,* III, xxiii, 4; III, xxiv, 17). Our Lord writes over the revelation of God as Judge, even as over that of Him as Father, "how much more" than any human type (Matt. 7:11; Luke 11:13, 18:6-7).

The justice of God is not to be denied because the pagans used a word from the same Greek root to mean vengeance, or

74. Cf. Acts 17:30 and O. Michel, *Der Brief an die Römer,* pp. 93-94.
75. K. Barth, *Kirchliche Dogmatik,* IV/1, p. 238.

a kind of fate that moved relentlessly over men and gods (cf. Acts 28:4, ARV). In the Old Testament God executes His righteousness by becoming the Father of the fatherless and the Judge of the widow, the Vindicator of the oppressed and the Support of the needy. For the philosopher, justice may be a blind, discarnate abstraction. In the New Testament God has committed all judgment to the Son because He is son of man (John 5:22, 27), who was tempted in all points like as we are, and thus can have compassion with the ignorant and erring (Heb. 4:14; 5:3).

For the pagan, man offers a sacrifice to appease the fury of an arbitrary god. For the Christian, "the sacrifice is the result of God's grace, not its cause. It is given *by* God before it is given *to* Him."[76] In the Gospel, the whole work of reconciliation is God's doing. It was consonant with God's holy character for a sacrifice to be offered to remove His wrath and to show forth His justice in justifying believing sinners.[77] But it was not less consonant with His heart of grace to provide that sacrifice — yes in the person of His Son to become that Lamb of God. God reconciled the world unto Himself by not imputing their trespasses unto them, that is, by making Him who knew no sin to be sin for us that we might be made the righteousness of God in Him. The Gospel is that the Judge came in Christ to bring us back to the arms of the Father. God is that particularly kind Judge who both gave His only Son to bear our sin and curse and committed all judgment to that Son.[77a] The Judge is the One who was Himself judged for us.

"It is not true that the New Testament speaks with any unharmonious voices on the death of Christ. One thought recurs again and again: that death is God's answer to and settlement with sin: In Christ's shedding His blood for the remission of sins, bearing sins, putting away sins, made sin, we are

76. P. T. Forsyth, *The Cruciality of the Cross*, p. 89.

77. In the Old Testament, first Moses (Ex. 32:10-14; Ps. 106:23) and then Phinehas (Num. 25:4-13; Ps. 106:30-31), turn away the wrath of God. In the New Testament times it was a common Jewish view that death expiates, that through substitutionary suffering one can propitiate God, or turn away His wrath, e.g., the Jewish martyrs (4 Macc. 17:22), Elias and Moses in Jewish apocalyptic literature (*TWZNT*, II, 942f., IV, 867f.), possibly the death of the Teacher of Righteousness. Cf. O. Michel, *op. cit.*, pp. 93, 95.

77a. Thus K. Barth, *Kirchliche Dogmatik*, IV, 1, 211-283, proclaims this tremendous transaction; but G. S. Hendry, *The Gospel of the Incarnation*, pp. 112, 119, opposes substitution and satisfaction in the presentations of Barth, of Calvin, and of Hodge.

brought to the moral center of things where the supreme righteousness of God is manifested, and God justifies Himself forever."[78] Under the shield of this righteousness we are forgiven
and the righteousness of God's dealings with the creatures of
His hand is vindicated. With wonder and amazement, angels
desire to behold and to worship as the Cross sets forth the
righteousness, the power, the wisdom, and the love of God.

As Romans 3 and the second half of chapter 5 show the
Gospel glorifying the righteousness of God, so chapter 4 magnifies the power of the God on whom Abraham and his spiritual
heirs believe. The two thoughts are brought even closer together
in Romans 1:16-17. The Gospel which reveals the righteousness
of God in dealing with believing sinners is the power of God
unto salvation. God is not mere reckless power, not arbitrary
almightiness. The Occamist presentation of God as bare almighty will disturbed Luther's view of predestination, until
he found God's overflowing love and kindness in Christ. For
Calvin "the notion of the Romish theologians concerning the
absolute and arbitrary power of God is profane and deserves
our detestation" (*Inst.* III, xxiii, 2; cf. I, xvii, 2). God can
no more fail to be good than He can fail to be God (*Inst.*,
II, iii, 5). God's will is the expression of His character, of His
justice, His wisdom and His love. Accordingly, the solution
of the problem of righteousness is the way to power, or as the
Apostle puts it, the Word of the Cross is the power of God
and the wisdom of God (I Cor. 1). Similarly, our Lord first
forgave the sin of the paralytic, and then sealed the pardon
with the power to rise up and walk (Mark 2:1-12). Likewise,
the Oral Gospel finds the power of God manifest in the Cross,
that is, His ability to turn the wrath of men to His praise and
the salvation of sinners (Acts 4:25).

Abraham gave all glory to God's power to fulfill His promises
when all natural ways of accomplishing them seemed out of
the question, when he and Sarah were too old to expect to
have a child, and later when he was called to sacrifice that
child of the covenant on the altar. He staggered not at the
promises of God through unbelief, but was strong in faith,
giving glory to God, being fully assured that what God had
promised He was able to perform. Abraham believed that
God was able to raise up Isaac from the dead and so fulfill
His promise to the Patriarch (Heb. 11:17-19). This is the faith

78. J. R. Mozley, *The Heart of the Gospel*, p. 38, cited by L. Morris,
The Wages of Sin, p. 24.

that was reckoned to Abraham for righteousness. "Now it was not written for his sake alone, that it was reckoned unto him, but for our sakes also unto whom it shall be reckoned, who believe on Him who raised Jesus our Lord from the dead, who was delivered up for our trespasses, and was raised for our justification" (Rom. 4:23-25).

The exceeding greatness of God's power to work in believers according to the energizings of the mastery of His strength is revealed in the working by which He raised Christ from the dead and lifted Him to His own right hand (Eph. 1:19-20). We are saved as we believe in our hearts that God raised Christ from the dead (Rom. 10:9). Our Christian life is strengthened with power through His Spirit in the inner man (Eph. 3:16); it is directed to knowing Christ in the power of His resurrection (Phil. 3:10), and, as it lays hold of this power, it gives glory to God in the Church in Christ Jesus (Eph. 3:20-21). The faith which gives God the glory is thus depicted by Luther:

> He who can say, "I am a child of God through Christ, who is my righteousness," and despairs not, though he be deficient in good works, which always fail us, he believes rightly. But grace is so great that it amazes a human creature, and is very difficult to be believed. Insomuch that faith gives the honor to God, that He can and will perform what He promised, namely, to make sinners righteous (Rom. 4), though it is an exceeding hard matter to believe that God is merciful unto us for the sake of Christ. O! man's heart is too straight and narrow to entertain or take hold of this.[79]

The faith of an Abraham, of a Paul, and of a Luther is "according to the power of God who saved us" (Titus 1:8-9). Faith is the unlimited willingness to give God all the glory of saving sinners.[80]

As Romans 3 shows that the Gospel vindicates God's righteousness, and Romans 4 that it magnifies His power, so Romans 5 finds it commending God's love. The Holy Spirit sheds abroad the love of God in our hearts, as God commends His own love toward us, in that while we were yet sinners Christ died for us (Rom. 5:5, 8). As the same Spirit helps our imperfect prayers with His own intercessions for us, He brings the Gospel assurance that nothing shall separate us from the love of Christ, or from the love of God which is in Christ Jesus our Lord (Rom.

79. Luther, *Table Talk,* p. 143.
80. G. Vos, *Biblical Theology.*

8:26, 35, 39). The revelation of the love of God in the death and resurrection of Christ is carried over into II Corinthians 5:14-16 and constrains us to live no longer unto ourselves but for those for whom He died. Similarly, John finds the love of God manifested in reference to us in that God sent the Son of His bosom into the world to be the propitiation for our sins, that we might live and love (I John 4:9-11; cf. John 3:16).

Ephesians is, perhaps, the greatest paean of praise to God for the graciousness of His love to us revealed in the Beloved. Here the several voices in the anthem proclaim: "God rich in mercy," "for His great love wherewith He loved us," "for by grace are ye saved," "the exceeding riches of His grace in His kindness toward us in Christ Jesus," "to the praise of the glory of His grace." In Ephesians 1:6-7 "grace" occurs three times, twice as a noun and once as a verb. Once it is strengthened to "the glory of His grace" and once to "the riches of His grace." In chapter 2 this phrase is repeated, namely, "for it is by *grace* that ye are saved." It is grace that in love foreordained our salvation, it is grace that wrought redemption in the blood of the Beloved, even the forgiveness of sins, that published salvation in the Gospel and sealed it with the earnest of the Spirit, that brought salvation to the children of wrath, making those who were dead in sin alive in Christ. Yes, the Epistle to the Ephesians is a shout of praise to the glory of the saving grace of God. It shows that "the whole glory of our salvation should be ascribed undividedly to God alone."[81]

Moreover, God is glorified by the fruit of the Gospel. The Apostle who speaks of himself as not yet made perfect, nay even as the chief of sinners, nevertheless prays that his churches may walk worthily of the Lord unto all pleasing, in every good work bearing fruit and increasing (Col. 1:10). We have noted how the Apostle carries over the righteousness of God into Romans 5, 6, and 8, showing that it brings us into the service of righteousness. God is glorified as we yield our bodies as instruments of righteousness, that grace may reign through righteousness. The Spirit who comes with the preaching of the Word of the Cross (I Cor. 1:18-2, 5; Gal. 3:2f.) brings forth the first fruits of the Spirit even in the present lives of believers (Rom. 8:23), and these fruits are such rich clusters as love, joy, peace, long-suffering, kindness, goodness, faithfulness, meekness

---

81. Calvin, *Commentary on Ephesians,* chap. 1.

or gentleness, self-control (Gal. 5:22-23). The Epistle which insists that we are justified not by the works of the law, but on the contrary by the faith of Christ Jesus (Gal. 2:16), nevertheless calls for this faith to work through love (Gal. 5:6). The paragraph that asserts that our salvation is not of works lest any man should boast reminds us that we are created in Christ Jesus unto good works (Eph. 2:9-10). Further, from Romans 12 through 15 the Apostle sees a fellowship developing in which each uses the gifts given him according to the measure of his faith (12:3, 6), for the good of the Body. Differences in faith permit detailed divergences in conduct (chapter 14), but love for those for whom Christ died (I Cor. 8:11) calls one to give up things which offend the weaker brother. The branch draws its life from the vine (John 15). The Christian fellowship draws her life from the Father and from His Son Jesus Christ (I John 1). As she does, she reflects the light that streams from the Sun of Righteousness, and men see her good works and glorify the Father in heaven (Matt. 5:16). Thus in some faint way, the several congregations of the body of Christ may be thought of as candelabra of the Lord supplied by the Spirit, shining to the glory of God.

Only, if we are true to the Reformers, these figures must not be read as modifying or qualifying their *soli Deo gloria.*

> What does it mean, in Luther's view, to give glory to God and to let God really be God? His answer may be summarily stated in what he calls the "article of justification," the doctrine of salvation by faith alone, or grace alone — for the two are the same. The glory of God is His grace, the unmerited and unmeritable love that meets us with absolute judgment and fathomless mercy in Jesus Christ. In the Cross of Christ, above all, Luther finds the full depth and majesty of the Godhead revealed — to faith, for it was not evident to sight, that God was in Christ reconciling the world unto Himself.[82]

For Calvin, nothing

> is more consistent with faith than to acknowledge ourselves naked of all virtue, that we may be clothed by God; empty of all good, that we may be filled by Him; lame, that we may be guided; weak, that we may be supported by Him; to divest ourselves of all ground of glorying, that He alone may be eminently glorious and that we may glory in Him.

82. P. S. Watson, *Let God be God!*, p. 61; cf. Luther on Jer. 9:23 in his *Table Talk.*
83. Calvin, Letter to Francis I.

5. SOLA SCRIPTURA

Deut. 4:2, 12:32; Mark 7:5-7; Matt. 15:7-9, citing Isa. 39:13;
Jer. 23:16; Acts 4:19, 5:29; Gal. 1:9; Heb. 4:12; II Tim. 3:16;
Rev. 22:18.

The content of the slogans we are discussing is the everlasting
and ever effective Gospel, revealed by God, recorded in the
Scriptures, preached in the Church, and applied by the Holy
Spirit for our salvation. In his work as Doctor or Professor of
Biblical Theology in Wittenberg, Luther discovered this true
meaning of the written Word of God, while Calvin insists that
everyone who would enjoy the light of true religion must begin
as a disciple of Scripture with the doctrine of heaven (*Inst.,*
I, vi, 3). The God of the Bible is the God of grace.

Galatians taught Luther that "righteousness is promised by
God, fulfilled by Christ without the law, given to us — out
of grace alone," while Romans showed that "faith is a living,
daring confidence in God's grace."[84] For Calvin, faith respects
every part of the Word of God, but it never stands firmly until
it comes to the gratuitous promise of God's mercy or loving
kindness. For the grace of God is the fountain from which
every species of blessing flows down to us (*Inst.,* III, ii, 30, 29,
28).

For Luther "all the scriptures point to Christ alone," while
the New Testament Gospel is "really a preaching of the benefits
of Christ" . . . "the preaching about Christ, Son of God and of
David, true God and man, who by His death and resurrection
has overcome for us the sin, death and hell of all who believe
in Him."[85] According to Calvin, the Word presents Christ
clothed with His Gospel that faith may behold God (*Inst.* III,
ii, 6), and as faith unites us to Christ we are reconciled to God
(III, ii, 30).

In Luther's *Liberty of a Christian Man* faith is a laying hold
of the promises of God set forth in His written Word, that the
blessings there promised may be received. Likewise, the best
and greatest part of all sacraments is the promise and the words
of God, for though God has prepared for our faith a pasture, a
table, and a feast, faith is not fed except on the Word of God
alone.[86] For Calvin, faith has a perpetual relation to the Word,

84. Prefaces to Galatians and to Romans, 1546.
85. *Avoiding the Doctrines of Men,* and *Preface to the New Testament,* 1546.
86. Luther, "Treatise on the NT, that is, The Holy Mass," *Luther's
Works,* ed. Pelikan and Lehmann, xxxv, 91-92.

and can no more be separated from it than the rays from the sun or the fruit from the root. Faith is so founded on the truth of the gratuitous promise in Christ that the removal of the Word indicates the departure of the Lord and the downfall of faith. As faith is the knowledge of God's gracious disposition towards us received from His Word, the same Divine Word is the foundation by which faith is sustained and supported (*Inst.*, III, ii, 6, 7, 31; II, v, 13).

As a form of humanism, current existentialism begins with man, and for the theology based thereon, faith is the actualization of man's self-understanding. The Reformers begin with God, and for them faith is primarily an understanding of God from His self-revelation. It is the believing acceptance of His lovingkindness, His merciful disposition toward us in Christ. It brings forth praise from forgiven hearts, and issues in a life of grateful obedience. A true Christian so preaches and praises Christ that the people learn that they are nothing and Christ is everything. For "the glory or honor or praise belongs only to God."[87] From its "deeper plunge into the meaning of the Gospel," the Reformation came up with a richer appreciation of the grace of God in Christ Jesus. That appreciation issued in a clearer echo of the Biblical anthem of praise to the glory of God's grace. The watchword of the Reformation fathers is ever a melodious sound in the ears of their authentic disciples: "The Word, nothing but the Word, the whole Word; grace, nothing but grace, God's all-sufficient grace."[88]

87. Luther, "On the Magnificat," and "On the Sermon on the Mount," *Luther's Works,* ed. Pelikan, xxi:322, 66, 148; Calvin, *Inst.*, III, ii, 6, 7, 28.
88. W. A. Langenohl, in *The Reformed Faith*, p. 157.

CHAPTER TWO

THE SIGNIFICANCE OF THE REFORMATION

Luther Rediscovers God

THE REFORMATION was a rediscovery of God. In place of the saints and angels, or the powers thought to lie in relics and indulgences, the Word of the one, only, living, and true God was heard. God manifested Himself to the Reformers in His holiness and His grace, in His mercy and in His might. The Holy Spirit made the Gospel the power of God unto salvation. Luther grasped the hand of God stretched out to him in Jesus Christ, and Europe awoke to the glad tidings of God our Saviour. The proclamation of the mighty acts of God heralded the years of God's right hand.

For the Reformers, God is at the center of life, God who acts, God who does, God who thinks, God who speaks, God who saves, God who reigns and rules here and now. When "every true Christian, whether living or dead, has a share given to him by God in all the benefits of Christ and the Church even without letters of pardon," then God advances for him into the foreground, and once more "the true treasure of the Church is the Holy Gospel of the grace and glory of God."[1]

1. THE NEED FOR A NEW DISCOVERY OF GOD

Perhaps an old Scottish story will illustrate this need. A Protestant tenant who rented a small farm from Alexander, the second Duke of Gordon, fell behind in his payments. In the Duke's absence, a vigilant steward seized the farmer's stock and advertised it to be sold on a fixed day. Happily his Grace returned in the interval and the tenant went to him to supplicate for mercy. As the farmer entered with a sad, downcast countenance the Duke asked, "What is the matter, Donald?" Donald told his tale in a natural and concise way. It touched the Duke's heart and procured a formal acquital of the debt.

1. Theses 37 and 62 of the Ninety-five Theses.

37

As Donald was happily withdrawing, he stared at the images and pictures in the castle. Noticing his bewilderment, the Roman Catholic Duke remarked, "These are the saints who intercede with God for me." "My lord Duke," said Donald, "would it not be better to apply yourself directly to God? I went to muckle [big] Sandy Gordon and to little Sandy Gordon; but if I had not come to your Grace's self, I would not have got my discharge, and both I and my bairns had been turned out of house and home."

Melrose Abbey boasted one hundred and forty-seven statues of saints; the Cathedral in Milan, some two thousand. The three bells of the Church in which Martin Luther was baptized bore the following inscription:

"God help us: Mary have mercy, 1499."

"Help us, Anna, also St. Peter, St. Paul, 1509."

"Help us God, Mary, Anna, St. Peter, Paul, Arnold, Stephan, Simon, 1509."[2]

The name of the Lord Jesus Christ does not appear.

When Procopius, the first of the martyrs of Palestine in the Diocletian persecution, was urged by Judge Flavian to sacrifice to the gods, he replied that there was but one God to whom he was willing to sacrifice, the Maker and Creator of all things. On being told that he should at least sacrifice to the four Emperors, he quoted a verse of Homer: "It is not good that there should be many lords. There is one Lord, one King."[3] As Augustine had twitted the pagan worshippers with their thirty thousand gods and goddesses, so the Reformers charged the Romanists with worshipping thousands of saints.

In the monastery, Monk Martin selected twenty-one of these for his special intercessors, three for each day in the week. Later, in expounding the first commandment, Luther complains that when one has a toothache he fasts in honor of St. Apollonia, that he turns to St. Lawrence as his patron saint against perils of fire, pays his vows to St. Sebastian when he fears the pestilence, or even covenants with Satan to give him abundance of wealth. "All these fix their trust elsewhere than in the true God. They look to Him for no favors, they seek nothing from Him."[4]

---

2. T. M. Lindsay, *A History of the Reformation*, I, 136.

3. Eusebius, *Martyrs of Palestine*, Ch. 1.

4. *Dr. Martin Luther's Large Catechism*, p. 4. For current examples, the personal column of *The New Orleans States and Items*, Friday, August 7, 1959, has expressions of thanks to "St. Anthony," "to the Blessed Mother," "to Almighty God, Blessed Mother, Sacred Heart, and Jesus Christ" for answered prayers.

In the place that should have been filled by the one Mediator between God and man, the Man Christ Jesus, there had grown up a network of objects of worship reaching from earth to heaven. There were *holy places,* such as the Holy Sepulcher, the Holy City of Rome, the Castle Church in Wittenberg, the altar in each church built over the tombs or the bones of martyrs. There were *holy things,* such as the relics of the saints, the holy lance, the holy ladder, the sacraments which continued and were the causes of the grace they signified,[5] and the indulgences granted for contributing to or devoutly visiting the holy places and contemplating the holy things. There were pictures and statues, some endued with special sanctity. There were *holy persons,* martyrs and saints, doctors of the Church and scholastics, priests, monks, bishops, archbishops and cardinals, the holy family with Joseph and Anna and the ever-virgin Mary who reigned in heaven as did the Pope on earth.

If one approaches the period from the side of Noyon, France, then "in truth, what an epoch was this in which the most wise were cultivating astrology, the most pious were adoring relics, and in which the Church, striking blows with anathemas and blows with fists upon the subject of the beard of Monsignor de Hangest and the pretended bones of St. Eloi, confided its benefices to children of twelve years and trafficked with a chaplaincy as one trafficks today a title of rent or an obligation to the bearer!"[6]

This vast, ecclesiastical structure that screened man from God had, moreover, become legalized, externalized and secularized by the early sixteenth century. When the Church should have spoken of God, she talked "so loudly of rights and claims, of war and money, that the Gospel was stiffled."[7] The curia was concerned for sordid ends, and the Renaissance was busy with classical antiquity. "By the rankest simony" the College of Cardinals elected Rodrigo Borgia as Pope, knowing that he was a cardinal living in concubinage, with several recognized children.[8] This Pope, Alexander VI, devoted his energies to carving from the patrimony of the Church estates for his children, and crushed Savonarola, the great Italian voice that

5. So Hugo of St. Victor and Peter Lombard. See A. Michel in *Dictionnaire de Theologie Catholique,* XIV, I, 577; cf. 496-497.

6. E. Doumergue, *Jean Calvin, L'Enfance,* I, 45; cf. 17-20, 39-40.

7. J. C. Wand, *A History of the Modern Church,* p. 11.

8. J. Paquier, in *Dictionnaire de Theologique Catholique,* I, 724-727; L. Pastor, *History of the Popes,* V, 362f., 385.

was calling men to fear God. Indeed, secularization went so far that Alexander VI allied himself with the unbelieving Turk against the "most Christian King of France," and he did so when Charles VIII professed to be embarking on an expedition that included the Crown of Jerusalem and a crusade for its recovery.

Julius II was highly successful in taking the territories unified by Caesar Borgia back into the estates of the Church. After the death of this "warrior pope," Erasmus wrote the satire *Julius Excluded from Heaven.* Leo X and Clement VII were patrons of the Renaissance and adepts in Medicean diplomacy. This absorption in politics and family interest deflected Clement from his early concern for church reform, and indeed from the spiritual task of the papacy.[9]

Even among religious people, most were obsessed with man's merits, man's heart contemplation, man's logical formulations. By her three ladders of moralistic piety, rational scholasticism, and ecstatic mysticism, the mediaeval Church called man to climb up to God. He must mount up to God either by the way of merit known as practical piety, or by the *anagoge* of mysticism, or by the *analogia entis* of speculative thought.[10] Scotus reasoned that since by nature man loves himself, a lower good, still more by his natural powers is he able to love God. With his fancied ability he is to grip his will and make himself love God with all. The later nominalists taught Luther that by his natural powers he was able to make a pure act of love to God, and thus merit the grace of congruity. Even the doctrine of a gift coming down from God sometimes found in the Eucharist, and thankful expressions for grace in the home life were not sufficient to counteract the anthropocentricity of this *eros* piety.[11] The altar and the mass speak of a sacrifice offered to propitiate God; the table and the supper testify first of God's gift to us, that is, of Christ the bread of life. In Luther's childhood and youth he heard many sermons on sin, law, duty, merit, fear, penance, but he found no Gospel in any of them. Over against all these efforts of man to raise himself up to God and have fellowship with the Most High in His holiness, the Reformation proclaimed the mercy of the Almighty who came all the way down to the Cross of Christ that He might

9. L. Pastor, *op. cit.,* X, 327-381.
10. A. Nygren, *Agape and Eros,* pp. 700-708.
11. T. M. Lindsay, *op. cit.,* I, 126.

have fellowship with us here where we are — in our sin and need and misery — and make us partakers of His victory over sin and hell, over death and the grave.

Scholasticism began with Anselm's assurance that he could prove the Christian faith by necessary reason. Thomas sought to construct a veritable Gothic cathedral of thought that would reconcile Aristotle and Augustine at least by probable reason. But Scotus and Occam with the later nominalists gave up the confidence that man could prove the faith by reason, so that scholasticism fell back on the acceptance of the faith by ecclesiastical positivism. The works of the later great schoolmen, Occam and Biel, were also cathedrals of human thought; but the dissensions between their disciples invited the mockery of the humanists. Amid this war of words the simple Gospel was obscured. When Luther got to Rome, he found priests officiating at the mass in flippant haste, their faith undermined by Renaissance skepticism. Into the vacuum left by bickering scholastics and pagan humanists, the living God came; and He did so by speaking to and through the Reformers.

The Renaissance turns on man; the Reformation exalts God. The Renaissance was a rediscovery of man, and the proclamation of the human god as the object of its concern. The Greek motto "Know thyself" and the Latin adage "I am a man and nothing that is true to man is alien to me" came again into their own. While ancient Platonism found the center of gravity in the Ideas, or the divine world above, the Platonic Academy which gathered about Marsilio Ficino in Florence sang the praises of empirical, earthly man. Glorying in the divine nature of the human soul, Ficino set it forth as the rival of God in arts and government, as lord over the four elements, as God's representative, yes, as God upon earth.[12] The humanist asks, How can the great I know that God exists? Sometimes he speaks as though he were conferring an inestimable favor on the universe, when so important a person as himself admits that perhaps God is personal. The agonized Reformer cries, How can I know that God, who unquestionably exists, is gracious to me, the sinner?

Likewise, Italian art turned from the glory of the gracious God to the beauty of the human body. "Titian's *Virgin Received into Heaven,* soaring midway between the archangel who descends to crown her and the apostles who yearn to follow her,

12. A. Nygren, *op. cit.,* pp. 688, 675.

is far less a Madonna Assunta than the apotheosis of humanity conceived as a radiant mother. Throughout the picture there is nothing ascetic, nothing mystic, nothing devotional."[13]

This turn from God to man during the Renaissance is illustrated by John Ruskin in his *Stones of Venice*. Of the façades on the Ducal Palace in Venice, he writes:

> The point I have here to notice is in the copy of the ninth capital which was decorated with the figures of the eight Virtues — Faith, Hope, Charity, Justice, Temperance, Prudence, Humility (the Venetian antiquaries call it Humanity!), and Fortitude. The Virtues of the fourteenth century are somewhat hard-featured; with vivid and living expression, and plain everyday clothes of the time. Charity has her lap full of apples (perhaps loaves), and is giving one to a little child, who stretches his arm for it across a gap in the leafage of the capital. Fortitude tears open a lion's jaws; Faith lays her hand on her breast, as she beholds the Cross; and Hope is praying, while above her a hand is seen emerging from sunbeams — the hand of God (according to that of Revelation, "The Lord God giveth them light"); and the inscription above is *"Spes optima in Deo."*
>
> This design, then, is rudely and with imperfect chiselling imitated by the fifteenth century workman: The Virtues have lost their hard features and living expression; they have now all got Roman noses, and have had their hair curled. Their actions and emblems are, however, preserved until we come to Hope: she is still praying, but she is praying to the sun only: *The hand of God is gone.*[14]

2. The Rediscovery of God

To Columbus's discovery of a new continent, to Copernicus's finding of a new center for the universe, and to Gutenberg's new communication by printing, the Reformation added the rediscovery of God.

As the Renaissance was man-centered, so the Reformation was God-centered. It was a flight from the clever ground of man to the surer ground of God, from man's works to God's deeds.[15] This flight took place as God dealt with Luther by His Word and in His spiritual presence.

Yet when God broke through the cloud of ecclesiasticism, humanism, and worldliness by making Himself known to Martin Luther, He was pleased to use the fruit of some of the Renais-

13. J. A. Symonds, *The Renaissance* in *The Great Events by Famous Historians*, VII, 122.

14. John Ruskin, *The Stones of Venice*, I, pp. 30-31.

15. L. Pinomaa, "Die Heilung bei Luther," *Theologische Zeitschrift*, Jan.-Feb., 1954, pp. 42-50.

sance scholarship as tools for His grace. With Erasmus there came a turn from good letters to sacred letters. Luther used Reuchlin's translation of the penitential Psalms and LeFevre's commentary on the Psalms, *Quincuplex Psalterium*. He compared the ancient languages to the sheath of the sword of the Spirit, while Melanchthon called them the swaddling-clothes of the Christ-child. Zwingli copied Erasmus's Greek New Testament, and Thomas Bilney was converted by reading it at Cambridge. At Bourges, Paris, and Orleans, Calvin studied the classics so well that his commentary on Seneca's *De Clementia* refers to fifty-six Latin and twenty-two Greek works. John Colet made the Epistles of Paul a personal message to the English students and inspired William Tyndale to translate the Bible into English. LeFevre translated the New Testament into French, and taught Guillaume Farel that salvation was all of grace, and that faith alone was sufficient in the case of the dying thief. Moreover, the earliest presses in Germany printed far more editions of the Bible and portions thereof in the vernacular than in the language of the classics. As a result, the common man had the Word of God in his hand. God did not set aside human learning, but as earnest scholars wrought with the rediscovered New Testament, God wrestled with them — with Luther, with Zwingli, with Calvin, with Bilney, with Tyndale, with Berquin, and with Knox. The result was the Reformation.

The Augustinian vicar general, Johann von Staupitz, commissioned Luther to take his own chair and teach Bible in the University of Wittenberg. As the monk, torn by a sense of sin and anguish, wrestled with the Word of God, the living God spoke to him. Luther's inner personal experience cannot be separated from his theological and Biblical studies. His 1515-16 commentary on Romans is saturated with Bible references. As he studied the Psalms, such as the twenty-second, the thirty-first, the thirty-second, and the seventy-first in the light of Romans, help came. Romans 1:16-18a was long a stone of stumbling and a rock of offense, but when the Holy Ghost opened to Luther the depths of that passage, it became to him the gate to paradise — the door into God's grace and Christ's peace.

> For I am not ashamed of the Gospel, for it is the power of God unto salvation to every one who believes ... for in it the righteousness of God [*justitia Dei*] is revealed through faith for faith. As it is written, the one who is just through faith shall live. For the

wrath of God is being continually revealed from heaven upon all ungodliness and unrighteousness of men.

The central thought was the righteousness of God, or as Luther's Latin read, *justitia Dei.* When Luther read *for the justice of God is revealed* in the light of its parallelism, *for the wrath of God is revealed,* or verse 17 in the light of verse 18, it struck terror to his agonized soul. Later he was enabled to see that this justice or righteousness of God becomes ours through faith, and mercy poured through the asperities of wrath; that is, Luther read verse 17a in the light of verse 17b: this *justitia Dei* is revealed for faith; yes, the man who is justified through faith shall live. Accordingly, faith is the sign of the new age of grace and mercy reigning in us through Jesus Christ, for the Gospel is the *power* of God unto salvation. That is, he finally read the *justitia Dei* in the light of verse 16 (cf. Rom. 15:13, 19), and found the Gospel not the mere presentation of an idea but the operation of a power. When the Gospel is preached, something occurs; God justifies the ungodly. Thus Romans 1:16-18 gives us the main heads of discourse, or the fundamental revelation of the one only, living and true God as He revealed Himself to Paul and to Luther: first, God in His wrath and judgment; secondly, God in His grace and mercy; thirdly, God in His power and saving action.[16]

First, then, God manifested Himself to Luther as the holy and just God. As God spoke from His Word, Luther came to a higher conception of the majesty and holiness of God and to a more serious view of the inability and unworthiness of man than prevailed in the Church of his day.

Easy accounts of penance gave no peace to the soul of this serious student. Seeing young lads made old by their Carthusian austerities, and noticing Prince William of Anhalt worn by fastings and vigils to skin and bone and carrying the beggar's sack like a donkey, Luther doubted whether he could do enough to win a gracious God unless he, too, became a monk. The vow and the rule of the monk were preached as the ark of salvation. His hold on the things of this life was shaken by the death of two friends and by the accidental cutting of an artery with a copious loss of blood. Then, while he was returning to the University of Erfurt, suddenly lightening struck him to the ground, and in fear of impending doom he cried out, "Hold, St. Anna, I will become a monk."

16. O. Michel, *Der Brief an die Römer,* pp. 49-50.

In the monastery, Luther was given a little red Latin Bible from which he learned the Psalms used in divine worship and other portions of the Scriptures. Ever and again he turned to his dear Paul. But as often as he did, these words of Romans confronted him:

> For therein is revealed the righteousness of God . . . for the wrath of God is being continually revealed from heaven against all ungodliness and unrighteousness of men . . . for God shall judge the secrets of men according to my Gospel by Jesus Christ.[17]

The more Luther studied Romans, the sharper became his terror. Here it was not only that God's justice condemned him for original sin and for breaches of the Ten Commandments. It was that even the Gospel included the wrath to come. Through the Gospel which God Himself has revealed from heaven, one knows that the wrath of God is over him, that before God all are in sin.[18] By means of the accusations of the law, the Gospel brings man under the Divine judgment. In this sense, Romans 1:18-32, 2:1-16 and 17-29 are necessary for the true understanding of Romans 1:17, 3:21-31, and 5:9.[19] The proclamation of the Cross is only understandable when the judgment of God which lies on man is taken in all seriousness.

Even later when Luther had learned to begin with the Gospel, he included the exhibition of the eschatological wrath of God in his preaching of the Gospel. Though the law and the wrath it entails be God's strange work (cf. Isa. 28:21), yet is it His work that has a part in bringing us to salvation. Accordingly, the painful way in which God was leading Luther was the way to the correct understanding of Paul's Gospel.[20] For the time, he was led as a horse with blinders over his eyes.

The wrath of God beset him behind and before; it was set against him uniquely with an awfulness that made of a wisp of straw an intolerable burden. Panic invaded his spirit; a nightmare gripped his soul. Before the anguished conscience of the monk, God lifted Himself in His holiness, His majesty, His justice and His wrath. Luther saw God as the One who rewards

17. H. Kraemer, *Religion and the Christian Faith*, pp. 286-293.

18. Luther, *Commentary on Psalms*, 1513-16; *W.A.*, iii, 174; cf. *W.A.*, 56, 10-11.

19. O. Michel, *op. cit.*, pp. 49-50.

20. John von Rohr, *Journal of Bible and Religion*, Jan. 1951.

the good and who punishes the wicked. His comments on the Psalms, 1513-16, are saturated with the sense of the wrath of God. Even the Lord Jesus appeared as the Judge coming on the clouds of heaven, the One to be feared as a jailor and a hangman.[21] Luther's conscience smote him with the realization of sin and its due desert. It was not that God was absent. He was present and had called the monk before Him as truly as He called Adam and Eve from their hiding place. Before Martin's anguished conscience, God established Himself in His majesty and holiness that can make a dried leaf the terror of an army (cf. Lev. 26:36). When God appears in His sovereignty, sin is unmasked as rebellion against Him. God is here; there is no hiding place from Him; and *coram Deo* man is conscious of nothing but his sin.

Sin is our own personal guilt in the face of the reality of God. God is angry with the wicked, and Luther knew in the depths of his soul that he was evil. He rebelled against the revelation of the wrath of God. At times he hated God. Yet nominalist theology taught him that in order to be saved he must have a *habitus* of love for God ever burning in his soul. Even Thomas Aquinas speaks of an ability to love God naturally of ourselves, and that without the presupposition of faith or of the hope of future blessedness.[22] Accordingly, Luther tortured his soul to get and keep this love. He tried to grip his will and make himself love God with all, but he could not.

Brother Martin kept the Augustinian rules with a zeal that won for his monastery acclaim for his scrupulosity. He went to confession, racking his memory to bring up every possible sin. At times he confessed for six hours, using the seven deadly sins and the Ten Commandments to bring each to light. But after such an ordeal, Luther would find that his memory had played him tricks and that he had not confessed all his sins.

Moreover, the form of absolution then used in the Augustinian order made forgiveness dependent on the adequacy of the contrition and the confession of the sinner. It ran, "I absolve thee from thy sins through the merits of our Lord Jesus Christ, for the sake of the contrition of thy heart, the confession of thy mouth, and the intercession of the saints." As

21. *Ibid.*
22. *Summa Theologicae*, II, 1 qu. 65, art. 5, 1.

Luther later came to see, "the condition was the cause of all calamity."[23]

When he was ordained and old Hans Luther returned to offer a handsome gift at his son's first mass, the young priest became stupefied and terror-stricken at the task of offering the sacrifice to the Divine Majesty of the Most High. "I am dust and ashes. I am full of sin. And I am speaking to the living, the eternal, the true God."[24]

In the presence of God, he knew himself a sinner; and the wrath of God gave his conscience no rest. At that time, the text did not seem to read, "If God be for us who can be against us?"; but rather, "If God be against us who can be for us?" The wrath of the eternal God was against him, and apparently against him alone. Before God he stood in the open with a full sense of his guilt and shame. At that moment, sin was the first, the last, the deepest and truest expression of his whole being.[25] Later, as a preacher, Luther sought to arouse the consciences of men to the multiple sins from which they supposed themselves free, to magnify sin as its gravity merits, to impress it upon his hearers in order to teach them that they need Christ and His righteousness to be free from sin. How unutterably great our sin must be if such a miracle — the sacrificial death of Christ — is necessary to save us. We are helpless and undone before the Holy One against whom we have sinned; and yet it is only the mercy and the might of that same God which can help.

At times Luther was carried by the nominalistic emphasis on the will to a sense of an arbitrary God, and then the concept of God added to the fears aroused by his own condition. At other times the *justitia Dei* took on the colors of the Hellenistic picture of justice, a blind discarnate principle such as he had presented in his lectures on Aristotle's ethics. Like the iron necessity of fate, justice seemed to tower over God Himself and hold man as a helpless pawn in its fearsome grasp (cf. Acts 28:4).

About 1510, Luther went to Rome on business for his order. While there, he rushed like a crazy saint to every place in the Holy City where merit or indulgence was offered. To get the soul of his grandfather out of purgatory, he climbed the *Scala*

23. U. Saarnivaara, *Luther Discovers the Gospel*, pp. 27-28.
24. Cited by R. Bainton, *Here I Stand*, p. 41.
25. E. Thurneysen, *Das Wort Gottes und die Kirche*, p. 14.

Sancta, offering a Paternoster on every step. But when he got to the top a doubt intruded. "Who knows whether it is true after all?"

Similarly, the easy solution offered by scholastic theory and church praxis gave no peace to his agonized conscience. The sinner who felt no genuine sorrow of heart on account of his sin against God was assured by the later schoolmen that the Church's penance could change his mere "Judas' rue" into real compunction, and that absolution and indulgences could clear the slate for him. But this was to forget that "the sinner who is primarily concerned to escape penalties is hopeless. He must be consumed with horror before he can be saved."[26] Luther learned by the hard road of experience that "those whom God would heal, He first wounds; whom He would make alive, He first kills; whom He would save, He first damns. He brings them to despair in themselves."

The modern humanist Jean Paul Sartre writes, "There is no human nature, because there is no God to conceive it . . . . Man is nothing but what he makes out of himself." In diametrical opposition stands Luther's faith: "It is God's nature to make something out of nothing. Hence, he who has not yet become nothing, out of him God will not make anything."

The more spiritually Luther understood the law, the more profoundly he realized that it both kills and damns. It makes clear that in themselves even just and pious men are before God's judgment most vile sinners. The mature Luther realized that, apart from Christ, no human righteousness can survive God's judgment, but that every man in himself is already judged with Satan and condemned as guilty of eternal hell. Man in himself is totally a sinner before God.[27] The whole weight of the Gospel of Romans 1:16-17 rests upon the *for* of verse 18: *for* God reveals His wrath against all unrighteousness and ungodliness of men. He is continually revealing from heaven that we are all sinners in His sight. Accordingly, the one who is justified is the one who believes that God's wrath is being poured over him. And whoever thinks that he can smile at the wrath of God will never praise Him eternally for the wonders of His grace. It is the man who condemns himself that justifies God, because like Job (42:6-7), David (Ps. 51:4), Paul (Rom. 3:4-23), he sentences himself in the same way

26. R. Bainton, *The Reformation of the Sixteenth Century,* p. 40.

27. F. E. Cranz, *Luther's Thought on Justice,* pp. 53, 57, 71, 79, 88 and 89, citing *W. A.,* IV, 699, 7, *passim.*

God does. Thus self-condemnation is the justification of God, but self-justification is the same as setting up our own judgment over or above the judgment of God (Isa. 40:27; Rom. 10:3). The confession of our unrighteousness commends the righteousness of God (Rom. 3:5). Our real righteousness, then, begins with the assertion of our own unrighteousness, for the righteousness of God is first experienced as the believer's penitent recognition of his own sinfulness (Ps. 51:17; Isa. 6:5, 57:15).

Thus, secondly, in and through the Gospel (Rom. 1:17, 3:22f.), *God revealed Himself to the tortured soul of Martin Luther as the God of forgiving grace, the Father of love and mercies.* After Martin, the monk, had tried by all the methods of monkery to do enough to make God gracious to him, Luther, the evangelical, was enabled to start with the fact that in Christ God was already reconciled and gracious to him. And thereafter, he needed only one thing to live by: the Gospel assurance of God's love and care.

Before developing this sequel, however, let us consider some of the helpers along Luther's way. There are evangelical opinions in the writings of Bernard of Clairvaux, for whom Jesus is honey in the mouth, melody in the ear, joy in the heart, so that any conversation which lacks His name is mere twaddle. Accordingly, Luther recognized that Bernard loved Jesus as much as any man can and preached Christ most excellently. According to Bernard, God assigns to man who has no righteousness of his own the righteousness of another (*justitia aliena*). In his *Discourse on the Annunciation* he says, "The testimony of the Holy Ghost in thy heart is this: *Thy sins are forgiven thee.*" Bernard found his final consolation not in his monkish mode of living, but in the promise of God not to despise a contrite and a broken heart.

In the notes on Romans, 1515-16, Luther cites Augustine, whose newly printed works were making his "the loudest voice" in the sixteenth century. For Augustine, as for Luther, Christ as man was the way to Christ as God. God broke the chains of Augustine's self-will through His word in Romans 13:13-14, and thus Augustine's conversion prepared for Luther's. At the crucial moment, Augustine *On the Spirit and the Letter* reminded Luther of an enemy whom Christ stopped on the way to Damascus. Saul deserved to be cast out, but Jesus took him in. The raging inquisitor who had no righteousness of his own was given the righteousness of the Lord whom he was persecuting. Thus was Luther encouraged to trust in the righteousness with which God endues us when He justifies.[28]

Most and first of all it was Luther's vicar general, Johann von Staupitz, who proved a good director of souls. From his doubts about the will of God in predestination, and doubts suggested by the inadequacy of his own contrition in penance, Luther's eyes were turned by Staupitz to the wounds of Christ. "Behold the wounds of Christ and His blood which is shed for you. Out of it shines the predestination of God. For God had also predestined that His Son should suffer for sinners . . . . Find yourself there, and predestination will be inexpressibly sweet." When Luther was distraught at the hollowness of his own contrition of heart in the act of penance, particularly when the form of absolution used by his order was conditioned upon the contrition and confession of the penitent, Staupitz showed him that *penitentia* was not an act — do penance — but a change of mind or of heart to that of love for the God of all grace. And this change is brought about as the Holy Spirit reveals the graciousness of God's love in Christ to our hearts and fills them with gratitude and consecration. "The commands of God become sweet when we understand that they are to be read not only in books but in the wounds of the sweetest Saviour." Staupitz told Luther that the creed taught the forgiveness of sins and that it was his duty to believe it. Against his morbidness, the director suggested, "My son, God is not angry with you, you are angry with Him. Hope in His mercy." Staupitz so taught salvation by grace alone and so led sinners to put their trust solely in the crucified Saviour that Luther later described him as "my first father, who bore me in Christ."[29]

28. For evangelical phrases in *On the Spirit and the Letter* note: "The righteousness of God is not that by which He is righteous, but that wherewith He clothes man when He justifies the ungodly," 15 (ix). "So in the Psalm which our Apostle quotes in testimony of this same grace, we read 'Blessed is he to whom the Lord hath not imputed sin, nor is there deceit in his mouth . . . . Then he [the Apostle] goes on to speak of that clothing with the righteousness of faith, clothed wherewith we shall not be found naked," 31 (xvii). "Alternatively, we must suppose that 'shall be justified' here means 'shall be held just,' 'shall be accounted just'; as in the case of the lawyer in Luke of whom we read, 'and he, willing to justify himself . . .', that is, with a view of being held or accounted just," 45. *Augustine's Later Writings*, ed. John Burnaby, pp. 205, 219, 229. That this is not, however, the main emphasis in Augustine is shown by F. E. Cranz, *Luther's Thoughts on Justice*, p. 60; and U. Saarnivaara, *Luther Discovers the Gospel*, pp. 5-9.

29. Saarnivaara, *op. cit.*, pp. 19-34.

Luther used a fourfold exegesis in studying the Psalms. As he understood it, the first, or literal and historical, was applicable to Christ; the allegorical to the Church; the tropological to God's moral and spiritual work in the soul; and the anagogical to its eschatological fulfillment. As he studied Psalms 22 and 31 and applied these to Christ, the tempted monk found Christ entering into his suffering with him. From Psalms 22:2 and 42:3 Luther deduced the thought that Christ wept much at night. From God's mighty acts in His Son, Luther moved to the soul. From Jesus' faith struggling to hold on to God amid the darkness of Calvary the light fell upon Luther's anguish of spirit. Instead of an abstract consideration of the righteousness of God such as he had earlier presented in his lectures on Aristotle's ethics, he again found the wounds of Jesus.

Perhaps the evangelical change in Luther may be dated between the study of Psalm 31, "O Lord, deliver me in thy righteousness," and Psalm 32, "Blessed is the man to whom the Lord imputeth not iniquity" — as these Psalms were studied in the light of Romans.[30] Here occurs Luther's note, "Thy righteousness of faith by which we are justified in Thy Presence." When Psalm 32 is read in the light of Romans 1 through 4 it means that God justifies us when *we justify God in His words* which condemn us all as sinners. When I kept silence, in refusing to confess my sins to God, my bones waxed old. Day and night Thy hand was heavy upon me. I had put my judgment above God's and agony sank me into the depths of despondency — anguish — *Anfechtungen.* But when I confessed my sin unto Thee — when I accepted Thy judgment, when I condemned myself as a wicked, hell-deserving sinner, when I acknowledged myself as the chief of sinners, when I thanked God that Christ came into the world to save *sinners* — when I knew that Christ died for us *ungodly people* and that thus God justifies *the ungodly* — then this faith in Christ was accepted for righteousness. Not that one who considers himself humble is justified, but the man who in his eyes is worthy of damnation and rejection, he is justified.[31] That is, he is not justified by his humility, nor by his self-condemnation. What the justice of God requires of His creatures, what we sinners can never render of ourselves, that God in His mercy gives. This is nothing less than the righteousness of God which Christ

---

30. Lefevre, *Quincuplex Psalterium,* 1573, Second Edition, pp. 45-47.
31. R. Thiel, *Luther,* pp. 145-146; L. Pinomaa, *Der existentielle Character der Theologie Luthers,* pp. 136-144.

wrought out for us in His own life and death that God might be just and the justifier of all those who entrust themselves to Jesus Christ. Faith is the algebraic formula for laying aside all trust in self and placing one's trust wholly in Christ, His obedience, His atonement. The believer, like Abraham the father of the faithful (Rom. 4:20), is the one who gives God all the glory of saving the sinner.

Thus the Lord who after testing and trying the Canaanite woman had healed her daughter, brought the monk torn with anxieties through self-distrust to faith. In Romans 1:17 the key word is *faith*, which occurs three times. The righteousness of God is from faith for faith, as it is written, "The one just by faith is the one who shall live." Luther saw the connection between the righteousness or justice of God and "the just shall live by faith." The righteousness of God for me, the sinner, is faith in Christ.

> The justice of God revealed through the Gospel is that righteousness by which through sheer mercy God justifies us through faith. . . . Thereupon I felt myself to be reborn and to have gone through open doors into paradise itself. The whole of Scripture took on a new meaning. Whereas before the phrase "the justice of God" had filled me with hate, now it became to me inexpressibly sweet in greater love. So to me that place in Paul was the gate to paradise.[32]

Through this very concept of justice there burst the saving intervention of a merciful God, a work wrought in Jesus Christ and freely bestowed on sinners.

The analogy of other terms strengthened his assurance. The *opus Dei* is what God works in us; the *virtus Dei* is that by which God makes us strong; the *sapientia Dei* is what makes us wise. These are not cold attributes of God standing over against us to condemn. They and with them the *justitia Dei* are blessed gifts with which God endows His trusting people. The righteousness of God has a passive sense; it is God's gift imputed to me. That is, Luther discovered that righteousness is given in the Word of the Gospel through which Christ comes and gives Himself to men, so that man can lay hold upon Him in faith, as the ring lays hold upon the precious stone.[33] And God's action in justifying sinners is the revelation of His pure love and grace working in Christ Jesus for fallen man.

God who had spoken in majesty and justice now spoke in

32. *W. A.*, 54, 186.
33. Luther, *Commentary on Galatians*.

mercy and grace. God came to our help in Jesus Christ. No, monk Martin, you can never do enough to win a gracious God at the end of life's way. But little monk, you can begin with a gracious God. God has Himself acted in Jesus Christ to strike out your sin and guilt. The Judge upon the rainbow has become the derelict on the Cross. God has made peace through the blood of His Cross. God has made Him to be sin for you that you may be made the righteousness of God in Him. Not in some far-off timeless eternity, but here in our own history God has wrought out His own righteousness for us in the obedience of Christ, and freely gives it to us of His pure grace. The wrath of God is fused with His righteousness and mercy in the Cross of Christ, the pivot of our salvation. God set Him forth there as the propitiatory sacrifice by which we are redeemed. Being now justified by His blood, we shall be saved from the wrath of God through Him. The nail-pierced hand tears away the clouds that have veiled the Father's face and lifts the sense of guilt from the sinner's conscience. The faith which grasps the Son of God who loved me and gave Himself up for me brings me into the pure grace and overflowing love of the Father's heart. In the Cross of Christ Luther found the one thing he needed to live by: the certainty that God was gracious and merciful toward him.[34]

> The Almighty is the All-Merciful. "Like as a father pitieth his children, so the Lord. . . ." But how shall I know this? In Christ, only in Christ. In the Lord of life, born in the squalor of a cow stall and dying as a malefactor under the desertion and derision of men, crying unto God and receiving for answer only the trembling of the earth and the blinding of the sun, even by God forsaken, and in that hour taking to Himself and annihilating our iniquity, trampling down the hosts of hell, and disclosing within the wrath of the All-Terrible the love that will not let us go.[35]

Thirdly, the Reformation was a rediscovery of God in His saving power. It proclaimed "the power of God who saved us and called us with a holy calling, not according to our works, but according to His own purpose and grace that was given us in Christ Jesus." It was the Divine initiative that made Luther conscious of God's presence and led him *coram Deo* to self-accusation, to humility, to distrust of self, to faith in Christ. When Romans 1:16-18 was a stone of stumbling and a rock of offense, then, as Luther testifies, "the Holy Spirit revealed to

34. H. Boehmer, *On the Road to Reformation.*
35. Condensed from R. Bainton, *Here I Stand!*, pp. 63f.

me the meaning of that text in the Black Tower at Wittenberg."
"Luther's re-discovery of the true meaning of the oneness of
God's righteousness to salvation, man's righteousness through
faith, and God's wrath . . . was an act of God, of the Holy
Spirit."[36]

Thus, the Gospel is the power of God unto salvation. It is not
merely a proclamation of ideas, "but God's mighty work, the
power of God whereby He snatches the victim of sin and death
from its master and sets him in the new relation of righteousness and life." "It is not man's faith that gives the Gospel its
power; quite the contrary, it is the power of the Gospel that
makes it possible for one to believe."[37] Through the Gospel,
God exercises His power and creates faith in us and this faith is
the evidence that God is for us and has brought us into His
new age of grace. It is the sign of His saving power.

Luther's faith is set upon the living God who is ever active.
He sees Abraham with the knife drawn and Isaac with his
neck laid bare. If God had slept but for a moment, the fatal
blow had been struck. But the hand of God stayed the hand
of the heart-rent father. The Word of God was living and
moving and acting, "even while I slept or while I drank with
my friend Philip and with Amsdorf." Against Erasmus, Luther
complains, "You put God and the devil at a distance as if
they were spectators . . . . But God has not gone off to an
Ethiopian banquet." Luther's *De Servo Arbitrio* was "the
finest and most powerful *Soli Deo Gloria* to be sung in the
whole Reformation period."[38] When threats accumulate, Luther
calls for the Book and has Justus Jonas read, "God is our
refuge and strength, a very present help in trouble," until
this Psalm of refuge takes wings in the battle-hymn of the
Reformation:

> *A mighty fortress is our God,*
> *A bulwark never failing.*
>
> . . . . .
>
> *That Word they never can dismay*
> *However much they batter,*
> *For God Himself is in the fray*
> *And nothing else can matter.*
>
> . . . . .
>
> *For God will win the battle.*

36. H. Kraemer, *Religion and the Christian Faith*, p. 291.
37. A. Nygren, *Commentary on Romans*, pp. 67, 77, 78, 72.
38. Bishop Normann of Oslo, cited by G. Rupp, *The Righteousness of
God*, p. 283.

On the occasion of the papal bull *Exsurge Domine*, Luther wrote to Spalatin:

> Let there be a new and great conflagration, who can resist the counsel of God? Who knows whether these insensate men are not predestined by Him as the means of revealing the truth? . . . God alone is in this business. We are carried away by Him. We are led rather than lead. . . . This is God's war. . . . You ought to beware of thinking that Christ will achieve things in the earth quietly and softly, when you see that He fought with His own blood and afterwards all the martyrs.[39]

As he prepared himself to face the Diet of Worms, Luther was overheard praying:

> O God, do thou help me against all the wisdom of the world. Do this: Thou shouldst do this . . . Thou alone . . . for this is not my work, but Thine . . . the cause is Thine . . . and it is a righteous and eternal cause. O Lord, help me! Faithful and unchangeable God, in no man do I put my trust. It would be vain. All that is of man is uncertain; all that comes of man fails. . . . Act, then, O God. . . . Stand at my side, for the sake of Thy well-beloved Jesus Christ who is my defense, my shield, and my strong tower.[40]

In his last letter Luther wrote: "Let us see what God will do."

The other Reformers traveled in the same direction. For a time Zwingli walked with Erasmus, treating Christianity as merely the most perfect of the religions of mankind. But the living God who had revealed Himself to Moses as "I will be who I will be" took the initiative and brought Ulrich to Himself. By the mouth of prophet and apostle God spoke, confounding the wisdom of the world. Dragged down to the depths of the pit by the plague, Zwingli was saved body and soul by the grace of God alone. Then religion ceased to be for him merely a human concept; it became the call of the living God, "Adam, where art thou?"[41] Thereafter, Zwingli exalted the agency of God who alone saves against the paganism which reigned in the images, saints and ceremonies of the papal Church.

Calvin says that "while I trusted in ceremonies, I was far removed from any certain peace of conscience. For as often as I descended into myself, or raised my heart to Thee, such an extreme horror surprised me that neither purifications nor satisfactions could heal me." "In obedience to the will of

---

39. G. Rupp, *Luther's Progress to the Diet of Worms*, p. 81.

40. E. M. Plass, *What Luther Says*, III, 1107-1108; Merle D'Aubigne, *op. cit.*, VII, viii.

41. J. Courvoisier, *Zwingli*, pp. 57, 67.

my father, I applied myself to the pursuit of law. But God, by the secret guidance of His Providence, at length gave a different direction of my course. At first, I was too obstinately devoted to the superstitions of popery to be easily extricated from so profound an abyss of mire, until God by a sudden conversion subdued and brought my mind to a teachable frame, which was more hardened in such matters than might have been expected from one at my early period of life." When this occurred, "I condemned with tears and groans the fashion of my past life and entrusted myself to Thee."[42]

If Calvin has been understood as teaching that God is a God afar off, who reigns in some absentee fashion by letting the world roll on according to decrees made ages ago, he has been misinterpreted. The sovereignty of God means that God's hand is at the helm. In His living Presence, He is reigning and ruling now. God is *activissimus*. There is nothing for which Calvin has more detestation than the notion that God is otiose, or an idler in heaven. He feared nothing more than a "distant" Christ. The *Christ in us* of sanctification is to be distinguished but never separated from the *Christ for us* of justification. "So long as Christ remains apart from us, His whole work for the benefit of men is useless for us . . . . Our victory over the world is only possible because we are inserted into Christ through faith. We begin to live when we are incorporated with Him and lead one life with Him . . . . Christ shares His gifts with us one after another — step by step — in the measure in which we receive them by faith."[43] The God of Elijah, who fed His prophet day by day at the brook Cherith through the ministry of ravens, daily feeds His believing people with the bread of life.

At Cambridge, while the doctors of the schools were emphasizing *man's* part in the work of redemption, Thomas Bilney laid energetic stress on *God's* part. There Hugh Latimer was taught by God to know Him, until he, too, came to regard all trust in human strength as a relic of paganism.[44] John Bradford, another of these Reformers and martyrs, declares that justification is God's work, in which we are only patients and not

---

42. Calvin, *Opera* V, 412-413; *Preface to Psalms; Reply to Sadolet;* Doumergue, *op. cit.,* I, 349-350.

43. W. Kolfhaus, *Vom Christlichen Leben nach J. Calvin,* pp. 97-98.

44. M. D'Aubigne, *History of the Reformation,* Bk. xviii, ch, ix. Cf. the boast of haughty Ajax, "Without the help of God, I can fight; and I will get the victory with my own strength." Sophocles, *Ajax,* 783.

agents. "For as to our first birth we bring nothing, so do we bring nothing that can help to our justification." From his death bed at Cambridge in 1551, Martin Bucer cried, "He reigns, He governs all." Under Elizabeth, *The Decades* of Henry Bullinger made the Church of England conscious of the grace of God working in the lives of believers.[45]

The Evangelicals have continued to recognize the hand of God acting directly in the salvation of His people. In His *Autobiography,* Thomas Halyburton gives the following account of his own conversion:

> I was at secret prayer, in very great extremity, not far from despair, when the Lord seasonably stepped in and gave a merciful turn to affairs. When I said there was none to help, then His arm brought salvation. God who commanded the light to shine out of darkness shined into my mind to give the light of the knowledge of the glory of God in the face of Jesus Christ. That which afforded me relief was a discovery of the Lord manifested in His Word . . . But it was not the Bible alone that conveyed the discovery for most of these passages whereby I was relieved I had formerly thought upon, without finding any relief in them. But now the Lord shined into my mind by them . . . and in His light I saw light.

John Wesley's account of his experience includes magnificent passives which recognize the act of God warming the evangelist's heart and giving him that assurance of salvation for which he had long sought:

> I went . . . where one was reading Luther's preface to the Epistle to the Romans. About a quarter before nine, while he was describing the change which God works in the heart through faith in Christ, I felt my heart strangely warmed. I felt I did trust in Christ, Christ alone, for salvation; and an assurance was given me that He had taken away my sins, even mine, and saved me from the law of sin and death.[46]

Thereafter, God mightily used John Wesley to offer Jesus Christ to men. And it is gloriously true that God is pleased to use even our hands in His service, after Christ has first met us and made us His own.

In this gracious encounter with us today, the "risen conquering Son" is pleased to use the testimony of His servants even as he used the martyrdom of Stephen to stir the conscience of Saul and the prayers of Monica to move Augustine. And yet the saving action was the power of the Lord Christ. It

---

45. Bullinger, *The Fourth Decade, Of the Gospel of the Grace of God.*
46. *The Heart of John Wesley's Journal,* p. 43.

was only after the Saviour had met Saul and told him what
he "must do," Acts 9:3-6, that Paul was able to say, "I was not
disobedient unto the heavenly vision", Acts 26:19. The un-
created light which shone from the face of the Lord blinded
Saul of Tarsus and changed the persecutor into the Apostle.

In a score of places,[47] the primitive Christian literature sets
forth our Lord Jesus Christ *at the right hand of God.* That is,
He is risen, living, active, reigning in all the plenitude of
Divine power and sovereign majesty. May the Hand that
wrought in Luther, the Hand that lifted Calvin, the Hand
that used Knox to bring Scotland to Himself, and Wesley to
save England from rationalism, act in His living power in your
life and mine, in your ministry and mine, in the hearts and
lives, in the faith and worship, of your people and of mine.

And for Luther, the Reformer, the Hand of the Almighty
was no longer thought of as abstract arbitrariness. The nominalist theology had taught him the absolute and arbitrary will of
God, thus positing the dominion of bare power apart from the
wisdom, justice, and goodness of God. But in rediscovering
God, Luther found the gracious, loving Father whose saving
intervention in Jesus Christ makes His sovereign will the de-
light of those who trust Him. The gracious reign of the God
and Father of our Lord Jesus Christ is our joy. At His right
hand sits the Son of David; therefore, rejoice, for the Lord
God omnipotent reigns, King of kings and Lord of lords. Amen.

47. Rom. 8:34; I Cor. 15:25; Col. 3:1; Eph. 1:20; Hebr. 1:3, 8:1, 10:13;
I Peter 3:12; Acts 2:34, 5:31, 7:55; Rev. 3:21; Matt. 22:44, 26:64; Mark
12:36, 14:62, 16:19; Luke 20:42, 22:69; I Clem. 36:5; Barn. 12:10; James as
cited by Hegesippus, Eusebius, *H. E.,* II, 22-23.

CHAPTER THREE

THE GOSPEL OF THE REFORMATION

Christ All-Sufficient

IN THE OLDEST CEMETERY IN CHARLOTTE there is a flat stone with two inscriptions upon it covering the grave of an Irishman. The head inscription in Latin asserts that the Cross of Christ is our only hope. If that were the only inscription upon the slab, and if that wholly and fully represented the Irishman's Church, a reformation of that Church would never have been needed. But at the foot of the stone there is another inscription which limits and changes the meaning of the first one. This other inscription, in English, states that it is a good thing to pray for the souls of the departed.

Thus the mediaeval Church wavered. With Anselm's *Cur Deus Homo* she taught dying men to put the Cross between themselves and their sins, and with John Gerson and Christoph von Utenheim she inculcated the motto *spes mea, crux Christi*. But the same Church undertook to supplement the Cross with penances, purgatory, masses, prayers to the saints, and the intercession of the Virgin Mary.

On the other hand, "the Reformation . . . was a deeper plunge into the meaning of the Gospel than even Augustine had made."[1] Luther found the Cross in the outskirts of the cathedral, often overshadowed by the statues of the Virgin, of Joseph, or of St. Anna. He replaced it in the center of the Church's Gospel and rested all his weight upon it. For the Reformers, "all Scripture teaches nothing but the Cross." Therefore, "glory be to the Man upon the Cross to all eternity!" "Christ alone — Christ all-sufficient for your soul."[2] "The commencement of salvation and the sum of Christianity is faith in Christ, who by His blood alone, and not by our works, has made atonement for sin and put an end to the dominion of death . . . . This faith

1. P. Schaff, *The Creeds of Christendom*, I, 204.
2. Luther on the Ten Commandments, 1516.

is a gift of God, that is created by the Holy Spirit in our hearts and not found by our labours."[3] "Only through the preaching of the Cross will a man find his way back to God as his Father."[4] "Having emerged from the depths of idolatry and superstition, we are borne to heaven in the chariot of the Cross, there by faith to apprehend the things that God has prepared for those who love Him."[5] "In His death, [Christ] is a sacrifice; in His resurrection, a conqueror; so is He in His ascension, a king; in making mediation and intercession, a high priest."[6] Luther's recognition of the revealing, reconciling, and redemptive reign of the crucified Christ was formally expressed by Calvin as the offices of Prophet, Priest, and King. The Cross is at the same time the school of the Prophet in which he teaches us the mystery of our salvation; the altar of the Priest in which He offers Himself in sacrifice to God; and the trophy of the King in which He triumphs over principalities and powers.[7]

The Gospel is the proclamation of an event and the invitation to an encounter.[8] On one occasion, Dr. John R. Mackay, an esteemed Scottish minister, said: "It seemed to me as I looked into my own heart that I could see nothing there but darkness, guilt, and pride. But then I remembered that Christ is a Prophet who can dispel my darkness, Christ is a Priest who can absolve my guilt, Christ is a King who can humble my pride. And I said, it were good that Christ and I should meet." The Gospel of the Reformation is the declaration of that event by which God became man and did for us what we could not do for ourselves and what we cannot do without. And it is a clarion call to an encounter with Him as our Prophet, our Priest, and our King.

1. Christ the All-Sufficient Prophet

First, then, let us meet Christ as our Prophet. Grace and truth came by Jesus Christ. He is the Word who lays bare in a human life the heart of the heavenly Father. For Luther, Christ himself is the key to the Scriptures, and there is enough of the revelation of God in the Cross of Christ to last a man all his life. Even when commenting on Genesis, Calvin bids

3. Luther to the Duke of Savoy, *W. A., Briefw.*, 3:150.
4. Calvin, *Inst.*, II, vi, 1.
5. Calvin, *Argument* to the *Commentary on Genesis*.
6. Luther, *Table Talk*, v. 82.
7. Francis Turretin, *Institutio Theologiae Elencticae*, 2, p. 428: XXIV, v. 13.
8. D. T. Niles, Address to Second Assembly, World Council of Churches.

the believer start, as does I Corinthians, "with the Gospel which sets Christ alone before us with his Cross."[9]

Protestantism is a down-to-earth religion, the religion of God who became man for us men and for our salvation. It has issued in an art that depicts the everyday life of the common man and reveals the hitherto unmeasured depths of the human heart. Its Rembrandt realism,[10] particularly as represented in his final picture, *Return of the Prodigal Son,* is distinct from the escapism of the Renaissance and the Jesuit baroque which lift us out of the actual world into the dreamland of fantasy. For Tillich, Protestantism means that we do not have to cover up anything, but we are to look at the human situation in the depths of estrangement and despair.[11]

We cannot build a tower of Babel that reaches up to heaven either with our works or with our ingenuity. The infinite majesty of God is too great for our feeble comprehension, so that "apart from Christ all knowledge is a vast abyss that swallows up our thoughts."[12] That God has come down to us in Christ ought to teach us to find Him where He has come to us, that is, in the arms of the Virgin Mary, in the feed-box of the donkey, in the refugee camp in Egypt, in the leather apron of the Carpenter, in the Teacher of the beatitudes, in the agonies of Calvary, in the victory of the Resurrection, in His intercession at the right hand of God, and in His coming with the clouds of Divine glory.

Since the brightness of God's face is too much for our sin-clouded eyes, He has clothed Himself in the *veil* of human flesh. God stoops to our weakness, speaking to us as a mother to her prattling babe. That we might know Him, God has put His eternal truth in the human words of the Good Book: "Here you will find the swaddling clothes and the manger in which Christ lies . . . . Plain and poor are the swaddling clothes, but precious is the treasure *Christ* that lies in them."[13]

When our Lord was tempted of Satan, He Himself stayed on the written Word, answering every thrust of the adversary with

9. Calvin, *Argument* to the *Commentary on Genesis.*

10. This realism is saved, however, from the purely empirical and sordid by the lines of the original plan and the revelation of future glory to be wrought by the Master-Artist. Cf. A. Kuyper, "Calvinism and Art" in *Calvinism,* pp. 233-235, 250-253.

11. P. Tillich, "Existentialist Aspects of Modern Art, in *Christianity and Existentialists,* pp. 128f.

12. Calvin, *Commentary on I Peter,* 1:21.

13. Luther, *Vorrede auf das Alte Testament.*

"It is written." Rather than yield to the temptation to make the stones into bread, He answered that man shall not live by bread alone, but by every Word that proceeds out of the mouth of God. Thus, He identified Himself in a community of trust with us, who walk by faith not by sight, knowing not the day or the hour of His coming in glory. Luther found comfort in Psalm 31. The words of this Psalm on the lips of the Crucified assure me that, "because of His tribulation and humiliation Christ inclines Himself to me in my distress." Again, the Reformer insisted that Christ used Psalm 22 of Himself, rather than merely of the Church, in the agonizing cry, "My God, my [own] God, why hast Thou forsaken me?"[14] This suffering of Christ *with* us was the path by which Luther learned to appropriate His sufferings *for* us. In the supreme crisis of His ministry, Jesus clung to God in the words of Psalm 22, Psalm 31 and Isaiah 53. He placed His hope and trust in God as the mockery indicates (Matt. 27:43), and as the Epistle to the Hebrews teaches (2:13). For Calvin, "it was no mean specimen of Christ's incomparable love to us, to contend with horrible fear, and amid those dreadful torments to neglect all care of Himself that He might promote our benefit" (*Inst.*, II, xvi, 5).

Indeed, to give anything like a comprehensive statement of our response to the Biblical testimony, we need to develop not only the three offices which summarize the work of Christ, but as well the correlatives of each. As the Lamb of God, He was sacrifice as well as priest. As the Servant of the Lord, He was subject as well as king. As the One who was given the Spirit and who lived by every Word that came from the mouth of God, He was believer as truly as prophet who proclaimed that Word. He, the Master Teacher, was also the docile learner. "The Saviour, the Man Christ Jesus, is Himself the brightest illustration of predestination and grace."[15] "He offered up strong cryings and tears unto Him who was able to save Him from death and was heard for His godly fear; though He were a son, yet learned He obedience by the things which He suffered" (Heb. 5:7-8).

While Rome has, in effect, qualified her acceptance of Chalcedon by reasoning from the hypostatic union that Christ could not have failed to know the day of His return, and could not have walked by faith, since there was nothing Christ did

---

14. Luther, *Commentary on the Psalms*, W.A., 3, 69.
15. Calvin, *Inst.*, III, xxii, i.; Augustine, *De predest. sanct.*, I, xv.

not know,[16] the Reformers have taken the words of Scripture concerning our Lord's full humanity at their face value. In so doing they have drawn Christ deeply into the flesh and found solace for anguished souls in His descent into hell — with us and for us.[17] He who was in the form of God took the form of a slave, that in His lowly life of service for us we might see the heart of God. Therein He humbled Himself and became obedient unto death, yea the death of the Cross, that by the obedience of the One the many might be saved. Our faith rests on His faithfulness. God in Christ is the perpetual object of Christian faith; but it is also true that in His human life and death our Lord walked by faith, leaving us an example that we should follow in His steps.

Luther compares Christ to a master craftsman or a great artist who teaches his apprentices. Sometimes he takes up their work, shows them the defects and chides them for their errors — as God does by His law. Sometimes he brings into the shop something of his own superb workmanship and puts it beside their bungling efforts — as God does in Christ's example. Best of all, he gives his own skill away, teaching the novices the tricks of the trade and his own skilled mysteries until they possess the perfection of the craft. So God in Christ has taken us into His eschatological plan of salvation by which He will make us workmen like our Master.[18]

God has put Himself into the stream of our own life, in the events of human history. He is in the mask of the manger, in the marred visage of the Crucified, in the blessed words of forgiveness that reach us through preaching, baptism and the Lord's Supper. Thus, God speaks to us through the proclamation of His Word, and seals us individually as His own in the sacraments.

The Pharisees murmured: This man receives sinners and eats with them the eschatological meal. Jesus answered with the parables of the lost sheep, the lost coin, and the prodigal son and his elder brother, across which one could write our Lord's Johannine word: he that has seen Me has seen the Father. Take God as He comes in the humiliated Christ and you will know

16. Thomas Aquinas, *Summa*, IV, 7, 8; cf. IV, 6, 8.

17. Luther, *W.A.*, 7, 450, 14: "I find indeed, according to the Scripture, that Christ, Abraham, Jacob, Moses, Job, David, Ezekiel and many others have experienced hell in this life."

18. Luther, *W. A.*, 56, 220-222; G. Rupp, *The Righteousness of God*, p. 181; cf. Belgic Confession, Art., 13.

Him as your forgiving heavenly Father. God tells the truth and God says He forgives my sins because Christ died for me. As the Holy Spirit enables me to put these simple affirmations together He bears witness with my spirit that God is my forgiving Father and I am His restored child.

The Apostle who began with Christ and Him crucified tells us that the *foundation* is laid, namely, Jesus Christ; no man can lay any other (I Cor. 3:11). While the scholastic theology begins with nature and brings in grace only to complete what nature has begun, the Reformation begins with grace and looks to God in Christ as the continual object of faith. Christ is not merely the second story built on Aristotelian foundations. He is the foundation, and the foundation always determines the lines of a structure. In Protestant thinking we begin where the light is brightest, and that means the light of the knowledge of the glory of God as it shines in the face of Jesus Christ. We begin intellectually where God has graciously placed us, that is, in Christ Jesus, who is made unto us wisdom from God. We would not pour the new wine of the Gospel into the old wineskins of either Greek or German idealism, nor sew the new skin of Christ's righteousness upon the worn-out rags of either Judaistic or medieval legalism.

For Luther, the ground on which we know ourselves and the law is the Gospel of the grace of God in Christ Jesus. "One who is saved and can only be saved in the person of another, he evidently is, in his own person, a lost man. Only in that positive belief will this negative knowledge come to pass. On the other hand it is not possible that in this belief, there shall not come to pass immediately and effectively the self-knowledge of man the sinner. The picture of the obedience of God's Son is the compulsion, no we prefer to say, the freeing to this self-knowledge."[19] Thus we begin with the grace and truth that are in Christ Jesus and read the Bible in the light that shines from His blessed countenance. Moreover, with the Reformation we put on the glasses of Scripture and read nature and our human nature with the light of God's covenant of grace falling upon it.

The Reformation answers the problem of knowledge thus: begin with Christ, read the Bible in the light of Christ, read all nature in the light of the Bible. Jesus Christ covers the whole face and heart of God, so that there are no dark spots

19. K. Barth, *Kirchliche Dogmatik*, IV/1, 458.

in the Almighty for which He does not go bail. He is God's heart laid bare, God's love made clear in a human life and a human death. Sinner, would you find the ladder that leads to God? It is the one by which He has come down to meet us where we live. Come and meet God in Jesus Christ. He is our Prophet who reveals to us, by His Word and Spirit, the will of God for our salvation. Meet God in Christ and your sins are forgiven you for His Name's sake.

A few years ago, a student with an unusually full philosophical training entered Columbia Theological Seminary. In the course of his studies he had tried to build an intellectual ladder up to heaven. The rungs in the structure were these: *If* certain things be true, *then* certain conclusions seem to follow. *If . . . then* were the steps by which one was to scale the parapets of glory. But Kierkegaard came with the reminder that one may not start with a finite premise and logically reason up to an infinite conclusion. Thus, even the *if . . . then* steps seemed to disintegrate. He was so skeptical that his presbytery hesitated about permitting him to attend the Seminary. In the study of the Reformers, however, he found God descending to him in Christ, God entering into our human history in the Word made flesh, God speaking to us in His Word and sacraments, confirmed by the inward witness of His Spirit. Accordingly, that student preached his faculty sermon on the theme, *The Faith of a Gambler, or the Faith of a Saint?* At its best the *if . . . then* ladder is but the faith of a gambler. Who knows whether it is true after all? But the faith that rests on Jesus Christ as the Holy Spirit opens our hearts to hear Him speaking in His Word and confirming the same by the sacraments that is the faith of a saint, the faith of assurance.

2. CHRIST THE ALL-SUFFICIENT PRIEST

Secondly, we may meet Christ as our Priest. We begin with a gracious God acting in the all-sufficiency of Christ as our priest. God is gracious to the sinner when He justifies the believer for Jesus' sake. "The salvation which is free to us," writes Luther, "cost Christ a dear price, who that he might purchase it for us was made under the law, and satisfied it for us both by life and also by death."[20] "For he might have satisfied for all the sins of the world by only one drop of his

20. Luther's *Works*, VII, pp. 281, 131, 132, 273, 272.

blood; but now has he shed it plentifully and has satisfied abundantly."[21] "His death not only signifies, but also accomplishes the remission of sins as a most sufficient satisfaction" (*satisfactio sufficientissima*).[22] "It is also impossible to separate our salvation, this article about justification before God through Christ, or satisfaction for sin, from the Person of Christ, who is God. For He alone, and no other, rendered eternal satisfaction for sin." "With His blood He rendered satisfaction for sin, death, and hell." And whoever believes in Him has rendered satisfaction through Christ alone.[23]

"By Christ does come unto us both satisfaction, which we owe to the justice of God, and the gift of salvation which we of ourselves can by no means merit." "Of His own will Christ made Himself subject to the punishment of the law for our sakes."[24] "The judgment which we deserved, He took upon Himself; He willingly suffered the punishment due unto us, making Himself subject to death and the curse, that is to eternal damnation not otherwise than if he had transgressed the whole law."[25] And He did this of no necessity, but of His great love toward us was made a curse for us. "God has sent His only begotten Son into the world, that we might live through Him. He was crucified for thee, and bore thy sins in His own body." This means that we should learn, in all our conflicts and terrors of conscience, "to turn our eyes wholly to the brazen serpent Jesus Christ crucified, and assuredly believe that He is our righteousness and life." For in the whole Gospel nothing else does Christ do but take us out of ourselves and put us under His wings "that we may trust wholly in His satisfaction and merit." As chickens are covered under the wings of the hen,

21. Luther, *On Galatians*, ed. P. Watson, p. 137.
22. Luther on Romans 4:25, *W.A.*, 56:296.
23. Luther on John 3:19, *Luther's Works*, 22, pp. 393, 392, 163f.
24. *Luther's Works*, VII, pp. 281, 131, 132, 273, 272.
25. Cf. Seeburg, *Dogmengeschichte*, IV, i, pp. 237f. Further citations from Luther in P. Watson, *Let God Be God*, p. 143, n. 114, pp. 124ff; and G. Rupp, *The Righteousness of God*, p. 157, citing T. Harnack and Pinomaa, and p. 146; also Luther's *Werke*, Weimar edition, 56:37, 38, 296, "God does not give grace freely in the sense that he will demand no satisfaction, but he gave Christ to be the satisfaction for us." In such places Luther teaches the "Latin" doctrine that the atonement is the satisfaction of Divine justice, even as he also elsewhere teaches the "classical" doctrine that it is the triumph over death, Satan and hell. T. Torrance, *Scottish Journal of Theology*, "The Atonement and the Oneness of the Church," VII, 3, p. 6, holds that we can only apply both the *anhypostasia* and the *enhypostasia* to Christ if we take both of these doctrines.

so we should shroud ourselves and our sin under the covering of the flesh of Christ, who is our pillar of cloud by day and our pillar of fire by night.[26] "Christ is the propitiation of God, who excuses our works and makes them possible to overlook, so that what is lacking in us, we supply by His fullness."[27]

Whence, then, is our defence? Nowhere save from Christ and in Christ. For if there shall come some reproach against the heart which believes in Christ, testifying against Him concerning some evil deed, then it turns away from itself, and turns to Christ (*ad Christum*) and says: But He made satisfaction. He is the Righteous One. This is my defence. He died for me, He made His righteousness to be mine, and made my sin to be His own. Because if He made my sin His own, then I can have it now no longer, and I am free. If, moreover, He has made His righteousness mine, I am righteous with the same righteousness as He is. But my sin cannot swallow Him up, but it is swallowed up in the infinite abyss of His righteousness, since He is God, blessed forever. And so, God is greater than our heart. Greater, infinitely greater, is the defender than the accuser. God is the defender, the heart is the accuser. What, is that the proportion? So, so, even so it is. "Who shall lay anything to the charge of God's Elect?" Nobody. Why? Because "it is Jesus Christ [who also is God] who died, nay rather, who is risen again." "If God be for us, then who can be against us?"[28]

The sacrifice of Jesus Christ is all-sufficient. It does not need to be supplemented with new sacrifices or masses, with purgatory, with penances, or with prayers for the dead. To us the Lord's Supper is neither a new sacrifice, nor a repetition of His one sacrifice. It is the sacrificial meal based on the one sacrifice made once for all by which God assures the believer that the sacrifice made by the Lamb of God on Calvary is sufficient to save him from sin, death and hell — and bring him to glory. Throwing ourselves wholly upon that one sacrifice we proclaim with the Apostle: "He was delivered up for our offenses and raised for our justification." "There is, therefore, no condemnation to those who are in Christ Jesus."

As in the Cross of Christ we have an all-sufficient sacrifice, so in His intercession we have an all-sufficient Priest. There is one God and one Mediator between God and men, the Man Christ Jesus (I Tim. 2:5). Whenever we sin we have an Advocate with the Father, Jesus Christ the Righteous, the

---

26. Luther, *On Galatians*, ed. P. Watson, pp. 131-132, 168, 225.
27. Luther on Job xlii, 8, *W.A.*, I, 370, 27.
28. *W. A.*, 56, 204, 14.

Propitiation for our sins (I John 2:1-2). He is able to save unto the uttermost all those who come unto God by Him, seeing He ever lives to make intercession for them (Heb. 7:25). No man knows the Father save the Son and He to whom the Son wills to reveal Him. Come unto Me, and ye shall find rest for your souls (Matt. 11:25-30).

> *Lo, the incarnate God ascended*
> *Pleads the merits of His blood;*
> *Venture on Him, venture wholly,*
> *Let no other trust intrude:*
> *None but Jesus can do the guilty sinner good.*

With Luther we cling to the righteousness by which Christ is well pleasing to God, intercedes for us as our Mediator, and gives Himself wholly to be our own as our High Priest and Protector. Jesus Christ is our Patron and our Priest, who is ever turning our sorrows into joy and leading us onward in His service. His intercessions are not insufficient. They do not need to be supplemented by the prayers of Mary or of the saints. They can be added to neither by pilgrimages to sacred places, nor by cherishing the bones of the martyrs, nor meditating before statues of the saints or imaginary pictures of Christ.

To pray in the Name of the Lord Jesus means to come to the Father, trusting in Christ's merits and looking to Him as our "mouth" to pray for us to the Most High (*Inst.*, III, xx, 21). Moreover, as invoking the Name of the Lord in the Old Testament meant God's presence with His people, so praying in the Name of Christ means our Lord's being with us. As Luther put it in his 1517 Exposition of the Seven Penitential Psalms, "Christ is God's grace, mercy, righteousness, strength, comfort, holiness, given to us by God quite apart from any merit" (of our own). Nor does this mean that Christ merely causes us to have righteousness while He Himself remains outside us. Such would be a dead righteousness. God gives us the righteousness of Christ only when Christ Himself is there, just as the brightness of the sun or the heat of the fire are never found where the sun and the fire are not.[29]

We proclaim the old, old story of Jesus and His love as historically true, but we cannot agree that the myth of the assumption of the body of the Virgin into heaven be turned into a Christian dogma.[30] We sing no Hail Marys; we rely

---

29. Luther, *Die sieben Busspsalmen,* I, 219, 30.
30. Cf. *Excursus on Mariolatry.*

not on her prayers for us either now or in the hour of death. We believe that He whom the Virgin bore is God, and that Mary's Greater Son has all the compassion and sympathy and sweetness which one associates with womanly virtue as well as all the strength and fortitude that goes with manly worth. Accordingly, we pray:

> *In the hour of trial,*
> *Jesus, plead for me,*
> *Lest by base denial*
> *I depart from Thee . . . .*
> *When my last hour cometh,*
> *Fraught with strife and pain,*
> *When my dust returneth*
> *To the dust again;*
> *On Thy truth relying,*
> *Through that mortal strife,*
> *Jesus, take me, dying,*
> *To eternal life.*

For, as Luther put it, except the living Christ stand at God's right hand and pour forth the Holy Spirit upon us continually, Satan would not allow a one of us to hold, for a single hour, to the Easter faith, or to our Christian confession.

3. CHRIST THE ALL-SUFFICIENT KING

Thirdly, the Gospel of the Reformation calls us to meet Christ, as our all-sufficient and ever-victorious King. In his Introduction to the New Testament, Luther reminds us that when David overcame the mighty Goliath, there was a shout of victory in Israel, and the ancient people of God were free and established in joy and peace. So the Gospel is the good news of the victory of our true David who has met and conquered sin, death and the devil. The glad tidings, proclaimed to the whole world by the Apostles, tell all those who were imprisoned in sin, plagued with death, overcome by the devil, that Christ has redeemed them without their merit, has justified them, made them alive and blessed. He has given them peace and brought them back to God, so that they sing, give thanks, praise God and are eternally glad as they remain fixed in this faith.

Christ is the Conqueror of the law, sin, and the devil; He reigns and rules over these so that they cannot hurt the believer.[31] His mighty victories are successively pictured in Luther's

---

31. Luther, *On Galatians*, ed. Watson, p. 138.

Commentary on Galatians, 3:13. **Thus,**

> Our most merciful Father, seeing us to be oppressed and over-
> whelmed with the curse of the law, and so holden under the
> same that we could never be delivered from it by our own power,
> sent His only Son into the world and laid on him the sins of all
> men, saying: Be thou Peter that denier; Paul that persecutor,
> blasphemer and cruel oppressor; David that adulterer; that sin-
> ner which did eat the apple in Paradise; that thief what hanged
> upon the cross; and briefly, be thou the person which has com-
> mitted the sins of all men; see therefore, that thou pay and satisfy
> for them . . . . So the law sets upon him and kills him. By this
> means is the whole world purged and cleansed from all sins, and
> so delivered from death and all evils. Now sin and death being
> abolished by this one man, God would see nothing else in the
> whole world, especially if it did believe, but a mere cleansing and
> righteousness. And if any remnants of sin should remain, yet for
> the light of that sun, Christ, God would not perceive them . . . .
> Therefore, feeling thy terrors and threatenings, O law, I plunge my
> conscience in the wounds, blood, death, resurrection and victory
> of Christ.
>
> If Christ be made guilty of all the sins that we have committed,
> then are we delivered utterly from all sins, not by ourselves, nor
> by our merits, but by Him . . . . Thanks be unto God who has
> given us the victory by our Lord Jesus Christ" . . . .
>
> Sin is a most mighty and cruel tyrant, ruling and reigning over
> the whole world, subduing and bringing all men into bondage . . .
> sin is a mighty and strong god, which devours all mankind, learned,
> unlearned, holy, mighty and wise men. This tyrant, I say, flies
> upon Christ, and will needs swallow Him up, as he does all other.
> But he sees not that He is a person of invincible and ever-lasting
> righteousness. Therefore, in this combat, sin must needs be van-
> quished and killed, and righteousness must overcome, live and
> reign. So in Christ all sin is vanquished, killed and buried, and
> righteousness remains a conqueror and reigns forever.[32]

Death is the king of terrors and the terror of kings. The
fear of death drove Luther into the monastery, and for him
death is the devil's henchman. The devil has raised a banner
on which is written, "I am a god and prince of this world, and
that it may be true, I have a fellow with me, death, who
devours the whole world."[33]

> In like manner death, which is an omnipotent queen and empress
> of the whole world, killing kings, princes and generally all men,
> does mightily encounter with life, thinking utterly to overcome it

32. *Ibid.,* pp. 272, 355.
33. Cited by Watson, *Let God Be God!* p. 145.

and swallow it up: and that which it goes about, it brings to pass indeed. But because life was immortal, therefore when it was overcome, yet did it overcome and get the victory, vanquishing and killing death . . . . Death, therefore, through Christ is vanquished and abolished throughout the whole world, so that it is now but a painted death, which, losing its sting, can no more hurt those that believe in Christ.

His death crucifies and swallows up my death.

So the curse, which is the wrath of God upon the whole world, has the like conflict with the blessing: that is to say, with grace and the eternal mercy of God in Christ. The curse, therefore, fights against the blessing and would condemn it and bring it to nought: but it cannot do so. For the blessing is divine and everlasting, and therefore the curse must needs give place. For if the blessing in Christ should be overcome, then should God Himself also be overcome. But this is impossible: therefore, Christ, the power of God, righteousness, blessing, grace, and life, overcomes and destroys these monsters, sin, death, and the curse, without war or weapons, in His own body, and in Himself . . . spoiling all principalities and powers, and triumphing over them in Himself . . . so that they cannot any more hurt those that believe."[34]

> *Both death and hell were stricken down*
> *When Thou didst for our sins atone,*
> *O Jesus, blessed Saviour.*[35]

In preaching the freedom of man from the thralldom of sin, Satan and death, the Reformation likewise proclaimed man's freedom from the exactions of men and the tyranny of a totalitarian church. In proclaiming justification by faith, Luther placed every man as man directly before God and made every believer, in his own conscience, a king with none over him save God in Christ. Thus the heteronomy of Rome was set aside not for the autonomy of man, but for the theonomy of the Lord Jesus. And the Reformation was not a revolt against authority, but a struggle for the scepter of Christ.[36]

As a sign thereof Luther replied to the efforts made to burn his books by hurling the canon law into the flames at Eyester Gate, Wittenberg, December 10, 1520. The lawyers stood aghast. Canon law had ruled Europe for a millennium. Luther likewise realized the import of what he had done. Returning to the classroom, he said to his students: You know what I have done.

---

34. Luther, *On Galatians*, ed. Watson, pp. 272-273, 162.
35. E. M. Carlson, *The Reinterpretation of Luther*, p. 65.
36. G. C. Berkouwer, "Reformation or Revolution," in *Modern Uncertainty and Christian Faith.*

If you follow me any longer it will mean martyrdom for you as for me. But you know the Gospel, and if you desert the Gospel, that means hell. The chips are down and the issue is: *martyrdom or hell.* Thus Luther took his stand with Isaiah who wrote, "The *Lord* is our Judge, the *Lord* is our King, the *Lord* is our Lawgiver; He will save us"; and with our Lord when He warned, "In vain do they worship Me, teaching for doctrines the commandments of men"; and with Peter, as he answered, "We must obey God rather than men." Following in the Reformer's train, the Scottish Covenanters gathered in 1638 under the blue banner with this inscription, *For Christ's Crown and Covenant.* Today one needs still to insist on a Church in which Christ is the sole King and the only Lawgiver in Zion. Freedom from ecclesiastical tyranny opened the door for political democracy and economic free enterprise. The human bulwarks against modern totalitarianism are the countries in which the evangelical churches flourish: Scandinavia, Great Britain, Holland, Switzerland, the United States, Australia, Canada.

Most of all, Christ has overcome our rebellious wills and made us His own. In *The Bondage of the Will* Luther shows how fallen man, though free in the things of earth, is fettered in reference to the things of God, by his own sinful affections. Then the Lord Jesus Christ, who died for our sins and rose for our justification, entered into the holy of holies and pleaded for our salvation. In answer to His intercession, the Father granted Him the might of the Spirit to break from our hearts the shackles of sin. "I believe that I cannot believe in or come to Jesus my Lord by my own wisdom or power, but the Holy Ghost calls me by the Gospel."[37] When the Spirit comes, He persuades and enables us to accept Jesus Christ as He is freely offered to us in the Gospel. Thus God delivers us from the thralldom of Satan and translates us into the Kingdom of the Son of His love. The Good Shepherd calls, and by the liberating grace of the Spirit, the sheep hear and respond. As man thus decides, he meets his responsibility and becomes really free.

> *My will is not my own*
> *Till Thou hast made it Thine;*
> *If it would reach a monarch's throne,*
> *It must its crown resign.*

The greatest good for man lies in serving God, who alone can make him truly free.

---

37. Luther's *Catechism.*

As Christ freed the soul from the bondage of Satan and the exactions of men and taught man moral responsibility by faith alone, so in love He bound the believer to the service of His brothers and released the dynamic of God for our social culture.[38] Indeed, justification through Christ alone and the purity of works are inseparably united. As long as one fancies that by his own good works he can adorn himself before God, the doing of these works has a selfish, perhaps even a mercenary, interest. Only when one stands before God justified by faith alone, can he work for his fellow man out of unselfish love for his neighbor. "Through emphasizing that justification occurs by faith alone, Luther wishes first to keep the God-relationship free from all thoughts of merit, and secondly to keep the relationship to the neighbor free from all religious selfishness . . . . Works are to be done here on earth with the neighbor as the only end. Therefore works must not be done by a person who veiledly pursues his own salvation, but they must be done by a person who already is saved, and who is certain of his own righteousness in Christ before God."[39] There is ever a Satanic hostile power tempting man to offer his own religiosity and moralism in order thereby to make himself righteous before, or establish a claim upon God; and in so doing, he unceasingly deprives the neighbor of those unselfish services which the neighbor needs and deprives Christ of the praise for justification which is due to Him alone.[40]

According to *The Liberty of a Christian Man*, the believer is the freest man of all and subject to none, and yet in love the Christian makes himself the servant of all. He follows the Saviour who came not to be served but to serve. He sets before himself the mind of Christ, who being in the form of God took the form of a slave, in order to serve us and give His life a ransom for us. All this Christ did to serve us. When God in His mercy and without any merit of mine has given me such unsearchable riches, shall I not then freely, joyously, wholeheartedly, without prompting, do everything I know will please Him? I will give myself as a sort of Christ to my neighbor as Christ gave Himself for me. I must even take to myself the sins of others, as Christ took mine to Himself. Thus we see that the Christian man lives not for himself, but to Christ and

38. Cf. Karl Holl, *Gesammelte Aufsätze z. K.g.*, I, Luther, 2, 473.
39. G. F. Wingren, "Justification by Faith" in *Scottish Journal of Theology*, 9:4:376-377.
40. *Ibid.*

to his neighbor. By faith he rises above himself to God and from God goes below himself in love and so remains always in God and in love.

Or, as it is pictured in Luther's *Little Prayer Book,* the whole of Christian truth is to be held in our hearts as if in two purses, namely, those of faith and love. "The purse of faith has two pockets. In one pocket is the faith or conviction that we are sinners, totally ruined and condemned by Adam's sin, Romans 5, Psalm 51. In the other pocket is the faith that we have all been redeemed through Jesus Christ from our ruined, sinful and damnable condition, Romans 5, John 3. The purse of love also has two pockets: in one is the faith that we must serve by doing good to everyone, as Christ did for us, Romans 13; in the other is the faith that we must gladly endure suffering and be patient."[41]

Christ truly reigns and triumphs in us, even when we are so weak we can scarcely groan. Then we have recourse afresh to the living Christ, and cry through him, "Abba, Father," so that the Holy Spirit helps our infirmities and assures our spirits that we are children of God. Although we are justified with the righteousness of Christ, this is never merely external to us. Rather, it is Christ's personal presence in the believer through faith and the Holy Spirit. "The popish school-divines dream that faith is a quality cleaving in the heart without Christ." But Luther insists, "Christ should be so set forth that you should see nothing beside him, and should think that nothing can be more near unto you, or more present within your heart than he is. For he sits not idly in heaven; but is present with us, working and living in us."[42]

Although we have only the first fruits of the Spirit, and sin still remains in us, yet are we nourished and cared for, as a sick patient by a good doctor, until we attain the fullness of the Spirit for Christ's sake. "We are that wounded man who fell into the hands of thieves, whose wounds the Good Samaritan bound up, pouring in oil and wine, and afterwards laying him upon his beast, he brought him into the inn, and made provision for him, saying to the host, Take care of him."[43] Christ is the Great Samaritan who comes to us, the damned, raises us from death's clutches and takes us to the hospital for

41. B. L. Woolf, *Reformation Writings of M. Luther,* II, 323.
42. Luther, *On Galatians,* ed. Watson, pp. 367, 343, 252.
43. G. Rupp, *The Righteousness of God,* pp. 169, 176, citing Luther on Romans. Cf. K. Barth, *Kirchliche Dogmatik,* I/2, 419.

medical treatment. He promises us most perfect health in the future life, and now does not impute sin unto us; but in the meantime in the hope of the promised cure, He forbids us to do those things that would hinder the cure and increase sin.[44] The Great Physician has taken us into His inn, the Shepherd King has brought us into His reign of grace, by faith-union with Christ God has inserted us into His own eschatological program. The Father has received us for Christ's sake; and in the fellowship of His sufferings and the power of His resurrection, the Holy Spirit is working to make us like Him, our all-sufficient Saviour.

> *Did we in our own strength confide,*
> *Our striving would be losing;*
> *Were not the right man on our side,*
> *The man of God's own choosing.*
> *Dost ask who that may be?*
> *Christ Jesus it is he,*
> *Lord Sabaoth his Name,*
> *From age to age the same,*
> *And he must win the battle.*[45]

Here is the Gospel, for the publication of which in England William Tyndale gave his life: Christ is our Redeemer, Deliverer, Reconciler, Mediator, Intercessor, Advocate, Attorney, Solicitor, our Hope, Comfort, Shield, Protection, Defender, Strength, Health, Satisfaction and Salvation. His blood, His death, all that He ever did, is ours. And in the power of His resurrection Christ Himself and all that He is or can do, is ours.[46]

EXCURSUS ON MARIOLATRY

In Rome itself, eighty out of some three hundred of the churches are dedicated to the Virgin Mary. These buildings

44. G. Rupp, *op. cit.*

45. This translation, made by F. H. Hedge, is closer to Luther's German than is Carlyle's rendering. Conrad Porter's version is nearer than either to Luther's, thus:

> *Christ Jesus! 'Tis he!*
> *Lord of Sabaoth,*
> *True God and Saviour both,*
> *Omnipotent in battle.*

The original runs:

> *Er heiest Jesus Christ,*
> *Der Herr Zebaoth,*
> *Und ist kein andrer Gott;*
> *Das Feld muss er behalten.*

46. Tyndale, "A Pathway into the Holy Scriptures," in *Doctrinal Treatises*, p. 19.

date from many ages of the Church's history. Already with the publication of *The Praise of Folly,* Erasmus warned that the people placed more confidence in the Virgin-mother of God than in her Son. The result of this stress upon Mary is to deflect dogma from the course it took in the early Church. The focus of the early ecumenical councils was Jesus Christ; the critical center of Roman Catholic dogma, at least since 1850, has been the Virgin Mary.

The first ecumenical council asserts that Christ is true and eternal God; the second that He became also complete man; the third that He is one Person; the fourth that this One Person exists in two natures.

In 1854 the Pope enunciated the dogma of the Immaculate Conception of Mary. The dogma of the Infallibility of the Pope necessarily followed, since his enunciation of dogma was now a *fait accompli.* In 1931, *Lux Veritatis* invited Protestants to return to the papal obedience and so share in the intercessions of Mary. In 1950, the Assumption of Mary's Body into heaven was enunciated as dogma. Visions of Mary were proclaimed in the autumn of 1951. The year 1954 was set aside as the Marian Year, with an encyclical dated October 11, and a coronation of an ancient image of the Virgin as Queen of Heaven and Earth on November 1. It is expected that the doctrine of the Baltimore Catechism[47] will soon be made a dogma and Mary set forth as the Co-redemptrix of the Human Race. "The proper theme of the mariology of the twentieth century is coredemption; that is, Mary's active collaboration with Christ in the redemption of the world."[48]

Concerning the Dogma of the Assumption, the Roman Catholic theologian Michael Smaus writes: "The Assumption of Mary into heaven naturally cannot attest itself by the historical, but only by the theological considerations. The Holy Scripture offers no express testimony."[49] Professor George A. Barrois, formerly of the Catholic University, now of Princeton Seminary, says that the Dogma of the Assumption "certainly obscures the uniqueness and all-sufficiency of Christ as Saviour."[50] For a Roman Catholic theologian, "She is our bridgehead in heaven"; but for the Reformed Heidelberg Catechism, "We have our flesh in heaven," by the ascension

47. *A Catechism of Christian Doctrine,* p. 65.
48. G. Miegge, *The Virgin Mary,* Ch. 8, "The Co-Redemptress."
49. M. Smaus, *Katholische Dogmatik,* II, 880.
50. G. A. Barrois, *Theology Today,* Jan., 1951, p. 456.

of Christ. The glory of the Lord Jesus Christ has been given Him by the Father; the position of honor ascribed to the Virgin is given her by the Roman Catholic Church. The one recognizes the hand of God, the other magnifies the authority of the papal church; the one proclaims the grace of God in Christ, the other only a human, feminine pity, that is, only humanity's pity for itself.

According to a lecture by Professor Owen Chadwick in the Michaelmas Term at Cambridge, 1955, the new emphasis upon the Virgin as well as the Cult of the Sacred Heart comes from the effort of Ultramontane piety to give our Lord the central place with a warm devotion to His humanity. On the other hand, a Latin American student finds that it results in the picturing of two hearts, with that of the Virgin pierced through by a sword (Luke 2:35), and the consequent implication that hers is the greater pain and the more significant suffering. Moreover, by focussing attention upon the physical heart, mariology depersonalizes Christ.

This same student, a graduate of the University of Puerto Rico, has supplied the following contrast in current Roman Catholic statements on this matter:

In the Spanish edition of the Holy Bible entitled "Nacar-Colunga" it is stated:

La expression *"culto de los angeles"* es prueba de que los falsos doctores predicaban una religion en que entraban los angeles como intermediarios entre Dios y los hombres, *en perjuicio del unico mediador,* Jesucristo.[51]

Translation of the above:

The expression "worship of the angels" is proof that the false doctors preached a religion in which the angels were considered as intermediaries between God and men, *in detriment to the only mediator,* Jesus Christ.

In opposition to this statement the Catholic Catechism states:

Why do we add the "Hail Mary" to the Lord's Prayer?
We add the "Hail Mary" to the Lord's Prayer in order that *through the intercession of the Blessed Virgin Mary* we may the more easily obtain from God the things we ask for in the Lord's prayer.[52]

This obvious contradiction in doctrine is undoubtedly aimed at equating the authority of Jesus Christ with that of Mary.

51. Nacar-Colunga Sagrada Biblia, La Editorial Catolica, S. A. (Box 466), Madrid, MCMLVIII, 8th. Edition (foot-note on page 1287).
52. *The Catholic Catechism* by Peter Cardinal Gasparri (only authorized English translation), pp. 150.

By so doing the Roman church succeeds in exerting *a control on the people*. The "priesthood of believers" is thus exchanged, contrary to Biblical authority, for "Mary-centered religion." What happens to the words: 'Whatsoever ye ask in my name . . ! (John 14:13) when faced with the reason given in the Catholic Catechism for the "Hail Mary"? It is obvious that one or the other must yield, and the authority of heaven is only of God.[53]

53. So Mario E. Rivera of Columbia Theological Seminary.

CHAPTER FOUR

THE ARTICLE OF THE REFORMATION
Justification

WHEN THERE WAS NO ROOM IN ENGLAND for William Tyndale to carry on his work of translating the Bible, the English evangelical fled to Luther at Wittenberg. There he interested John Bugenhagen in the progress of the Reformation in England. Bugenhagen's *Letter to the English* is the first tract in behalf of the Reformation written to the English people. In it the author says:

> We could not but rejoice, dear brethren, when we heard that in England also the gospel of the grace of God has had a good report. But we are informed also that many have turned away from it because of slanderous stories against us and our way of living. We shall not stop to answer these calumnies. Know, therefore, that whatsoever ye may have heard and however simply minds may be puzzled and confused by the flood of controversy, we have only one doctrine: *Christ is our righteousness.*[1]

When Bugenhagen wrote, the Gospel of the free grace of God and of faith as justifying solely by the power of its object was having good report among the little group of Cambridge dons gathered at White Horse Inn. That gathering furnished a thin line of Reformation witnesses: William Tyndale, Thomas Bilney, Robert Barnes — martyred under Henry VIII, John Rogers, Hugh Latimer, Nicholas Ridley and Thomas Cranmer — burned under Queen Mary. The Gospel found a way even under Henry VIII, faced an open door under Edward VI, and was firmly established under Elizabeth I. At that time the echoes of Bugenhagen's one doctrine were sent reverberating through the churches of England. In the *Homilies of 1562*, "A Sermon of Salvation" proclaims that, "Christ is now the righteousness of all them that truly believe in Him."

1. J. P. Mozley, *William Tyndale*, p. 54.

1. The Cardinal Place of Justification in the Reformation

Luther describes justification as the heart of the Church, *articulus stantis et cadentis ecclesiae,* which "keeps and rules all teachings of the Church and raises up our conscience in God's presence." He warns that if the article of justification is lost the whole Christian doctrine is lost.[2] According to the Reformer, the beginning of the preaching of the doctrine of faith had a most happy course, and if all had continued to teach and urge diligently the article of justification — neither by the righteousness of the law nor by our own righteousness — this one article would have overthrown the papacy.[3] As early as 1516 he writes to Spenlein, "You will never find true peace until you find it and keep it in this . . . that Christ takes all your sins upon Himself, and bestows all His righteousness upon you."[4] To another his word is: "Our Lord Jesus Christ alone is the garment of grace that is put upon us, that God our Father may not look upon us as sinners but receive us as righteous, holy, godly children and give us eternal life." Again, "In my heart one article alone reigns supreme, that of faith in Christ, by whom, through whom and in whom all my theological thinking flows back and forth day and night. And still I find that I have grasped this so high and broad and deep a wisdom in a weak and poor and fragmentary manner."[5]

Following Luther, Melanchthon and Flacius struggled against Osiandrianism for the doctrine of justification. The teaching of such Lutheran disciples as Claus Harms, E. W. Hengstenberg, F. A. Philippi, H. Cremer, L. Ihmels, P. Althaus, A. Nygren, and R. Prenter has kept the banner of justification flying. For these and a host of others, in the words of Karl Holl, "justification is not a doctrine that has had its day, it is the *eternal gospel.*"

On the Reformed side, John Calvin was "in all respects a true disciple of the early Reformers," a biblical theologian who read the Word in the light of the doctrine of justification by faith.[6] He "comprehended the Gospel of Luther in its whole depth and distinctivity, as scarcely any other man of the Reformation."[7] Accordingly, for Calvin justification is the prin-

2. *Schmalkaldic Articles, W. A.,* 39, 1205.

3. Luther, *On Galatians,* ed. Watson, pp. 217, 218.

4. *W.A., Briefw.,* 1, 35.

5. R. Preus, "Justification of a Sinner Before God," *Scottish Journal of Theology,* 13, 3, 263.

6. W. Pauck, *The Heritage of the Reformation,* pp. 55, 57.

7. R. Seeberg, *Dogmengeschichte,* IV, 2, 558-559.

cipal hinge by which religion is supported, and wherever the knowledge of it is taken away, the glory of Christ is extinguished, religion is abolished, the Church is destroyed, and the hope of salvation is utterly overthrown.[8] This means that believers receive righteousness such as the people of God may obtain in this life; that is, only by imputation, because the Lord in His mercy accepts them as righteous and innocent solely by the intervention of Christ. "For our righteousness is not in ourselves but in Christ."[9]

The meaning and significance of justification receive adequate recognition in the Heidelberg Catechism and in the liturgical sermon provided for the celebration of the Lord's Supper in the Reformed Church of the Netherlands and in its daughter the Reformed Church in America. In the last century H. F. Kohlbrügge stood for its truth; and his son-in-law, Eduard Böhl, proclaimed justification by faith as the lever of the entire movement of the Reformation.[10] For H. Kraemer, justification "is no outmodish dogma, but one of the grandest expressions of what the Christian faith means." In the first eight chapters of Romans, where biblical realism rises to its heights, this belongs to the core of the Christian faith.[11] From Amsterdam G. C. Berkouwer is vigorously setting forth the biblical basis of justification and insisting on the full accord between the Reformed *soli Deo gloria* and the Lutheran *sola fide* statements of it.[12]

In the current disintegration of Bultmann's school, Heinrich Schleier has branded the views of his former mentor as the heresy Paul opposed, and he defends his own defection to Rome in a recent commentary on Ephesians. In reply, Ernst Käseman has undertaken the writing of a new commentary on Romans in the *Handbuch* series to show that the normative purification and preservation of primitive Christian theology is in the Protestant doctrine of justification.[13]

Professor Gordon Rupp has shown the accord of the British divines from William Tyndale to Richard Hooker with the

8. *Inst.*, III, xi, 2. *Tracts*, I, 41, "Reply to Sadoleto."
9. *Inst.*, III, xi, 23. Likewise for Calvin the infant children of believers, by baptism on the basis of the promises of the Lord, receive righteousness, but only by imputation (IV, xv, 10).
10. E. Böhl, *The Reformed Doctrine of Justification*, p. 23.
11. H. Kraemer, *The Christian Message in a Non-Christian World*, p. 74.
12. G. C. Berkouwer, *Faith and Justification*.
13. James M. Robinson, "Basic Shifts in German Theology," *Interpretation*, 1962.

German and Swiss Reformers.[14] The Protestant doctrine of justification is ably set forth in the Thirty-nine Articles, in a Sermon of Salvation in the Homilies of 1562, in Hooker's work on justification in 1585, as well as in the Westminster Confession and Catechisms. According to Hooker, "Christ has merited righteousness for as many as are found in Him. And in Him God finds us if we be believers: for by believing we are incorporated into Christ." Even the man who is full of sin, "being found in Christ through faith and having his sin in hatred through repentance, him God beholds with a gracious eye and accepts him in Jesus Christ as perfectly righteous as if he had fulfilled all that is commanded in the holy law of God." For John Owen of Oxford, justification gave the first occasion to the whole work of the Reformation. According to *Grace Abounding for the Chief of Sinners,* John Bunyan found peace for his troubled heart in a vision of Christ as our righteousness at God's right hand. E. Fisher wrote *The Marrow of Modern Divinity* about the middle of the seventeenth century, and Thomas Boston with the Erskines defended it in Scotland in the next century. These Marrow Men insisted on the free offer of the gracious Gospel of the imputation of the righteousness of Christ to needy sinners, against the tenet that the sinner must first prepare himself by forsaking his sin before coming to Christ. For Robert Traill faith justifies as a mere instrument receiving the imputed righteousness of Christ. Thomas Adam taught the evangelicals to see "sin and Christ, ill desert and no condemnation" at one and the same time.[15]

In England the evangelical emphasis was continued in John Wesley's *The Lord Our Righteousness,* by Charles Simeon of Cambridge and by Charles Spurgeon of London; in Scotland by William Cunningham in *The Reformers and the Theology of the Reformation,* by James Buchanan in *The Doctrine of Justification,* and by Alexander Whyte in *A Commentary on the Shorter Catechism.*

In America, Jonathan Edwards's sermons on justification in 1734 led to the Great Awakening, which was carried forward by George Whitefield. John Witherspoon and Archibald Alexander brought the torch to Princeton with their writings on justification. The light was lifted in Charles Hodge's *Systematic Theology* and in the works of his two sons and grandson, as

14. G. Rupp, *The English Protestant Tradition,* p. 171.
15. T. Adam, *Private Thoughts on Religion,* p. 225.

of the latters' colleague B. B. Warfield in *Perfectionism* and *Imputation*. One of the last acts of Dr. Joseph Hromadka at Princeton was to recommend E. Boehl's classic on justification to a Latin-American student.

At Columbia Theological Seminary, Thomas Goulding regarded the doctrine of justification as the epitome of the Christian system and James H. Thornwell made it the architectonic principle of all theology. It occupies large space in Wm. S. Plumer's *The Grace of Christ,* in John L. Girardeau's *Calvinism and Evangelical Arminianism,* in Thornton Whaling's *Questions on Theology,* in J. B. Green's *Harmony of the Westminster Standards,* as it does in this series of lectures. R. L. Dabney of Union Theological Seminary (Richmond, Va.) delivered his final addresses at Columbia on the theme, Christ Our Substitute and Sacrifice for Imputed Guilt. That this note is typical of the great institution with which Dabney's name is indissolubly connected is seen in the excellent words to be cited later from Thomas Cary Johnson's *John Calvin and the Genevan Reformation;* while for R. A. Webb (Presbyterian Seminary, Louisville, Ky.) "there is no more important doctrine, no more distinguished blessing, in all the Christian system than justification."[16]

2. The Relevancy of Justification for Our Day

Ultimately, justification will never be treated as relevant by those who have not encountered the risen Redeemer in the forgiveness of their sins. And it will ever be the pearl of great price to those whom He has effectually called unto Himself and into His standing before God. Yet there are considerations which indicate how justification is integral to current thought.

In order to be accepted as relevant by the theology of today, a Christian truth must, on the one hand, manifest its connection with the teaching of Jesus and the Kingdom of God, and on the other hand, show its germaneness to the personal call of the kerygma of the Church.

After a period in which the different approaches of the several writers of the New Testament were magnified, biblical theology has turned towards a synthesis of these several positions, or to what Professor A. M. Hunter designates as *The Unity of the New Testament.* Professor C. H. Dodd has found that whether

16. R. A. Webb, *Christian Salvation,* pp. 359, 388f.

one consider the Epistle to the Romans or Exodus 20, God's order is *Gospel and Law*, or *kerygma and didache*.

Some rapprochement between the Sermon on the Mount and the Epistle to the Romans is suggested in Pastor Eduard Thurneysen's *Die Bergpredigt* and by the article on *dikaiosune* and *dikaioo* by Professor G. Schrenk in Kittel's theological dictionary.[17] More recently, Professor J. Jeremias of Göttingen has found that the connection between Paul and Jesus is nowhere so clear as here in justification. Thus,

> The Pauline doctrine of justification has its origin in the conflict with Judaism, i.e. with the attempt to save oneself. The same conflict appears in the conflict of Jesus with the Pharisees in regard to their self-righteousness. Both Jesus and Paul are sure that nobody is so far from Jesus as the self-righteous person. The Pauline doctrine of justification is the development of the preaching of salvation by our Lord: "blessed are the poor" (Mt. 5:3) ; "I am not come to call the righteous but sinners" (Mt. 9:13) ; it is also the central message of His parables. This is the character of God. He is the God of the poor and needy, of the despairing and them who have no merit. Both Jesus and Paul proclaim God's great gift. Jesus says: "The beggars before God are blessed"; Paul says: "The ungodly ones are justified." It is the same message, only the terms are changed.
>
> Regarding the origin of the language, Lk. 18:14 is to be consulted: "This man went down to his house justified rather than the other." Has Luke made use of the Pauline terminology? This was formerly my view. But against this hypothesis is the semitizing construction *dedikaiomenos par'ekeinon* where (1) the passive is used as a circumlocution for the Divine name; (2) and the *para* is the rendering of an Aramaic exclusive "min". "God has justified him, and not the other." These Semitisms exclude the possibility that Lk. 18:14 is a Paulinizing formulation, since it is impossible that Luke should have altered a thesis of Paul formulated in fluent Greek to a bad semitizing Greek. Rather Luke 18:14 has the priority. Jesus was the first to designate the acceptance of the sinner by God as *dikaiousthai*, i.e. as an anticipated eschatological acquittal. Paul's doctrine of Justification is then, in matter and in language, simply a development of our Lord's teaching."[18]

The parables of the lost sheep, the lost coin, and the lost son were spoken by Jesus to defend His own conduct in receiving and celebrating the eschatological feast with sinners who apart from Him would have to flee from God. In these

17. G. Schrenk, *TWZNT*, II, 200, 219.
18. J. Jeremias, Lecture on Justification at St. Andrews, published in *The Expository Times*, September, 1955.

parables of grace, Jesus witnesses to Himself as the One who dares to act in God's stead, and vindicates His own conduct as God's goodness in action.[19] Accordingly, through the revelation of the Father's heart recorded in Luke 15, there echoes Jesus' Johannine word, "He who has seen Me has seen the Father," or as A. M. Hunter puts it, "Over the whole Parable of the Prodigal Son, or the Gracious Father, might be inscribed as a subtitle Paul's words, 'God who justifies the ungodly.' This was the heart of Paul's theology, but it was the Lord's before it was Paul's."[20] According to our Lord Jesus also, the Gospel is this: God be merciful to me, the sinner! And this man — the publican, the prodigal, the woman of the city — went home justified rather than the other — the Pharisee, the elder brother, Simon the critical host. For the first blessing in the Kingdom of Heaven falls upon those who recognize their own poverty of spirit (Matt. 5:3).

For Judaism, justification and all eschatology waits the final judgment and the Kingdom ensuing thereon. For Paul, Christ was raised for our justification, and thereby a piece of realized eschatology was read back from the final judgment into the present. This realized eschatology in Paul's doctrine of present justification points the way to an understanding of the Kingdom. In Christ's Resurrection, Ascension, and Pentecost, the Kingdom conquered so that we live under its invisible sway. But only at His parousia will the Kingdom be consummated in visible glory when those now justified in secret shall be openly acclaimed and reign with Him.

Moreover, the Kingdom is not without its forensic procedure. According to the biblical accounts, Satan formerly stood at God's right hand as the accuser of the brethren. Now by His Resurrection and Ascension, the Lord Jesus Christ sits at the right hand of the Majesty on High as our Representative and Advocate. Thus justification is integral to the biblical account of the Kingdom.

Exception has, at times, been taken against the terms and phrases used to set forth this doctrine. They are charged with being too abstract or impersonal. The technical terms *impute* and *imputation* which define the Protestant position have been the objects of recurring attacks. H. Boehmer, in *Luther in the*

---

19. So E. Fuches and J. Jeremias as cited by J. M. Robinson in *A New Quest of the Historical Jesus*, pp. 14, 15, 106.
20. *Interpretation*, XIV:2; 185.

Light of Recent Research, thought that Luther got the concept of the non-imputation of sins from William Occam, the giant of later Scholasticism. The word *impute,* however, occurs in the biblical passages Luther was studying — Psalm 32 (31) and Romans 4. The Reformer simply took what lay before him in his Vulgate Bible. The papal theologians who oppose the Protestant vocabulary at this point ought to attack Jerome. In the English antinomian controversy, John Owen gave a section of his work on *Justification* to the defense of these terms. When "liberalism" objected to the legal or forensic elements in the Protestant Confessions, Alexander Whyte took the high ground that the Holy Spirit had given and was pleased to use the word *impute.*[21] Imputed righteousness is asserted in the case of Abraham (Gen. 15:6), of Phinehas (Ps. 106:30; cf. Num. 25:11f.), and of David (Rom. 4:6-8); Christ is made unto us righteousness from God (I Cor. 1:30; Rom. 10:4), our sins being reckoned to Him (II Cor. 5:21; Gal. 3:13) and His obedience being imputed to us (Rom. 5:18-19; Phil. 2:8, 3:6-9; Rev. 7:14). In the article on "Imputation" in the *New Schaff-Herzog Encyclopaedia,* B. B. Warfield shows that Adam's sin is imputed to his posterity (Rom. 5:12-21); that our sin or curse, in grace to us, was imputed to Christ (II Cor. 5:21; Gal. 3:13); and that His obedience is imputed to us as our righteousness (II Cor. 5:21; I Cor. 1:30; Rom. 5:19, 10:4). C. W. Hodge, Jr., again vindicated the biblical basis of the doctrine in the article thereon in the *International Standard Bible Encyclopedia,* while Professor Hans W. Heidland shows that the Apostle uses *logizesthai* to describe a gracious gift, a saving act of God to sinners, and especially that saving act by which sins are not imputed for this reason: because Christ has become sin for us.[22]

The phrase *justification by faith alone* has been called in question from more than one point of view. Neo-Protestants have used it to assure men of their justification on the ground of their sincerity or genuine faith regardless of the content of that conviction. We are happy to admit or rather to proclaim that heart-trust is not identical with intellectual formulations. We recognize that the existential decision for a national leader, the consuming devotion of a monk toward his Buddhist rule, the passionate subjective loyalty of a Communist to the Party, all give a direction and drive to life that shames many a

21. A. Whyte, *A Commentary on the Shorter Catechism.*
22. *TWNT,* IV, 292f., 295, II Cor. 5:19, 21.

nominal Christian. But if one contend that it is either our passionate subjectivity or Christ's atoning act, we cannot reject the latter in the interest of the former. God did not reconcile the world unto Himself by the passion of our existential decision, but by the death of His Son. "To Him all the prophets bear witness that through His Name everyone that believes on Him shall receive the remission of sins" (Acts 10:43).

Writing from another point of view, F. D. Maurice charged that the phrase *justification by faith* was being substituted for faith in Christ, the Justifier. Though the phrase is well meant and has been properly used by many, in itself justification by faith may be too abstract and impersonal a contraction. Our day is concerned that persons be exalted above mere abstract ideas.[23] The truth we seek to proclaim is the personal relation of the sinner to God through Christ. For Luther, the righteousness which has been begun is not enough unless it cling to Christ and flow from Him; nor is just any kind of faith sufficient but only the faith which hides itself beneath the wings of Christ and glories in His righteousness.[24] Thus faith in justification must not be substituted for faith in Jesus Christ. We must not say *sola fide, sed sola fide Jesu Christi*.[25] "Justification by faith is clearly the same thing as justification through Christ."[26] "Of the three factors: Faith — Justification — Christ, it is the last which is both fundamental and regulative."[27] Faith is the naked hand of the beggar that putteth on Christ for justification.

> *In my hand no price I bring,*
> *Simply to Thy cross I cling.*

A new recognition of the relevance of justification comes from a critical appraisal of Christian missions today. The new situation calls "first" for "the Christian realism of sinners forgiven by God," a grasp "of the doctrine of justification, of the fact that God can use sinners for His own glory."[28]

The dialectical theologians have "struck afresh at the heart of all questions — the relation between God and man — and so set the whole field of religious thought in motion." The

23. A. M. Stibbs, Lecture on Justification given at Tyndale House, Cambridge, 1955.
24. Cranz, *Luther's Thoughts on Justice*, citing *W.A.*, VIII, 111, 31; 112, 2.
25. H. Thielicke, *Kerygma und Mythos*, 160.
26. G. F. Wingren, in *Scottish Journal of Theology*, 9:4:274.
27. K. Barth, *K.D.*, IV/1, 714.
28. David M. Paton, *Christian Missions and the Judgment of God*, p. 23.

man who interests the new theology is "not the man striving
for goodness, but man under the free judgment of God."[29]
When God encounters a man, there arises a cry of confession
and a supplication for mercy. Therefore, justification forms
the first center of this theological concern.

Current psychiatry is recognizing man's deep need for acceptance as he condemns himself and plunges into the abyss of
despondency. Where can this sinner who hopelessly and help-
lessly hates himself find acceptance? Only one who has been
loved can love; only one who has been trusted can trust; only
one who has experienced self-surrender in another can surrender
himself. We are set free to give ourselves to God through the
fact that He has given Himself for us. As we know ourselves
loved by God we love Him. As we find Him opening His
heart to us in Christ we open ourselves to Him. As we enter
into the fellowship of His sufferings for us, we receive grace
to give ourselves to Him who first gave Himself to and for us.
It is as we find God trusting us with His only-begotten Son
that we in turn entrust ourselves to Him who withheld not
this unspeakable gift but freely offered Him up for us.

3. THE FORMULATION OF THE DOCTRINE OF JUSTIFICATION

Luther's first guide toward the evangelical doctrine of justification was Augustine's *The Spirit and the Letter.* In places
Augustine touches on the forensic sense of "justify," that is, of
being held or accounted just. God graciously justifies by faith,
the divine mercy does not impute sin (Ps. 32:2; Rom. 4:3) ;
God clothes a man with righteousness when He justifies him.[30]
But the more usual teaching is that the word justify is equivalent
to "make righteous," that the Spirit of God shed love abroad
in our hearts and that by His gifts we gradually become righteous. Indeed the ambiguities of Augustine led to a disputation
between Melanchthon and Luther in 1536. Melanchthon charged
Augustine with teaching that justification by faith meant that
we are justified by our renewal by grace. Luther rejected this
doctrine but quoted a sentence from Augustine in agreement
with Luther's own mature doctrine.[31]

For Augustine, the love of God shed abroad in our hearts by
the Holy Spirit (Rom. 5:5) is our love to God, whereas the
context and the usage of Paul show it to be God's love for us

29. G. C. Berkouwer, *Faith and Justification,* pp. 11-12.
30. *Augustine's Later Writings,* ed. J. Burnaby, pp. 205, 219, 229.
31. F. E. Cranz, *op. cit.,* p. 60.

in that while we were yet sinners Christ died for us. When God is said to be justified in His words and vindicated when He judges (Ps. 51:4; Rom. 3:4), this cannot mean make righteous. Certainly the publicans do not make God righteous when they are said to justify Him (Luke 7:29). Luther came to see that the Greek verb *dikaioo* has the sense of vindicate, or declare righteous when used of God; and so it may have the sense of acquit in those places used by God with reference to men.

Augustine's fundamental position is that God's gracious action gradually makes righteous by the Spirit, while imputation or forensic procedure is a kind of supplement until the process of making righteous is complete.

Karl Holl's effort to construe Luther's doctrine as an analytical rather than as a synthetical judgment is a return from the Protestant Luther to the earlier, more Augustinian Luther. Holl's interpretation means that God declares us righteous because of the good work He has begun in us, which He sees developing in fellowship with Himself. Because we are righteous in germ or in process, because there is a beginning *in re,* therefore we are righteous *in spe;* what is present is a promise of fulfillment.[32] Now Holl's view has received some support from R. Seeberg, *Dogmengeschichte*, IV, 1, 238f., W. Koehler, *Dogmengeschichte*, 5, 369, E. Hirsch, *Die Theologie des Andreas Osianders*, pp. 229f., James Mackinnon, *Luther and the Reformation*, I, 210f., E. Vogelsang, *Die Anfänge von Luthers Christologie;* and it has elements in it akin to R. Baxter's *Aphorisms of Justification,* to H. E. Fosdick's *The Meaning of Faith,* and to many fundamentalistic pietists. Holl is an authority on the earlier writings of Luther, and found in these first evangelical efforts suggestions that man is partially righteous or righteous in spirit, while not in flesh, and that this antecedent partial righteousness is the promise that he will eventually be totally righteous in the final judgment of God.[33]

Luther moved from an Augustinian to the fully evangelical position that justification is a declarative act in which God pronounces the sinner righteous by graciously imputing or reckoning to him the merits of Christ whom he receives by faith. In this maturing of his understanding, Luther saw the believer completely righteous before God as he is in Christ, and completely a sinner as he is in himself. The subject *sinner* is

32. K. Holl, *Gesammelte Aufsätze zum Kirchengeschichte,* I, iiif.; III, 525f.
33. F. E. Cranz, *op. cit.,* pp. 11-12.

not annulled by the predicate *righteous.* "Hence in different respects we are said to be righteous and sinners at one and the same time." All his life the believer harbors a contradiction. "The Christian is free by faith, but in relation to the flesh, he is the slave of sin. These two things, though contraries, are nevertheless reconciled in Christ, so that the same Christian is holy and a sinner, dead and alive. There is no sin at all, and all is sin; there is hell and there is heaven."[34] In this mature position the Christian's complete justification already accomplished in Christ is the basis for his gradual sanctification in life. Here complete antecedent righteousness in Christ is the basis for the partial and progressive sanctification in life. In the light of Luther's *Commentary on Galatians,* the *Schmalkaldic Articles,* and such sermons as "On Salvation by Grace Without Works," and "Of the Works God Has Wrought for Us," our opinion concurs with those Luther scholars such as P. Althaus, W. Walther, I. Ihmels, G. Aulen, K. Barth, J. L. Neve, E. Böhl, R. Prenter, U. Saarnivara, and F. E. Cranz, who hold that Protestant justification is a synthetic judgment accounting us who are sinners in ourselves righteous in Christ. The believer's sins are no longer his but Christ's, and in Christ sins cannot conquer righteousness but are themselves conquered by it; therefore in Christ, sins are abolished, and the righteousness of Christ is now not only Christ's, but also belongs to His Christian.[35]

In the definitive *Commentary on Galatians* Luther has arrived at the view that justification is by a passive righteousness, that in faith Christ is present conveying His righteousness to us by the power of the Holy Spirit, while we and our works are receptive, passive. According to I Corinthians 1:30, Christ is our righteousness, but this means more than that He is the cause of our justification as if He were to give us righteousness and Himself remain outside us. The believer's righteousness is never given except where Christ is Himself present, just as the heat of the fire is only where the fire is. As faith receives Christ He moves and acts in us so that we become one by incorporation into Christ and in the energy of His name. Thus for Luther the reckoning or imputation of Christ's righteousness is never a divine decision with no real effect upon the sinner. By God's own Word the world was made, by His Word He calls the things that are not, and being called, they are. His own Word

34. *Ibid.,* p. 69, citing *W.A.,* XXXIX, 1, p. 564, 3; XXXIX, 1, p. 523, 19.
35. Cranz, *op. cit.,* p. 77, citing *W.A.,* II, 503, 36.

justifying the sinner is not a non-entity but is greater than the whole world. Often men speak empty words, but God's fiats are mighty, effective, standing when heaven and earth pass away.

Luther deduces from the passive righteousness of justification the obligation in sanctification to promote active righteousness in the several spheres of human life: domestic, civic, economic, ecclesiastical. Out of the blessed indicative comes the dynamic imperative. Because of what God has done, is doing, and will do for us, let us eagerly do for Him. Grace evokes gratitude, the man who is righteous by faith engages in good works. The faith which justifies is never alone, but the living Christ produces the fruits of the Spirit in those who are His. Good works are thus not the root, but the fruit or effect of justification (Eph. 2:9-10).

The Reformers were reared in an intellectual atmosphere dominated by "that mad pagan Aristotle," and necessarily had to relate their teaching to and distinguish it from this frame. Scholasticism regarded philosophy as the handmaiden of theology. In Christian theology current dialectics seek to use the instruments supplied by philosophy only after they have been thoroughly sterilized. Since God's thoughts are higher than ours (Isa. 55:8-9), every use of human philosophy must be carefully screened lest the shadow of puny man hide the riches of grace in Christ Jesus.

Luther found the schoolmen treating our faith as the shell or matter, and our love as the form which beautifies or perfects faith according to their familiar formula, *fides formata caritate*. Instead of "the monstrous dreams" of these scholastics, salvation begins for Luther not with our love for God but with His love for us. Accordingly, if faith be the body or the shell or the matter, then is Christ — apprehended by faith and dwelling in the heart — the kernel, the form, the beauty, the righteousness of the Christian. These three things, faith, Christ, acceptation or imputation must be joined together. Faith takes hold of Christ and has Him present and holds Him enclosed as the ring does the precious stone. For Christ's sake, God accepts us as righteous, covering or not imputing to us our sin. Our faith in Christ is reckoned for righteousness, but with our faith must always go the imputation of His righteousness, for our faith is imperfect and His righteousness is perfect.[36]

---

36. Luther, *On Galatians*, ed. Watson, pp. 134, 137-138.

Thus the sinner can believe that he is righteous solely through the atoning work of Christ and its gracious imputation to him.

Calvin uses the four Aristotelian causes as a teaching device to establish the theocentric character and the unity of salvation in a repeated recognition of God as our Saviour (cf. Titus 3:4-7). Thus, the gracious love of God the Father is the efficient cause of our salvation; the obedience of God the Son is the material cause; the illumination of God the Spirit, that is faith, is the instrumental cause; and the glory of God is the final cause (*Inst.*, III, xiv, 17, 21). As here used these causes are neither physical nor mechanical, but personal. As the Triune God acts in His infinite personality, so He brings man to a consciousness of himself as a responsible person in rebellion, and graciously calls him through a vital decision into a new personal relation as God's forgiven child. No one of these four causes is consistent with any merit on our part in salvation, as John 3:5, 6, 16; Romans 3:23f.; Ephesians 1:5-7, 2:10; Titus 3:4-6, and II Timothy 1:9-10 clearly show. Hence, in his commentary on Ephesians, Calvin writes, *"Christi nomen omne meritum excludit."*

In the *Institutes* (II, xvii), Calvin uses this formulation to answer the Socinian objection that if justification is to be free to us, there can be no satisfaction made or ransom-price paid for it. On the contrary, the mercy of God as the primary cause and the merit of the Mediator as the subservient cause are equally opposed, in their respective places, to our works. It is a matter of concern that "a contemporary interpretation" again divorces the grace of God from the redemption wrought by the propitiatory sacrifice of Christ which shows God to be just when He justifies the sinner who entrusts himself to Jesus.[37] These two things are properly joined together by the Word

37. G. S. Hendry, *The Westminster Confession of Faith for Today*, pp. 111-112, 135-137. In describing the view that Christ by His obedience and sacrifice satisfied the justice of God as a view "first propounded" by Anselm and "reflected in the Confession," this book overlooks significant elements in the patristic interpretation of Scripture, as may be conveniently seen in J. N. D. Kelly's *Early Christian Doctrines*, pp. 174, 186, 379, 380, 382, 385, 388, 389, 392-393; of such Eastern Fathers as Origen, Athanasius, Eusebius, Cyril and Gregory of Nyssa, and such Western ones as Irenaeus, Augustine, Ambrose, Hilary, and even Gregory the Great. The Reformers and the Confession drew both from these patristic insights into the work of Christ Godward and from *Cur Deus Homo?*, but both reached a more evangelical formulation.

of God (Rom. 3:24-26, 4:25, 5:10-11, 8:3, 31-34, for God's distributive justice Rom. 2:5-8; II Cor. 5:18, 21; Gal. 3:13; Eph. 1:6-7; I Tim. 2:5-6; I John 4:10; I Peter 1:3, 19, 2:24, 3:18), by Luther and Calvin; by Tyndale[38] and the 1562 English "Homily of Salvation"; by the Westminster Standards and the older interpreters thereof, e.g., A. A. Hodge, *Commentary on the Confession of Faith,* C. C. Hodge, *Systematic Theology;* as well as by such current scholars as Leon Morris, *The Apostolic Preaching of the Cross,* Paul van Buren, *Christ in our Place,* G. C. Berkouwer, *Faith and Justification,* J. I. Packer, "Justification" in Baker's *Dictionary of Theology,* John Stott on Protestant Radio Hour (3/4/62, sermon entitled "Suffered Under Pontius Pilate"), Fritz Rienecker, "The Cross and Demythologizing" in *Christianity Today* (3/16/62). For us, salvation is free; for God it was not cheap. His was the awesome cost; He gave His own Son as the propitiation for our sins (I John 4:10, 2:2; Rom. 3:25; Heb. 2:17).[38a]

In Calvin even the instrumental cause is strictly speaking God, that is, faith is the gift and illumination of the Spirit. Too often this has been so changed as to make faith the condition or even the meritorious cause. Some have fancied that God was required by some kind of bilateral covenant to save the man who met the condition thereof by his human faith. A. Nygren in his commentary on Romans is nearer Paul and the Reformers when he presents faith as the sign of the new order, the evidence that the Gospel as the power of God unto salvation is working in the believer. Warfield warns that, strictly speaking, it is not even faith in Christ that saves, but Christ saves through faith. The saving power rests exclusively, not in the act of faith or the attitude of faith, but in the object of faith; and in this the whole biblical representation centers, so that we could not more radically misconceive it than by transferring to faith even the smallest fraction of that saving energy which is attributed in the Scripture solely to Christ Himself.[39] Likewise for Webb, "faith in itself is not the basis upon which God declares the sinner not guilty but righteous; but it is what faith holds in its hand, namely the

---

38. Tyndale, *Doctrinal Treatises,* pp. 15, 17, 19ff., 395. "It is the blood of Christ that opens the gates of heaven, not thy works."

38a. Cf. J. Denney, *The Christian Doctrine of Reconciliation,* pp. 31, 74, 104, 142-162, 236, 239.

39. B. B. Warfield, *Biblical and Theological Studies,* p. 425.

righteousness of Christ, which is the premise of the Divine judgment."[40]

Thomas Carey Johnson comes to the same conclusion from a study of the nature of faith itself.

> If our salvation is by grace alone it follows that it is by faith alone, for to rely on grace alone is to give up any trust in our own capabilities or capacities for salvation. For faith is the acknowledgement of our own poverty and the prayer for God's riches.[41]

Without recourse to Aristotle, "The Homily on Salvation" for the Church of England, 1562, draws directly from Romans 3:22-26 that:

> Three things must go together in our justification; upon God's part, His great mercy and grace; upon Christ's part, justice, that is the satisfaction of God's justice, or the price of our redemption by the offering of His body and the shedding of His blood with the fulfilling of the law perfectly and thoroughly; and upon our part true and lively faith in the merits of Jesus Christ; which yet is not ours but God's working in us.

As the several aspects of justification are kept together, one is prevented from regarding the justifying righteousness of Christ as a legal abstraction separated from the life of faith, and on the other hand kept from transforming faith into a virtue or quality such as courage or prudence. Faith is man ever taking refuge from his sin and insufficiency in the faithfulness of God our Saviour — the faithfulness of God brought from heaven to earth and wrought out in the life and death of Jesus Christ for us. Our faith feeds upon His faithfulness (Ps. 37:3, ASV), as the solid ground of confidence in God's saving action.[42] God's word of forgiveness is at the same time both forensic and creative, for it moves in the fellowship of His Son Jesus Christ, our Lord (I Cor. 1:4-9). It is given as God in Christ confronts us in judgment, speaks to us in pardon, acts in us in grace. For Luther, as for his authentic disciples in the Lutheran, the Reformed and the Anglican Churches,

> Justification by faith is not a gradual process of renewal or becoming righteous. It is rather the bestowal of the righteousness of Christ by imputation. God justifies the sinner by forgiving his sins and reckoning him innocent and blameless for the sake of the atoning work of Christ. This acquittal God pronounces through

40. R. A. Webb, *Christian Salvation,* pp. 388-389.
41. T. C. Johnson, *John Calvin and the Reformation.*
42. Cf. G. Hebert, *Theology,* LXVIII:378.

the Gospel promises proclaimed by the ministry of reconciliation. By faith the sinner receives the divine gift promised and offered to him. The foundation of justification and also the object of the believer's faith and trust is not what God has done and does *in* him, but what God has done *for* him . . . According to Scripture the sinner is justified by grace alone, through faith in Christ, when he trustfully lays hold of the Gospel promise and offer of forgiveness of sins.[43]

That is, we would interpret, when he lays hold of Christ clothed with His Gospel. And, of course, he thus grasps Christ only because Christ has first grasped him by His Spirit through the means of the preached Word. In the living event of preaching, the justification of the ungodly through faith by grace alone is not merely taught, but it actually occurs as there is imputed to the hearer a righteousness which lies not in his own merits but in the merits of Christ *extra nos*.[44]

---

43. U. Saarnivaara, *Luther Discovers the Gospel*, pp. 123, 124, 125.
44. So H. Diem, *Dogmatics*, pp. 232, 233.

CHAPTER FIVE

THE THEOLOGIAN OF THE REFORMATION

John Calvin, Interpreter of God's Word

"THE REFORMATION WAS first and foremost a theological revival."[1] Consequently, the Reformers are witnesses to theology, to a biblical theology, as the very life of the Church. In October 1512, Luther received the degree of Doctor of Divinity and thereafter devoted himself to the establishment of a biblical in place of a scholastic theology. While he was in seclusion in the Wartburg, the glory of reviving theology was ascribed to Zwingli. It fell, however, to their two great successors, Philip Melanchthon and John Calvin, to build theological structures of the mighty stones which they quarried from the Word. For his friend Melanchthon, Calvin published in French the *Loci Communes,* describing this book as a summary in simplest terms and by a learned man of the things a Christian should know in the way of salvation. When Calvin worsted Dean Robert Mosham of Passau at the Second Disputation in Worms, he was acclaimed by Melanchthon as *the theologian.* Melanchthon's tribute, as well as the high intellectual standing which *The Institutes of the Christian Religion* gave Protestantism, justify the treatment of Calvin as *par excellence* the theologian of the Reformation.

Just what, however, is a theologian, or what is theology? A philosopher of religion describes it as

> that human inquiry which undertakes to present in intelligible form a coherent and comprehensive statement of truths which are of ultimate concern to man.[2]

This makes theology the queen of the sciences, but it makes no direct mention of God or of His Word. For Calvin, however, human speculation is a maze in which one is lost unless he have the Word to guide him out of the labyrinth, as Theseus

---

1. T. H. L. Parker, *Portrait of Calvin,* p. 12.
2. E. Ashby Johnson, *The Crucial Task of Theology,* p. 24.

found his way by the thread Ariadne had given him. Barth has more recently shown that if I only speak of myself, some Feuerbach may dismiss "my theology" as wishful thinking or as a religious phantasmagoria.[3] One can only speak of the living God when he proclaims what God has first revealed of Himself, that is *apo tou Theou*. Theology ought to have both a humbler and a higher task than *regina scientiarum*, she should be *ancilla Domini*, the handmaiden holding the torch for her Lord.

The classical Calvinist has often built on the etymology of the term theology. *Theos* means God and *logos* word, reason, or discourse: thus theology is a unified discourse about God. This definition brings in God and implies His special revelation. For, as such a keen "liberal" scholar as K. Lake of Harvard pointed out, only a special revelation can supply data accordant enough to be unified.[4] Yet this implication of one organizing principle has, at times, led Calvin's classical followers to force the Reformed faith into a pattern unified by human logic. As a matter of fact, "The Second Patriarch of the Reformation" took care never to become infatuated "with a rigid dogmatism and a diabolical logic."[5]

As Luther and others re-established the crucial position that the Church must be a *listening* Church, not listening to its own interior monologue, but to the voice of God it hears in Scripture,[6] so Calvin insisted that the believer is a disciple in the school of Christ, studying the Bible under the illumination of the Holy Spirit (*Inst.*, I, vi, 2; vii, 5; ix, 3; III, i). He is ever

> listening to the Word of God and again and again listening! Not as a system builder who already knows all things, but as a captive of that Word that marks the way through the brush of the world.[7]

This continuous listening to the Word issues in a believing reflection upon the truth of the Christian faith.[8] Just because he is not so much the systematic thinker as he is the Reformer

---

3. K. Barth, *Kirchliche Dogmatik*, I, 289; *Church Dogmatics*, I/2.

4. Rejecting special revelation, Lake opposed calling his institution a divinity or a theological school in the University.

5. A. M. Schmidt, *Jean Calvin et la tradition Calvinienne*, p. 93.

6. So R. A. Brown, *The Spirit of Protestantism*, p. 69.

7. G. C. Berkouwer, in *Contemporary Prophet*, p. 195.

8. Cf. Th. L. Haitjema's definition of theology as "the thought of faith springing from revelation," as cited by Th. C. Vriezen in *An Outline of OT Theology*, p. 120, and Vriezen's own description as "a personal exercise in listening and spiritual understanding," p. 123.

of strong faith, a faith which because it rests on the Word is able to bear in itself the theological tensions,[9] therefore there is in Calvin a clarity of individual themes, but an incomprehensibility of their relations.[10]

1. CALVIN AS BIBLICAL THEOLOGIAN

First, then, Calvin, like his Reformation colleagues, is a biblical rather than a speculative theologian. He is an exegete of Holy Scripture, and he interprets it by no one organizing principle but in the light of the tremendous reality of Him whom it sets forth, that is, he is a biblical realist. Standing in mighty majesty and high holiness above our sinful race, God has graciously condescended to put His Word nigh us, in our mouths and in our hearts (Rom. 10:8), that it might be a lamp unto our feet and a light to our pathway (Ps. 119:105). Calvin spent his life studying this Word, and like an Old Testament prophet he proclaimed it both by his words and his actions.[11]

In Calvin's *Reply to Sadoleto,* he declares that the light of saving truth is kindled by the Word of God alone, and he objects to the introduction of human inventions into the Church as sacriligious presumption. Calvin then gives an account which seems to be his understanding of the order of his own conversion:

> O Lord, Thou hast enlightened me by the clarity of Thy Spirit. . . .
> Thou hast put Thy Word before me as a torch . . . . Finally, Thou
> hast touched my heart that I might hold these things in the
> abomination they rightly deserve.[12]

God suddenly subdued Calvin to Himself so that his belief in biblical inspiration led him not to worry about all the logical connections in the thoughts he derived from God's Word.[13] Moreover, for Calvin the knowledge of faith is given by the Holy Spirit from the Word, and as such consists more in certainty than in logical comprehension.[14] "And men betray astonishing madness in desiring to comprehend immensity within the limits of their reason" (*Inst.,* III, xxiii, 4). There are

---

9. W. A. Hauch, *Vorsehung und Freiheit nach Calvin,* 3, 39.
10. E. A. Dowey, *The Knowledge of God,* p. 204.
11. T. H. L. Parker, *Portrait of Calvin,* p. 9.
12. *Oeuvres de Jean Calvin,* II, *Trois Traites,* p. 82.
13. W. S. Reid, in *The Westminster Theological Review,* xvii; 2; 177.
14. *Inst.,* III, ii, 14, 18; A. Lecerf, *Etudes Calvinistes,* p. 57.

things "which God would have us to adore and not comprehend" (III, xxi, I).

The fundamental error in theological thinking is to begin with man as though he were the original and to treat God as the copy. This is found in the pagan thesis that man is the measure of all things, in the Arian sophistry that whatever is true in human relations is *ipso facto* true of divine relations, in Feuerbach's psychology that God is an eject of man's subjective fear complex, and in Bultmann's placing of the acts of God in the light and within the limits of the existentialist's prior understanding of man (*Vorverständnis*). *Finis origine pendet.* The frame limits the picture that hangs in it. In the beginning of the *Institutes,* Calvin resolutely refuses to consider man apart from God. For him, the *Vorverständnis* does not consist in the knowledge of man but in the knowledge of God revealed in the Cross and Resurrection of Christ. Then man is seen in the light of God and His mighty deeds in Jesus Christ, and thereby brought to a true self-knowledge.[15]

Calvin refuses to subject the dogmas of the Christian religion to a particular scheme; rather he "begins with the question as to what data Scripture offers concerning the subject at hand. He never infers one dogma from another."[16]

"Calvin's true legacy is, indeed, not a system but a method, the method of striving to see everything — man, Christ, faith, the world, the Bible, religion, life — not from man's point of view but from the viewpoint of God."[17] "The business of reason is, not to think God according to its own lights, but to think God's thoughts after him."[18] It is to mind the things of God, not the things of men (Matt. 16:23). "What Christian faith declares is that the true understanding of history can be had solely from a point of view supplied by God Himself."[19]

"Calvin's thought has its whole existence within the realm of God as revealer and man as knower."[20] "All true knowledge of God is born of obedience" (*Inst.,* I, vi, 2). And as a result of the fall, with its darkening effects on man, the Creator can be known in the first place only through the Scriptures (I, vi,

15. H. Ridderbos, in *Christianity Today,* May 22, 1961; cf. J. Rodman Williams, in *Austin Seminary Bulletin,* LXXVI:1.
16. A. D. R. Polman, *Barth,* pp. 33-35.
17. P. T. Fuhrmann, *God-Centered Religion,* p. 23.
18. P. H. Lehmann, *Theology Today,* XIII, 3, 344.
19. H. R. Mackintosh, *Types of Modern Theology,* p. 204.
20. Edward A. Dowey, Jr., *op. cit.,* p. 3.

1, 2). All the knowledge of God as Creator would be useless unless it were succeeded by faith exhibiting Him to us as a Father in Christ (II, vi, 1). What is hidden from the unbeliever because of his blindness is unveiled to the believer by the Scriptures.[21] Accordingly, Scripture covers the whole field of God's revelation, introducing the believer to the revelation of God in nature and supplying the special redemptive revelation.[22]

The sermons in Geneva were expositions of Scripture, even as the *Institutes* are biblical theology, and as such they are a key for students in reading the Word. Calvin became the interpreter of God's Word with commentaries on almost the whole of the Bible, and "one understands Calvin best as a biblical theologian."[23]

The underside of Calvin's confidence in the Word of God is his realization of the darkening effects of sin, not only on the affections and will, but also on the intellect or reason. Indeed, Warfield has found here the organizing principle of the first sections of both the first and the second book of the *Institutes*.[24] The same realistic treatment of the noetic effects of sin is evident as well in the third and the fourth books. The wisdom of God is too high for the puny thoughts of man. We must never use the reason of the lesser to judge the greater; nor the logic of the sin-blinded to obscure the glory of the Holy One of Israel (III, xxiv, 17). Indeed, for Calvin, "apart from Christ, all knowledge is a vast abyss that swallows up thought."

As a biblical theologian, John Calvin stands in the great line of theocentric theologians. And compared with others in that line He is less philosophical and more biblical. When Augustine came to the puerile question about what God was doing before He created the universe, the Latin doctor gave the Platonic answer that time was part of the creation. When Calvin came to the same question he pushed aside this philosophical answer and gave instead a wisecrack: God was making hell for over-inquisitive people. While Zwingli tended to think of God as the object of human speculation, Calvin regarded God as the object of worship. Thus Calvin placed himself more be-

---

21. T. H. L. Parker, *The Evangelical Quarterly*, xxvi:4.
22. G. C. Berkouwer, *General Revelation*.
23. W. Pauck, *The Heritage of the Reformation*, p. 66.
24. B. B. Warfield, *Calvin and Calvinism*, pp. 42-44; Cf. T. Torrance, *Calvin's Doctrine of Man*.

49745

neath the Lord in the obedience of faith. Treating of Providence, Calvin rejected as a Stoic idea a concatenated series of causes. He disavowed Stoicism thus:

> For ourselves we have nothing to do with this iron philosophy which our Lord and Master condemned not only in word but also by His example, Matt. 5:4 (*Inst.*, I, xvi, 8; II, vii, 9).

He based the bondage of the will on the fall and ascribed the blame thereof solely to man (II, i, 10). The followers of Jonathan Edwards, however, present a psychological scheme in which the human will always chooses the greatest apparent good, so that both before and after the fall man has free agency but no free will. God predestined beforehand, so that by this series of causes He is the cause of the fall in the same sense as of creation.

The architectonic principle of Calvin's theology is not, then, the bare sovereignty of God as such. For Calvin, the Scotist doctrine of the absolute and arbitrary will of God deserves our detestation on account of its profaneness (*Inst.*, III, xxiii, 2; I, xvii, 2). God is not almighty arbitrariness apart from law (*ex lege*). He is a law unto Himself. Since "God can no more cease to be good than He can cease to be God," therefore the Divine will is "the highest standard of perfection" and "the highest rule of justice" (*Inst.*, III, xxiii, 2, 4, 5; III, xxiv, 17; II, iii, 5). And the invariable standard by which to interpret the will of God revealed in Scripture is the Father's "unspeakable love towards us which went so far that it spared not His own Son but delivered Him up for us."[25]

As an abstract rationalistic principle, the sovereignty of God can lead to Mohammedan fatalism, to a concatenated system in which God is the cause of Adam's sin just as He is the cause of the existence of the world, to a naturalism which equates God's will with physical laws, or to any other form of arid determinism. The Reformed faith is a faith and a life reformed and ever to be more fully reformed by the Word of God. "Without the Word, all our conceptions of the power and works of God are unprofitable and transient" (*Inst.*, III, ii, 13). Consequently, the sovereignty of God must be clarified in two ways before it can be grasped in its proper perspective. First, the Calvinist is concerned for the sovereignty, not of a philosophical deity, but of the God and Father of our Lord Jesus Christ; and secondly, he maintains that this God is Lord,

25. Calvin, Letter to Francis I.

not in the ways in which man can reason out God's sovereignty, but according to the manner in which the living God reveals His own Lordship in His Word. This means that one does not start with an *a priori* principle of the sovereignty of God and deduce from it a logical system of theology.

> The way of speculation always leads to confusion. The Reformation took position against this confusion. It refused to go beyond the limits of revelation to construct a rational "unity" which would endanger the reality of guilt and its historical reconciliation.[26]

It went to the Word of God to find out how He has revealed that God is the *Lord,* how the living God acted in Creation and in Reconciliation, and how He is acting and will act in Salvation and in Consummation.

For the Reformers, election is not in the hidden God but in Jesus Christ, the revealed God, and is "the ultimate expression of the evangelical doctrine of grace."[27] It was Beza, not Calvin, who presumed to operate with an order of divine decrees.[28] For Calvin, those who speculate about the decrees of God without the Word plunge themselves into a fatal abyss (*Inst.,* III, xxiv, 4).

Half a century after Calvin "the five points of Calvinism" were formulated at the Synod of Dort, and their logic so sharpened in the T-U-L-I-P acrostic that they suggest to the popular mind implications that go beyond the Canons of that Synod and differ from the teachings of John Calvin. *Efficacious redemption* is more precisely the language of the Canons of Dort as it is of Calvin on I John 2:2 than is limited atonement, and it is more expressive of God's saving action. More than irresistible, *invincible grace* brings out the personal character of the Divine-human encounter in which man makes excuses (Exodus 3) or kicks against the goads (Acts 26:14), but God ultimately triumphs. A believer's security is not in some fancied ability of a saint to persevere, but in our Father's faithfulness to His *purpose of grace* for us even when we fall into grievous sins against Him (Psalms 51 and 32; Luke 22:31-34).

The deepest source of the life of Christianity is the grace of God in Christ for lost souls, and the Reformation fathers learned this from God's own mouth through the Holy Scriptures.[29]

26. G. C. Berkouwer, *The Triumph of Grace,* p. 382.
27. W. Niesel, *The Theology of Calvin.*
28. Berkouwer, *op. cit.,* p. 283.
29. W. Kolfhaus, *Vom Christlichen Leben nach J. Calvin,* pp. 14-15.

The Word is the foundation by which faith is sustained and supported (*Inst.*, III, ii, 6), and this faith consists in a knowledge of God and of Christ (III, ii, 3). Thus the content overflows the container, and "the channel which conveys to us such a copious stream to satisfy our thirst must not deprive the fountainhead of the honor which belongs to it" (III, xxiv, 3).

2. CALVIN AS BIBLICAL INTERPRETER

Secondly, then, Calvin interpreted the Word in the light of the living God who in the Bible confronted him as his Father and his Lord. The basic structure of the Christian faith shines forth through sundry fundamental facets.[30] For Calvin, God's saving self-revelation distinguishes itself in several ways.

A. *The revelation of the holy God strips the sinner of every ground of glorying and gives all the praise to the glory of God's grace.*

The invariable standard by which all interpretations of Scripture ought to be tried is "the analogy of the faith." This is that all of man's goodness and wisdom comes from God (*Inst.*, I, ii, 1), and consequently all the praise of the glory of His grace belongs to God.

> For what is more consistent with faith than to acknowledge ourselves naked of all virtue that we may be clothed by God; empty of all good that we may be filled by Him; slaves of sin, that we may be liberated by Him; blind, that we may be enlightened by Him; lame, that we may be guided; weak, that we may be supported by Him; to divest ourselves of all ground of glorying, that He alone may be eminently glorious, and that we may glory in Him (Calvin, Letter to Francis I).
>
> We shall never entrust ourselves sufficiently to God, unless we completely put from ourselves all trust in ourselves. We shall never elevate our souls sufficiently to Him, unless we first beat ourselves completely down. Never shall we be sufficiently consoled in Him, except we are completely disconsolate in ourselves. Never shall we glory enough in Him, unless we lay aside all gloryings in ourselves. (Calvin, *Opera*, I, 48; cf. *Inst.*, III, xii, 8).
>
> Wherefore, the best and only worthiness which we can bring to God, is to offer Him our vileness, and, if I may so speak, our unworthiness, that His mercy may make us worthy; to despond in ourselves, that we may be consoled in Him; to humble ourselves,

30. Cf. H. Kraemer, *The Christian Message in a Non-Christian World,* pp. 61-85.

that we may be elevated by Him; to accuse ourselves, that we may be justified by Him (*Inst.,* IV, xvii, 43) .

The Christian life is one of increasing dissatisfaction with ourselves, and one of increasing satisfaction in God our Saviour. For Professor T. F. Torrance, the grace of God in Christ is the fundamental principle in Calvin, the one which underlies the original creation in the image of God and the perversion of the fall, as well as the supreme act of grace in Jesus Christ for our salvation.

Calvin's description of God's gratuitous mercy in Christ as gratuitous-goodness, gratuitous-mercy, gratuitous-love has been substantially re-affirmed by Nygren's description of love (*agape*) as "grace" or sovereign, uncaused love, spontaneous and un-motivated love.[31]

Accordingly, for Calvin the mercy of God is the true logic of religion.[32] As we divest ourselves of all ground of glorying that God may be eminently glorious in the saving grace of Christ, both the theological principle *Soli Deo Gloria* and the soteriological principle *Sola Fide* coalesce, and we are saved from a separation which leads on the one hand to a secularized Calvinism and on the other to a sterile mysticism.[33]

A current theologian insists that "forgiving love is the only way of fulfilling the intrinsic claim of every being, namely its claim to be reaccepted into the unity to which it belongs. Creative justice demands that this claim be accepted."[34] But for Calvin this would disturb the utter graciousness of God's free and sovereign dealing with sinners. In Calvin's teaching "it is beyond all controversy, that no man is loved by God but in Christ; He is the beloved Son in whom the love of the Father perpetually rests, and then diffuses itself to us; so that we are accepted in the beloved" (Eph. 1:6; *Inst.,* III, ii, 32; III, xxiv, 5; II, xvi, 4, on Eph. 1:4, 5, 2:7) . Tillich posits not a moral, but an ontological worth or value or claim on justice.

31. A. Nygren, *Agape and Eros,* I, 119, 52f., 61, 72, 117, 158; cf. Dowey, *op. cit.,* pp. 208-209, 220. There are, however, differences between Calvin and Nygren which can be overlooked if one presses Dr. Dowey's "precisely." For Calvin, the love of God is directed to man not primarily because of any worth in man; rather this love is a revelation of God's heart. Every value man has comes from God, but some comes by creation. Nor does God's love remove His distributive justice or stand counter to His law.

32. T. F. Torrance, *Calvin's Doctrine of Man,* p. 19, n. 8; p. 20. Cf. Calvin on Ps. 136; Ps. 103:8; Mic. 7:19.

33. J. van den Berg in *The Evangelical Quarterly,* July, 1950.

34. P. Tillich, *Love, Justice and Power,* p. 86.

Calvin goes back with Paul to election in eternity and finds that "in adopting us, therefore, God does not inquire what we are, and is not reconciled to us by any personal worth."[35] According to the Geneva Catechism, there is no worthiness in us why God should either show His power to help us, or use His merciful goodness to save us. In the *Institutes* (III, xii, 7), "the heart is not open to the reception of God's mercy unless it be divested of all idea of its own dignity," and "we shall never have sufficient confidence in Christ, unless we entirely lose all confidence in ourselves" (*ibid.* 8).

Similarly, Thomas Boston in *The Fourfold State of Man* finds that even when the sinner comes to Christ's door begging mercy, "he comes as a proud beggar standing on Personal Worth," until the Spirit brings conviction and the sinner "sees himself entirely unworthy," and Christ comes to him naked of all worth and grafts him into the true vine. With Berkouwer, "meritorial worth is ostracized as much from the realm of penitence as from that of faith."[36]

Treating of regeneration, Calvin agrees with Paul that God is the author of our spiritual life from its commencement to its end, that man has not the smallest particle in which he can glory, and that all of our salvation is gratuitous because the beginning of all good is from the second creation which we obtain in Christ (Eph. 1:10; *Inst.*, II, iii, 6).

> The Reformation doctrine not only entails but strenuously asserts that there is nothing in sinful man on which deliverance can "take hold," and that he is therefore incapable of deliverance save by the recreation of his dead soul by the almighty power of the Holy Spirit.[37]

As it was God's initiative which conquered Calvin's own stubbornness, so he testifies that God does not graciously accept us because He sees our change for the better, but that He comes into our lives and takes us just as we are, out of pure mercy.[38]

Writing of our reconciliation by Christ's death, Calvin says that God would not lose what remains of the good He placed in man by creation, despite the fact that He is properly incensed

---

35. Calvin, on Eph. 1:5; cf. on I Pet. 1, and on II Tim. 1:9-10, and *Tracts Containing Treatises on the Sacraments*, II, 133.

36. G. C. Berkouwer, *Faith and Justification*, p. 183.

37. B. B. Warfield, *Perfectionism*, I, 20. Cf. also *Thornwell's Collected Writings*, II, 388-389.

38. So G. E. McClellan, in "Dazzled by Grace and Glory," *Presbyterian Life*, June 1, 1959, p. 10; cf. *Inst.*, II, xvi, 3; Calvin on II Cor. 5:19.

against us for our sin and guilt. "Notwithstanding we have brought death upon ourselves, yet He had created us for life. Thus by a pure and gratuitous love towards us, He is excited to receive us into favour." And because He first — always — loved us, therefore He reconciles us to Himself in Christ (*Inst.*, II, xvi, 3). "Nor are we to be divested of vain glory for any other reason than that we may learn to glory in the Lord."[39]

B. *The light of the knowledge of the glory of God shines in the face of Jesus Christ.*

"The genuine Calvinist makes the redeeming love of God the Alpha and the Omega, the ultimate reality on which the universe rests, and which, in ways we cannot fathom, must be working through it all."[40]

> In a word, with all his emphasis on the sovereignty of God, Calvin throws an even stronger emphasis on His love; and his doctrine of God is preeminent among the doctrines of God given expression in the Reformation age in the commanding place it gives to Divine Fatherhood."[41]

Calvin not only proposed to read the revelation of God in nature through the glasses of Scripture, he also interpreted the revelation of God in Scripture by the light of the knowledge of the glory of God that shines in the face of Jesus Christ, that is, by God's self-revelation in Jesus Christ.[42] The second principle by which he undertook to state the evangelical understanding of Scripture to King Francis I is this:

> Again, what is more consistent with faith, than to assure ourselves of God's being a propitious Father, where Christ is acknowledged as a brother and Mediator? than securely to expect prosperity and happiness from Him, whose unspeakable love toward us went so far, that "He spared not His own Son, but delivered Him up for us?" than to rest in the certain expectation of salvation and eternal life, when we reflect upon the Father's gift in Christ, in whom such treasures are hidden?

So also in Calvin's *Catechism* God utters His mercy in Christ, in his *Instruction in Faith* God in Christ is the perpetual object of faith, and in his *Institutes* (III, ii, 30) we are reconciled to God only as faith unites us to Christ. In the "Argument" pre-

---

39. Calvin, Letter to Francis I.
40. *Letters of James Denney*, p. 110.
41. B. B. Warfield, *Calvin and Calvinism*, p. 176; Doumergue, *op. cit.*, **IV**, 89, citing *Opera*, xxvi, 90.
42. W. Niesel, *The Theology of Calvin*, p. 432.

ceding his commentary on Genesis, Calvin says we must not begin with the elements of this world, but with the Gospel which sets forth Christ with His Cross (I Cor. 1:21f.). According to his commentary on the Pastoral Epistles: "Till we know the divine majesty that is in Jesus Christ, and our human weakness which He has taken upon Him, it is impossible for us to have any hope, or to be capable of having recourse to the goodness of God." Only "thus do we emerge from the depths of idolatry and superstition and are borne to heaven in the chariot of the Cross, there by faith to apprehend the things God has prepared for those who love Him."[43] Indeed, "everything which faith ought to contemplate is exhibited to us in Christ."[44] He is the beginning, the middle, the end, and from Him all things must be sought, since nothing is, or can be found, apart from Him.[45]

The sixth chapter of the second book of *The Institutes* has convinced W. A. Hauch that for Calvin faith in God equals faith in Christ.[46] In this significant chapter all knowledge of the Creator as Father is denied to fallen man until knowledge is succeeded by faith that exhibits God to us as Father in Christ. For, "faith ascends from Christ to the Father." To that end one must begin with the preaching of the Cross. "The happiness of the Church has always been founded upon the person of Christ." Likewise "the hope of the pious has never been placed anywhere but in Christ . . . . There can be no saving knowledge of God without Christ . . . . When I say Christ, I include the doctrine of the Gospel which is sealed with His blood."[47] "The saints in former ages, therefore, had no other knowledge of God than what they obtained by beholding him in the Son, as in a mirror" (*Inst.*, IV, viii, 5, based on Matt. 11:27).

There is nothing that Satan so much endeavors to accomplish as to bring on mists with a view of obscuring Christ, for this is his way of opening up every kind of falsehood.[48] And we are *removed from Christ* when we fall into those views that are inconsistent with His mediatorial office, that is, when the Papists divide and mangle Christ:[49]

---

43. Argument to the *Commentary on Genesis*.
44. *Commentary on Ephesians* 3:12.
45. *Commentary on Colossians* 1:12.
46. W. A. Hauch, *op. cit.*, p. 57.
47. Calvin, *Commentary on Galatians* 1:6.
48. Calvin, *Commentary on Colossians* 1:12.
49. Calvin, *On the Necessity of Reforming the Church*.

by calling upon the saints to intercede when Jesus Christ is the one Mediator between God and man; by adoring the Virgin, when Christ alone should be adored; by offering a continual sacrifice in the Mass, when the sacrifice of Christ upon the Cross is complete and sufficient.[50]

Likewise is Christ the focal center of election. "We shall find no assurance of our election in ourselves; nor even in God the Father, considered alone, abstractedly from the Son." Rather our eyes must be directed to Christ, because it was impossible for the Father to love us except in Him. For Calvin as for Luther, Christ the Mediator is the mirror of election (*Inst.,* III, xxiv, 5); for Calvin, as later for Barth, Christ as God the Son is the Author of election (III, xxii, 7); and for Calvin following Augustine, Christ as a mortal man of the seed of David is the brightest example of gratuitous election (III, xxii, 1). Moreover, Calvin prays that "we may be led to Christ only as the fountain of election."[51] Thus "the Reformers, no less than Barth, willed every believer bound to Christ and every path that turned away from Him rejected as speculation." In that God's mercy comes to us in history, we are guarded against speculation. "For confronting us is the mirror of our election, Jesus Christ." This is "the deepest intent of the thought of both Luther and Calvin."[52]

Accordingly, the current effort to foist upon Calvin the doctrine *gratiam praecedit electio*[53] is a clear case of using a text as a pretext by taking it out of its context. What Calvin actually said in the sentence in question (*Inst.,* III, xxii, 1) is this:

> If election precede that grace of God by which we are made fit to obtain the glory of eternal life, what then can God find in us by which He is moved to elect us?

This rhetorical question in a conditional sentence means (as do the earlier sentences in the same paragraph) that only as the Father in His grace looks upon us in Christ can He choose us for His children. If election preceded grace, no sinner would be elected. "God loves us in Christ with the love that He has

50. T. H. L. Parker, *Portrait of Calvin,* p. 108.
51. Calvin's prayer in connection with his exposition of Mal. 1:2 as given by C. E. Edwards, *Devotions and Prayers of John Calvin,* p. 113.
52. G. C. Berkouwer, *Faith and Justification,* pp. 164, 165, 168.
53. J. K. S. Reid, "The Office of Christ in Predestination" in *Scottish Journal of Theology,* 1, 12; for contrary view cf. G. C. Berkouwer, *Divine Election,* 1960, p. 141.

for the Son." And "apart from Christ, we should be lost, for 'no man is loved by God out of Christ.' "[54]

For Calvin, the redemption wrought by Christ was *voluntary*. "His voluntary submission is the principal circumstance in His death; because the sacrifice unless freely offered would have been unavailable to the acquisition of righteousness" (*Inst.*, II, xvi, 5). Likewise was it *vicarious*. "In every respect, He substituted Himself in our room to pay the price of our redemption" (II, xvi, 7). "On this righteous person was inflicted the punishment which belonged to us" (II, xvi, 5). At the same time, it was *victorious*. "Paul magnificently proclaims the triumph which Christ obtained for us on the cross; as though the cross, which was full of ignominy, had been converted into a triumphal chariot," in which by submitting to the power of the curse and of death, He rode victoriously over them and delivered His people from the thralldom of the Devil (II, xvi, 6, 7).

In the last paragraph of the sixteenth chapter of the second book of the *Institutes*, Calvin summarizes our obligation to our Saviour thus:

> The whole of our salvation and all the branches of it are comprehended in Christ . . . . If we seek salvation we are taught by the name of *Jesus* that it is found in him; if we seek any other gifts of the Spirit they will be found in his unction; strength in his dominion; purity in his conception; indulgence discovers itself in his nativity, by which he was made like us in all things that he might learn to condole with us; if we seek redemption, it will be found in his suffering; absolution, in his condemnation; remission of the curse, in his cross; satisfaction in his sacrifice; purification in his blood; reconciliation in his descent into hell; mortification of the flesh, in his sepulchre; newness of life and immortality, in his resurrection; the inheritance of the celestial kingdom, in his entrance into heaven; protection, security, abundance, and the enjoyment of all blessings, in his kingdom; a fearless expectation of the judgment, in the judicial authority committed to him . . . . Blessings of every kind are deposited in him, let us draw from his treasury, and from no other source, till our desires are satisfied.[55]

Moreover, Calvin gave an enrichment to the content of the work of Christ as the Redeemer by re-establishing in the Church the representation of His saving ministry under the threefold

54. Paul Van Buren, *Christ in Our Place,* pp. 9, 121, citing Calvin on Rom. 5:10, and *Inst.,* III, ii, 32.
55. Cf. commentary and sermon on Titus 3:6.

offices of Prophet, Priest, and King. At the same time Calvin
stressed the actuality of Jesus' humanity in the temptation in
the wilderness and at Gethsemane. Jesus shared our lot. He
resembled us in fear, sorrow, and dread. Through the vehe-
mence of His agonies drops of blood flowed from His face.
He felt a greater degree of consternation, as He contended with
horrible fear and dreadful torments, while neglecting all care
of Himself that He might endure the punishment which belonged to us. The incredible bitterness of soul shows how much
our salvation cost the Son of God.[56] Thus Calvin did not follow
Thomas Aquinas and the Roman theologians who permitted
their reasoning about the hypostatic union to cancel or modify
the plain statements of Scripture as to the reality of our Lord's
human life with its trust in and fear of God.

Schleiermacher made Jesus the example for our faith or our
dependence upon God. In reaction thereto, P. T. Forsyth presents God in Christ exclusively as the One on whom our faith
depends. For Calvin, He is both the Lord in whom we believe,
and the believer whose faith we are to emulate. Accordingly,
it is in entire agreement with Calvin's Christology that these
studies suggest that the threefold offices be further enriched and
Christ drawn more deeply into the flesh by expressly bringing
out the correlatives of these offices. He who was priest was
also sacrifice, the Lamb of God. He who is our one rightful
King served as the only completely obedient subject of the
Kingdom. He who is the Prophet of whom Moses and his
successors were types lived as a believer by every Word that
proceeds from the mouth of God (Matt. 4:4, 27:43; Heb. 2:13;
cf. Ps. 22). It is out of the whole course of His obedience and
the agonies of His heart and His flesh that God established
among men that righteousness which becomes ours by faith.[57]
Moreover, that same obedience by which we are justified is our
example in temptation and our consolation in humiliation. The
house of comfort, as well as the ark of salvation, is built of
the wood of His Cross.

C. *As Christ is the theme of Scripture, so the Holy Spirit is the
internal Teacher whose illumination opens the eyes of our faith
to understand, and the trust of our hearts to appropriate the
promises of salvation.*

---

56. *Inst.*, II, xvi, 5, 12; *Harmony of the Gospels; Commentary on Hebrews.*
57. Cf. T. F. Torrance, *The School of Faith,* pp. lxxxf.

As long as there is a separation between Christ and us, all that He suffered and did for man's salvation is useless and unavailing for us. We look upon Him as a fact of past history, or an object of cold speculation at a great distance from ourselves. "The Holy Spirit is the bond by which Christ efficaciously unites us to Himself." It is by the communion of the Spirit that we enjoy the love of God and the grace of the Lord Jesus Christ. For the love of God for us is shed abroad in our hearts by the Holy Ghost who is given unto us. The Spirit is "the hand of God" by which He exerts His power to draw us unto Himself. We are made partakers of the salvation found in Christ as the Spirit enlightens us to believe in Him and at the same time engrafts us into His body that we may become partakers of all His benefits (*Inst.,* III, i; III, ii, 35).

Christ promised the Spirit of truth to the disciples that they might be capable of attaining heavenly wisdom.

> For in vain would the light present itself to the blind, unless this Spirit of understanding would open their mental eyes: so that He may be justly called the key, with which the treasures of heaven are unlocked to us; and His illumination constitutes our mental eyes to behold them (*Inst.,* III, i, 4). In this manner Christ opened the understanding of His two disciples (on the way to Emmaus); not that, rejecting the Scriptures, they might be wise enough of themselves; but that they might understand the Scriptures. So when Paul exhorts the Thessalonians to "quench not the Spirit" he does not lead them to empty speculations independent of the Word; for he immediately adds, "despise not prophesying: clearly intimating that the light of the Spirit is extinguished, when prophecies fall into contempt (*Inst.,* I, ix, 3).

An interesting commentary on the light of the Spirit in interpreting the Word is found in the experience of Professor G. A. Barrois, who has written that as soon as he was willing to read the Word in the light of the Spirit he became a Protestant. "The Book of Life would not be living for me were it not for the Living Spirit."[58]

The Internal Teacher not only brings us to Christ and illumines our minds to understand the Word, the Spirit also inwardly teaches us to feel an entire acquiescence in the Scripture as the Word of God. "It is such a persuasion, therefore, as requires no reasons; such a knowledge as is supported by the highest reason, in which indeed the mind rests with greater security and constancy than in any reasons; it is, finally, such

---

58. G. A. Barrois, *The Christian Century,* June 1, 1949.

a sentiment as cannot be produced but by a revelation from heaven" (*Inst.*, I, vii, 5). It is no limitation on the Spirit to believe that He uses the Word of His own forging as the instrument of His saving work, for He is in all things consistent with Himself (I, ix, 2).

> The Lord has established a kind of mutual connexion between the certainty of His Word and of His Spirit; so that our minds are filled with a solid reverence for the Word, when by the light of the Spirit we are enabled therein to behold the divine countenance; and, on the other hand, without the least fear of mistake, we gladly receive the Spirit when we recognize Him in His image, that is, in the Word . . . . God did not publish His Word to mankind for the sake of momentary ostentation, with a design to destroy or annul it immediately on the advent of the Spirit; but He afterwards sent the same Spirit, by whose agency He had dispensed His Word, to complete His work by an efficacious confirmation of that Word (I, ix, 3).

As faith rests on the gracious promise in Christ so it is both revealed to our minds and confirmed to our hearts by the Holy Spirit (III, ii, 7). As the Holy Scripture is the external source of knowledge, so is faith, the work of the Spirit, the inward principle by which the truth of God is received. As such it is more of the heart than of the head (III, ii, 8), and more of certainty than of comprehension (III, ii, 14). It is an assurance that leads from anxiety and diffidence in ourselves to confidence in the Divine mercy (III, ii, 17). Moreover, this inward work of the Spirit leads to "the obedience of faith" (III, ii, 8); so that while the law of the Lord slays the reader when it is separated from the grace of Christ (I, ix, 3), yet "the state of Christians under the law of grace consists not in unbounded license, uncontrolled by any law, but in being ingrafted into Christ, by whose grace they are delivered from the curse of the law, and by whose Spirit they have the law inscribed on their hearts" (II, viii, 57). Our knowledge is very imperfect and our faith is likewise imperfect (III, ii, 4, 18); accordingly, the gracious ministry of the Spirit is indispensable to the right understanding of the Word.

The ultimate inward guide in interpreting Scripture is the illumination of the Holy Spirit. God has established an inviolable union and a mutual connection between the Word and the Spirit. As, in one sense, the Spirit dispenses the Word, so, in another, the Word is the instrument by which the Lord dispenses to believers the illumination of the Spirit (I, ix, 3; I, vi, 1). Calvin distinguishes but does not separate the work of the Word and of the Spirit (cf. Isa. 59:21). Because Christ is in us by His Spirit we know that Christ is for us. Calvin avoids a theology of the Word only, which would dry up into a metaphysics, and equally avoids a theology of the Spirit alone, which would disintegrate into mysticism.[59] By emphasizing both the Deity of the risen, present living Christ and the Deity of the Holy Spirit, Calvin presents a theocentric theology based on the presence and activity of the living and self-revealing God rather than one based on the "mutilated" principles of human rationalization.[60] Gathering up the great work of his predecessors, Calvin gave

> to the Church the entire doctrine of the Work of the Holy Spirit, profoundly conceived and wrought out in its details, of noetic, aesthetic, and thelematic effects, — a gift, we venture to think, so great, so pregnant with benefit to the Church as fairly to give him a place by the sides of Augustine and Anselm and Luther, as the Theologian of the Holy Spirit, as they were respectively the Theologian of Grace, of the Atonement, and of Justification.[61]

Moreover, for Calvin a meeting with the living Christ by the power of the Holy Spirit is essential to the interpretation of the Word. But this confrontation is not a mere momentary mystical experience. Thereafter, the believer still needs the illumination of the Spirit, and by this illumination to read the revelation of God given in His Word. As he yields obedience to that Word, he accepts the mastery of the Holy Spirit and is fitted into the program of God's all-embracing purpose.

D. *As God confronted Calvin, by His Word and Spirit, He spoke forgiveness to the sinner.*

In the Protestant formulation, Holy Scripture is the rule of faith, and justification by faith alone is the decisive doctrine in interpreting it.[62] Calvin was "a biblical theologian who read the Word in the light of the doctrine of justification by faith."[63] The Lutheran doctrine of justification forms the heart of Calvin's *Institutes;* and Calvin expressed these doctrines "in their purest systematic form."[64] G. C. Berkouwer agrees

---

59. K. Barth, *Die Protestantische Theologie im 19. Jahrhundert*, p. 410.
60. Cf. E. Schaeder, *Theozentrische Theologie*, II.
61. B. B. Warfield, *Calvin and Calvinism*, p. 21.
62. W. P. Paterson, *The Rule of Faith*, 1932.
63. W. Pauck, *The Heritage of the Reformation.*
64. K. Holl, *Calvinstudien*, p. 116; E. Troeltsch, *The Social Teachings of the Churches*, II, 580.

that Calvin was "a Lutheran from the beginning" and was always conscious of being "heir to Luther," at least as far as the doctrine of justification is concerned.[65] With Luther and Melanchthon, Calvin teaches justification by the mercy of God through the imputation of the righteousness of Christ received by faith alone. The *Institutes* give one chapter to the illumination of the Spirit, a following one to faith, and eight chapters to justification. The same theme looms large in the Commentaries and the Tracts, especially in the "Reply to Sadoleto" and the "Refutation of the Council of Trent." For Calvin, justification is the principal hinge by which religion is supported, and wherever the knowledge of it is taken away there the glory of Christ is extinguished, religion abolished, the Church destroyed, and the hope of salvation utterly overthrown.[66]

The question is not how can we be righteous, but how though unrighteous can we be considered as righteous. And the answer is: "Christ alone must be proposed for righteousness, who exceeds all the perfection of the law." We who are unrighteous in ourselves are considered as righteous in Christ (*Inst.*, III, xi, 3). The believing man is to think on everlasting righteousness, not on the basis of the good works to which he devotes himself, but solely on the intervention of the righteousness of Christ given one by the mercy of God (III, xi, 2, 11, 12, 13, 16). A believer is not righteous in himself, nor by faith, because faith receives the Spirit by whom he is made righteous, but because the righteousness of Christ is communicated to him by imputation (III, xi, 23). Facing the tribunal of God, one must dismiss all thought of his own works in reference to justification and embrace the Divine mercy alone. He must turn his eyes from himself and fix them solely on Christ (III, xix, 2; cf. II, xvii, 5; II, xviii, 5). Since we are saved by grace alone it can only be by faith alone, the faith which throws one upon, entrusts one as an undeserving sinner wholly to, the mercy of God in Christ. Faith strips a man of all commendation and brings him empty to God. Yet this faith is necessary, for it is the instrument of receiving Christ in whom righteousness is communicated to us.[67]

65. G. C. Berkouwer, *Faith and Justification*, p. 50 n. 4.
66. *Inst.*, III, xi, 1; "Reply to Sadoleto."
67. *Inst.*, III, xiv, 17; Commentary on Romans 3:22.

E. *This confrontation likewise brought Calvin to read the Word with a profound sense of God's presence and a passionate devotion to the glory of his gracious Lord, his sovereign Father.*

According to Pauck, Calvin read the Word in the light of the doctrine of justification and in terms of the absolute Lordship of God. His crest is a hand holding out a burning heart and bearing this inscription: "I offer my heart to Thee, O Lord, as a slain victim, eagerly and sincerely." To this Calvin adds in a letter to Farel in October 1540, "I yield my soul chained and bound unto obedience to God." The *Institutes* (I, ii, 2) define religion as consisting in faith united with a serious fear of God, comprehending a voluntary obedience, and producing a legitimate worship agreeable to the injunctions of the law. Paul Wernle suggests that if one would know Calvin, how he lived with and for God and the world, let him read first of all in the *Institutes* the section on "The Life of the Christian Man," for "it is the portrait of himself."

> What men chiefly saw in him was the intense concentration that arose from his basic conception of the Christian life as a self-denying labor and a whole-hearted embracing of the divine will.[68]

One ought also to note in the *Institutes* the illuminating chapter on "Prayer," the one on "Christian Liberty," and that on "The Ten Commandments," which have forever made ethics authentic to Reformed theology.

For Calvin, justification and sanctification must always be distinguished, but never separated. The faith by which God justifies is the faith which apprehends Christ, who is made unto us both righteousness (justification) and sanctification (I Cor. 1:30). By the power of His Spirit, Christ is working in the lives of those who have been grafted into the Lord to the end that the image of God may again be mirrored in the creature.[69]

In his sermon on "The Lord Our Righteousness," John Wesley professed to be and was in accord with Calvin on justification.[70] At other times, under the influence of Richard Baxter's *Aphorisms on Justification,* he gave our obedience such a place in the final justification of a sinner that sanctification

---

68. John T. McNeill, *Calvinism,* p. 233.
69. Kolfhaus, *op. cit.,* pp. 94-101.
70. *The Works of Rev. John Wesley,* I, 169-177.

tended to obscure justification by the merits of Christ alone.[71] And in this aspect of his teaching Wesley has been followed by many advocates of perfectionism and the victorious life.[72] On the other side of the matter, some who followed Kohlbrugge of Elberfeld allowed justification to overshadow sanctification.[73] In the second half of the fourth volume of his *Kirchliche Dogmatik,* Barth cites and endorses the astute arrangement of the *Institutes* by which Calvin balances justification and sanctification — the Christian's standing and the Christian's living before God.

Treating of how the things of Christ become ours, Calvin opens the third book of the *Institutes* with a chapter on the illumination of the Holy Spirit and follows that by one on the effect of this illumination, that is, on faith. Then follow sundry chapters on repentance and the Christian life. Thereafter justification receives some eight chapters. Thus for Calvin no justified sinner is ever in a purely legal relationship with God. By the illumination of the Holy Spirit he has been brought to Christ in a living faith and a vital Christian life. At the beginning and all through the course of this life he is held in covenant fellowship with God by the daily forgiveness of sins, and gratitude therefore motivates him in a voluntary obedience.

Calvin's purpose was not to attain a niche in the hall of philosophy but to serve the Church of God. Among his last words to Farel are the avowal that in the measure in which their union has been useful to the Church of God "its fruits abide for us in heaven."

> The unflinching intention of Farel and Calvin was to form again New Testament Christianity in Geneva, to restate it as faith, to re-create it as life, to re-establish it as Church.[74]

In the Church of the living God the Word is the primary pillar of the faith, and the faithful exposition of that Word glorifies God and blesses men. Indeed, out of that exposition comes

---

71. F. J. Powicke, *Life of R. Baxter,* p. 240; cf. Lindström, *Wesley and Sanctification,* pp. 93, 94, 97, 100, 101; and the doctor's thesis by Professor John Deschner of Southern Methodist University presented to University of Basel, 1956.

72. B. B. Warfield, *Perfectionism,* II.

73. K. Barth, *Die Protestantische Theologie im 19. Jahrhundert,* p. 586; G. C. Berkouwer, *The Triumph of Grace in the Theology of K. Barth,* p. 48.

74. P. T. Fuhrmann, *Instruction in Faith,* p. 8.

the Church, and the society and civilization that gather about it.[75]

About a century ago a dozen hymns by Calvin, mostly translations of Psalms, were discovered in an old Geneva prayer-book. These were published in the edition of Calvin's *Works* by Baum, Cunitz and Reuss in 1868. The same year, one of them, *Salutation à Jesus-Christ,* was translated by Mrs. H. B. Smith of New York, and is here appended as Calvin's testimony that the things we need are to be found in Christ.

> *I greet Thee, who my sure Redeemer art,*
> *My only Trust, and Saviour of my heart!*
> *Who so much toil and woe*
> *And pain didst undergo,*
> *For my poor, worthless sake;*
> *And pray Thee, from our hearts,*
> *All idle griefs and smarts,*
> *And foolish cares to take.*
>
> *Thou art the King of mercy and of grace,*
> *Reigning omnipotent in every place;*
> *So come, O King! and deign*
> *Within our hearts to reign,*
> *And our whole being sway;*
> *Shine in us by Thy light,*
> *And lead us to the height*
> *Of Thy pure, heavenly day.*
>
> *Thou art the Life by which alone we live,*
> *And all our substance and our strength receive:*
> *Comfort us by Thy faith*
> *Against the pains of death;*
> *Sustain us by Thy power;*
> *Let not our fears prevail,*
> *Nor our hearts faint or fail,*
> *When comes the trying hour.*
>
> *Thou art the true and perfect gentleness,*
> *No harshness hast Thou and no bitterness:*
> *Make us to taste and prove,*
> *Make us to adore and love*
> *The sweet grace found in Thee;*
> *With longing to abide*
> *Ever at Thy dear side,*
> *In Thy sweet unity.*

75. Abraham Kuyper, *Calvinism.* The Stone Lectures.

Our hope is in no other save in Thee,
Our faith is built upon Thy promise free;
  Come, and our hope increase,
  Comfort and give us peace,
Make us strong and sure,
  That we shall conquerors be,
  And well and patiently
Shall every ill endure.

Poor, banished exiles, wretched sons of Eve,
Full of all sorrows, unto Thee we grieve!
  To Thee we bring our sighs,
  Our groanings, and our cries:
Take pity, Lord, we crave;
  We take the sinner's place,
  And pray Thee, of Thy grace,
To pardon and to save.

Turn Thy sweet eyes upon our low estate,
Our Mediator and our Advocate,
  Propitiator best!
  Give us that vision blest,
The God of gods Most High!
  And let us, by Thy right,
  Enter the blessed light
And glories of the sky!

Oh, piteous and gracious as Thou art,
The lovely Bridegroom of the humble heart,
  Lord Jesus Christ, meet Thou
  The Antichrist our foe,
In this his cruel ruth!
  Thy Spirit give, that we
  May, in true verity,
Follow Thy word of truth.[76]

---

76. Philip Schaff, *Christ in Song*, pp. 678-680; A. M. Hunter, *The Teaching of Calvin*, p. 275; J. T. McNeill, *Calvinism*, p. 148.

CHAPTER SIX

THE INSTRUMENT OF THE REFORMATION

The Preached Word

Speaking on "The Preaching of the Word in the Reformation" Professor Oberman of Harvard offers a fresh characterization of this movement:

> The genius of the Reformation is best described as the rediscovery of the Holy Spirit . . . . The Reformation returned to an understanding of the Holy Spirit as the dynamic presence of God in Jesus Christ . . . under the veil of the preached word.[1]

The Holy Spirit gathers the Church through the proclamation of the Gospel as He opens the Bible both to the understanding of the preacher and to the heart of the hearer, making the sermon a corporate action that links speaking and listening. It is "the apocalyptic event" which "moves the doors of heaven and hell." For Jesus Christ becomes present under the veil of this God-ordained way. The risen Lord Jesus proclaims Himself through the Spirit-wrought exposition and application of His Word, evoking trust and obedience in the Church of Christ.

From her convent at Königsfeldt, Margaret Watteville wrote to Zwingli, praising the everlasting God "for enlightening us anew, and sending us by His Holy Spirit so many heralds of His blessed Word", and praying that "He will cause His Divine Word to grow in all men."[2]

William Tyndale, the man who gave his life that the plow boys of England might have the Bible in their own tongue, teaches:

> As the scripture is nothing else but that which the Spirit of God hath spoken by the prophets and apostles, and cannot be understood but of the same Spirit, let every man pray to God to send him His Spirit to loose him from his natural blindness and ignorance.[3]

1. H. A. Oberman, in *Harvard Divinity Bulletin*, Oct., 1961.
2. M. D'Aubigne, *History of the Reformation*, XI, vii; Zwingli, *Opera*, p. 280.

119

As the Spirit is the Divine author of Scripture, so is He its proper interpreter; and as He interprets Scripture it becomes a line leading to Christ, and a mirror in which faith beholds God.

Conversely, when Martin Bucer finds in Strasburg a congregation that loves, hears and observes the Word which pictures unto us Christ Jesus our Saviour, he assures them that they are born of God. For through the Spirit we recognize ourselves as children of God, our dear Father, and serve men as our brethren. For, "the divine Word brings faith, faith brings love, love brings good deeds."[4]

1. God Made the Light of His Preached Word To Shine through the Reformers

Speaking to the 1960 General Assembly of the Kirk of Scotland, Queen Elizabeth declared,

> The Gospel which had been revered as a record handed down from primitive Christianity was once more seen as a living light by which men ought to direct their lives and remold their institutions.

The Queen's verdict reaffirms the teaching of William Whitaker, the first Elizabeth's Professor of Divinity in Cambridge, that as the blind cannot perceive the light of the sun, neither can those whose minds are not divinely illuminated distinguish the splendor of the Scriptures. Only those who have the eyes of faith behold this light, and recognize in the Scripture the voice of God — even as one recognizes that of a familiar friend.[5]

In His mercy, God brought the Reformers into the light of the Gospel and assured them that not even the flames of martyrdom would be able to bury the light that God had made to shine in them. *Post tenebras lux.*[6] This light shone in

> the lively preaching and the simple revelation of Christ as the same is hid and promised in Scripture; for the Gospel teaches not otherwise than Christ, and Scripture likewise is nothing else than Christ.[7]

The way was prepared by the recovery of the ancient languages. "Greece rose from the dead with the New Testament

---

3. W. Tyndale, *Doctrinal Treatises*, p. 88.

4. M. Bucer, *Instruction in Christian Love*, ed. Fuhrmann, pp. 16, 44, 52.

5. W. Whitaker, *Disputation on Holy Scriptures, Homilies*, p. 290, *W. Th. B.*, xxiii, p. 133.

6. So Calvin, *Letter to the Five Martyrs of Lyons, Reply to Sadoleto, Introduction to the Psalms, Last Will.*

7. *Luther's Works*, 22, 477.

in her hands."[8] The Reformation proceeded from a serious exposition of the old Word. For the scholars this was Erasmus' Greek New Testament, for the common people the translations thereof. The Scottish Reformers owed their power to a living revival of biblical religion which brought a knowledge of Christ, from whose face the light of God radiates.[9]

A. *In giving them the light of His Word, God turned the Reformers away from the darkness of men.*

The necessity for this revelation is found in a loss of confidence in human reason and man's natural theology. In Luther's earliest statements, his marginal notes on the *Sentences* of Peter Lombard, he insists that the vapors of earth do not illumine the heavens, rather they hold back the light from the earth. All light must come from the biblical revelation, for the human reason is unable to understand supernatural matters. His early lectures on Romans show his extreme pessimism about human nature. After fifteen hundred years of Christianity there has been no improvement since the days of Paul. It is foolish to inquire about the image of God since it has been effaced by sin and will only be restored at the resurrection of the dead.[10]

For Thomism, man by his sin has lost the *similitudo* but not the *imago Dei*. This means that his unaided reason is still able to discern the first principles, practise the cardinal virtues, prove the existence of God, and build a natural theology. He needs the superadded gifts only to complete by grace what nature has already begun; that is, to exercise the theological virtues of faith, hope and love. For the Reformers, the image of God is not a mere superadded gift but is inherent in the very nature of man. According to Luther, man is fallen in his total being. He no longer reflects the image of God in spontaneous love; egocentricity has replaced filial trust.[11]

Calvin likewise rejects the Thomist doctrine of a difference between the image and the likeness of God (*Inst.*, I, xv, 3).

8. P. Schaff, *History*, III, 286.

9. J. Bullock, *The Kirk in Scotland*, pp. 13-14.

10. M. Reu, *Luther and the Scriptures*, p. 16; M. J. Heinecken, *Christ Frees and Unites*, pp. 30-31, together with a gracious letter from Professor Heinecken in which he qualifies and elaborates the views set forth in his book.

11. Similarly, John Wesley says that every single individual has totally lost, not only the favour, but likewise the image of God. "The Heavenly Treasure in Earthen Vessels," CXXVII in *The Works of John Wesley*. Cf. "On Original Sin."

With Augustine, he holds that fallen man has been wholly deprived of his supernatural talents, while the natural ones have been corrupted (II, ii, 4, 12). When his eye is fastened upon the former, Calvin describes the defection of the first man as sufficient to obliterate the divine image (III, ii, 12; *Instruction in Faith,* par. 4). Likewise the Scots' Confession speaks of it as *penitus obliterata,* the Gallic finds man's whole nature corrupt, while the Westminster Confession represents man as dead in sin and defiled in all his faculties, having lost all ability of any spiritual good accompanying salvation. Treating of John 8:44, Calvin can even speak of the impious degenerating into the likeness of the devil (*Inst.,* I, xiv, 18; II, ii, 11; cf. also Bullinger, *Decades,* I, 42). For Calvin, the image of God becomes partly visible in the elect, when they are regenerated by the Spirit. Yet it will only obtain its full glory in heaven (I, xv, 4).

While Luther held that the image of God will not be restored until the resurrection, he taught that in a believing person, regenerated and enlightened by the Holy Spirit through the Word, reason is a fair and glorious instrument and a work of God.[12] He recognized a civil righteousness even in the unsaved. Calvin speaks of the mind of fallen man as still invested with excellent talents in such matters as civil polity, domestic economy, mechanical and liberal arts (II, ii, 13-17). We should do good to all men on the ground that we can still contemplate the Divine image in them (III, vii, 6; *On Genesis* 9:6), that is, it was not utterly annihilated and effaced (I, xv, 4). While Luther's concept of civic righteousness left the state largely to human reason, Calvin brought all of man's relations more fully under the infinite personality of God. This militated against the remnants of impersonalism which had come into Christian thinking through scholasticism. When God made man in His own image, man functioned in a wholly personalistic manner; and as he is remade and seeks again the glory of God, he acts more and more in this personal way, living and moving and having his being in the infinite personality of God.

Even the opposition bore witness to the Reformation turn from rationalistic and ecclesiastical to biblical and Christological terminology. Against Zwingli's evangelical theses, Faber, the vicar-general of the bishop of Constance, sneered: "The Gospel! always the Gospel! . . . Men might live in holiness, peace and

12. *Table Talks,* transl. by Hazlitt, lxxvi.

charity, even if there were no Gospel."[13] On November 1, 1533, when Cop presented the case for the Reformed faith in his address to the University of Paris on "The Christian Philosophy," two Franciscans were heard to complain:

> Grace, pardon of God, Holy Spirit, that's all this speech is filled with. Nothing about indulgences, good works — where will it lead to?[14]

In a letter to the Pope's secretary, written to accompany a copy of his book on *Free Will*, Erasmus said:

> Some Frenchmen are still more out of their wits than even the Germans. They have five expressions always in their mouths: Gospel, Word of God, Faith, Christ, Holy Ghost; yet I doubt whether they be not urged on by the spirit of Satan.[15]

In his letter to Francis I, Calvin defends the Evangelicals against the complaints of the Romanists that we "overturn I know not what blind light of nature." "In order to enjoy the light of true religion, it is necessary to begin with the heavenly teaching, and no man can have the smallest taste [*minimum gustum*] of true and sound doctrine without being a disciple of Scripture" (*Inst.*, I, vi, 2). In the knowledge of God and especially His fatherly kindness toward us on which our salvation depends, the most sagacious of men are blinder than moles (II, ii, 18). We must seek in the Holy Scripture and not anywhere else the wisdom which is sufficient for salvation.[16] J. G. Hamann was nearer the position of the Reformers than were most of his contemporaries in the Age of Reason when he wrote:

> Was Reason given to make us wise? Just as little as the Law was given to the Jews to make them just. Rather [it was given] to convince us of the opposite, [to show us] how irrational our Reason is, and that our errors may be increased through Reason, as sins were increased through the Law.[16a]

B. *In the light that leaped from the proclamation of the Word God carried forward the Reformation.*

The Reformers did not fall into rationalism's ditch. They did not first in theology affirm that man is fallen as a totality, and then in apologetics draw up a series of principles from the

---

13. M. D'Aubigne, *History of the Reformation*, XI, i; Zwingli, *Opera*, I, 152.

14. E. Steckelberger, *Calvin, A Life*, p. 21.

15. M. D'Aubigne, *History of the Reformation*, III, xii, 10.

16. *Commentary on II Timothy*, 3:15.

16a. Cited by R. G. Smith, *J. G. Hamann*, p. 50; W. Lowrie. *J. G. Hamann*, p. 12.

reason or from the inner experience of this fallen man and force the revelation of the living God, the great events of His saving intervention, to conform to these puny presuppositions. Instead, they listened to the Word and set their compasses where the light is brightest; that is, where the faithful exposition of the written Word is illuminated by the living Word. Every Scripture is to be tested as to whether "it sets forth Christ or not" (Luther). In His own Word, they found Christ as their Saviour and Lord, then they reread that Word in the light from His countenance, and contemplated man and nature in the light of the Word. Of course, the mere letter of the Scripture is dead,

> and the law of the Lord slays the readers of it, where it is separated from the grace of Christ, and only sounds in the ears without effecting the heart. But if it be efficaciously impressed on our hearts by the Spirit; if it exhibit Christ; it is the Word of life converting the soul" (*Inst.*, I, ix, 3).

Through the instrumentality of the ministers of the Spirit, "Christ illuminates the minds of men, renews their hearts, and in short regenerates them wholly."[17] The zeal with which the Reformers gave themselves to proclaiming the Word accords with Ludwig Hofacker's declaration that the Gospel is like a trumpet "more powerful and piercing when it does not follow the range of the scale but keeps to one penetrating note."

Luther gave his life to preaching the Gospel from the Word and to translating that Word into a language that the people could understand and appropriate. To the demand of the Diet at Worms that he recant, the Reformer replied with the ringing declaration that his conscience was bound by the Word of God, the most precious thing in the world.

Thereafter, he lived in constant expectation of being called on to give his life for his proclamation of that Word. Indeed, he was thrown into fits of melancholy when certain of his disciples were making this sacrifice while he remained untouched. At the Marburg Colloquy, Melanchthon may have been influenced by political considerations, but Luther was held back from the Swiss Reformers by his understanding of the Word of God. In Saxony the letters VDMIAE (*verbum Dei manet in aeternitate*) were inscribed on the coach and harness as the insignia of the evangelical electoral house. The more Luther was attacked, the more he sank himself into the Word, especially the Epistle to the Galatians. He named this

---

17. Calvin on II Cor. 3:6; cf. on I Cor. 3:6.

book his Catherine von Bora. In his commentary thereon, the Reformer discerned that "the world owes the Gospel a grudge, because the Gospel condemns the religious wisdom of the world." In Scotland, the martyrdom of that noble Lutheran scholar, Patrick Hamilton, inspired a preaching of the Word in many parts of the land.

"In Zurich, as everywhere, the Reformation proceeded by means of a preaching closely drawn from the Bible".[18] On January 1, 1519, Zwingli began his ministry in the Zurich Munster with a series of sermons which carried straight through the Gospel of Matthew. After preaching through the Gospel, he took up Acts and then Romans, using the Psalms for lectures on feast days when the country people gathered in the city. The Great Munster was transformed into a theological college for the training of ministers to expound the Word of God. Here Pellicanus issued the first complete Protestant commentary on the Holy Scriptures. The Swiss Reformation came to articulate statement in the theses of Ilanz in 1526, and in those of Bern in 1528, both of which begin:

> The Holy Church of God, of which Christ is the only Head, is born of the Word of God, abides in it, and hears not the voice of strangers.[19]

One who listens can hear the overtones of this appeal to the tenth chapter of John echoed in the recent Theses of Barmen.

In England, William Tyndale complained that the boys in Oxford and Cambridge were nozzled on Aristotle for years before they were allowed to read the Word. Tyndale and John Rogers put the Bible into the English tongue that even the plow boys might hear its glorious cadences, and they paid with their lives for so doing. The preaching of Hugh Latimer and John Knox proclaimed that Word, the use of Thomas Cranmer's liturgy taught Englishmen to plead its promises, and the reading of Henry Bullinger's *Decades* expounded to them its Gospel.

John Calvin found the sheep of the Lord scattered on a thousand hills, and he lifted a banner to gather them, not a new banner but the old banner of God's Word. As a result, the asthmatic whispers of this gasping preacher had the authority of trumpets. Calvin was not a philosophical theologian but an expounder of the Word. His theology is found

18. J. T. McNeill, *History and Character of Calvinism*, p. 44.
19. *Ibid.*, pp. 59, 64; cf. P. Schaff, *Creeds of Christendom*, I, 365.

in his commentaries and sermons preached in the great churches of Geneva.

At the meeting of the Diet of Augsburg, the Protestant party rose in power and strength as long as the Word of God was being preached by the evangelicals. Then it was that the courageous old margrave of Brandenburg, Duke George, knelt before the Emperor and declared that he would rather have his own head struck off than have the Word of God taken from him. It was then that the evangelical princes refused to walk with the Emperor in the *corpus Christi* procession. But when the preaching of the Word was silenced and the Gospel stilled, then Protestant retreat set in.

The Word was primary because it was God's Word. For Calvin it was the mouth of the Lord that spake, and His Spirit now testifies to our hearts as He employs these Scriptures to instruct us. Since the preached Word becomes God's Word to the hearer, we ought not so much to consider man as speaking, as Christ by His own mouth.[20] Luther makes the matter even more concrete:

> God, the Creator of heaven and earth, speaks with thee through His preachers, baptizes, catechises, absolves thee through the ministry of His own sacraments. These are not the words of Plato or Aristotle: It is God Himself Who speaks.

For the Reformers, God was speaking, God was making Himself their God, God was daily forgiving their sins.

Thus did the Reformation advance. How can a sinner know that God is gracious to Him? Only on the authority of God's own Word. How can I be assured that God is truly reconciled to me, a guilty, hell-deserving sinner? Only because God tells me in His own Word that He has made peace by the blood of Christ's Cross. How can one be sure that his sins are forgiven? On the authority of the Word: "Son, be of good cheer, thy sins are forgiven thee." Can one be sure that only faith, faith alone — simply to Thy Cross I cling, naked come to Thee for dress, casting myself helpless and undone on the mercy of God, on the merit of Christ — is sufficient? Yes, sinner, you can, I can, be sure — for God graciously says so. God declares forgiveness in the proclamation of His Word and seals it in the fellowship of His people as they continue in the unity of Christ's body and true members of His Church.[21] We have

20. Calvin on II Tim. 3:16 and on John 10:4; *Second Helvetic Confession,* I.
21. Calvin, *Geneva Catechism,* a. 104.

put our trust in Jesus Christ that we may be justified by faith in Him, apart from the works of the law. Luther needed but one thing to live by: the assurance that God was gracious to him, the assurance which God gave him by His own Word. Calvin knew God's tender love toward us, for He has plainly uttered in His Gospel that He will be both a Father and a Saviour unto us through the means of Jesus Christ.[22]

2. ACCORDINGLY, THE REFORMERS RECEIVED THE WORD AS THE MOUTH OF GOD,[23] WIELDED IT AS THE SWORD OF THE SPIRIT, AND HONORED IT AS THE PRIMARY MEANS OF GRACE.

A. *The Word is the sword of the Spirit.*

In opposing those who separate the preached Word from the Spirit, Luther insists that "God's Word is an instrument and tool, through which the Holy Spirit works . . . and makes a beginning to justification." "God works through His Word, which is like a vehicle or tool whereby we learn to know Him in our heart." Consequently when an honest preacher speaks God's Word at His command "he is God's mouthpiece or tool."[24] Turning to the people of God, he admonishes those who feel any love or desire for the Word to acknowledge, with thankfulness, that this affection is poured into them by the Holy Spirit; and conversely that the Holy Ghost who comes with the Word preached purifies our hearts by faith and brings forth in us spiritual actions.[25] Or, as his position has been summarized,

> Now the Word is seen as an instrument in the hands of the Spirit by which the merits of Christ are given or the Church sanctified, and then it is seen as an instrument in the hands of the Triune God by which the Spirit is given. Thus in the one case the Spirit is *over* the Word, and in the other the Spirit is *in* the Word.[26]

As the Word without the Spirit would not be the saving Word of God, so the Spirit without the Word would not be the revealing Spirit. The Word is thus the door or the window through which the Spirit comes to us, or the bridge or path

22. Calvin, *Geneva Catechism*, a. 111, cf. *Commentary on Romans.*
23. Luther, *W. A.*, IV, 535, 1ff.; Calvin, *Inst.*, I, vii, 5; *Commentary on Deut.*, CR, xxv, 666-667; *Preface to Scots' Confession;* Collect for second Sunday in Advent, *The Book of Common Prayer.*
24. *Tischreden, W. A.*, iii, 672-674.
25. Luther, *On Galatians* 4:6 and 3:2.
26. R. Prenter, *Spiritus Creator*, pp. 256, 124.

on which He moves.[27] This means both the *necessity* of the
Word, and its insufficiency apart from *the Holy Spirit.*

> Thus Scripture is such a book that to it belongs not only the
> reading but also the proper Expounder and Revealer, namely, the
> Holy Ghost. Where He does not open the Scripture, there indeed
> it is not understood.[28]

Calvin teaches both the real presence of the Holy Spirit with
the preaching of the Word and also the witness of the Holy
Spirit in the heart of the believer, thus uniting the testimony
of Luther and that of Bullinger; that is, the Spirit acts both
per verbum and also *cum verbo.* The minister of the Word
is so to preach "that God may speak to us by the mouth of
a man." God uses the human words of the preacher in His
exposition of Scripture. As the preacher expounds the Bible,
God speaking through his human words uses them as the
vehicle of His grace, "the instrument by which Jesus Christ
with all His graces is dispensed to us." Thus the word we
hear is the Word by which we are saved. God adds to the
human voice the power of His Holy Spirit, or "the Spirit
puts forth His power in the Word preached" so that preaching
becomes revelation.[29] For Calvin as for Luther, "It is no less
unreasonable to boast of the Spirit without the Word, than
it would be an absurd thing to bring forward the Word without
the Spirit."[30] Commenting on the action of God both by
the Voice and by the Spirit of God in Ezekiel 2:1-2, Calvin adds

> This work of the Spirit is, therefore, joined with the Word of
> God. But a distinction is made that we may know that the
> eternal Word is of no avail by itself, unless animated by the
> power of the Spirit.

The close union which Isaiah 59:21 makes between the Spirit
and the Word leads Calvin to speak of their "inviolable union"
and "mutual connection" and to condemn as "detestable sacri-
lege" the separating of these two which God has joined together
(*Inst.*, I, ix, 1) .

Even when preaching is the Word of God it is not efficacious
unless the way to the heart be laid open by the internal teaching
of the Spirit. The Spirit by a wonderful and peculiar power

27. *Ibid.,* pp. 256, 124.
28. Luther on Luke 24:13f. cited by Barth, *Kirchliche Dogmatik,* I/2, 563.
29. T. H. L. Parker, *The Oracles of God,* pp. 54-57, citing Calvin, *Sermon
on Deut., Sermon on I Tim., Short Treatise on the Lord's Supper, On
Heb.* 4:12.
30. Calvin, *Opera Selecta* (ed. Barth, Niesel) , I, 466.

pierces the ears to hear and the mind to understand (*Inst.,* II, ii, 20).

> Regeneration is wrought by the power of the Holy Ghost, working in the hearts of the elect of God an assured faith in the promise of God revealed to us in His Word, by which faith we apprehend Christ Jesus.[31]

In this work of creating faith the Spirit works alongside the Word and not apart from it as Calvin's formal definition of faith makes clear (*Inst.,* III, ii, 7). Faith in God's goodness to us is founded on the gracious promise in Christ and is both revealed to our minds and confirmed in our hearts by the Holy Spirit. By this faith I am persuaded that Christ is mine and that the Father is propitious to me in Him (cf. III, ii, 2).

By His Spirit, the living Lord Jesus illumines my mind to know and my heart to confide in Him as the Word of the Gospel presents Him. The Spirit seals remission of sins in the elect (III, ii, 11). Thus by His Word and His Spirit, God brings the sinner into a most personal relationship to his Saviour. The objective revelation of God in Jesus Christ, and the inward working of the Holy Spirit, both in our hearts and in the proclamation of the Word, are the two arms of the heavenly Father by which He draws us back to His forgiving bosom.

Calvin uses our Lord's comparison of the preached Word to a seed, thus:

> For as seed, if it fall on a desert and neglected spot of ground, will die without producing a crop; but if it be cast upon a well manured and cultivated field, it brings forth its fruit with an abundant increase: so the Word of God, if it fall upon some stiff neck, it will be as unproductive as seed dropped upon the sea-shore; but if it light upon a soul cultivated by the agency of the heavenly Spirit, it will be abundantly fruitful. Now if the Word be justly compared to seed — as we say that from seed corn grows, increases and comes to maturity — may we not say that faith derives its commencement, increase and perfection from the Word of God? . . . Paul glories in having the ministry of the Spirit, as if there were an indissoluble connexion between his preaching and the power of the Holy Spirit operating to the illumination of their minds, and the incitement of their hearts, I Cor. 2: 4; II Cor. 3:6-8 . . . . The apostles, then, in their preaching, exerted the power of the Spirit, as far as God made use of the instruments appointed by Himself for the exhibition of His spiritual grace (*Inst.,* IV, xiv, 11).

31. *Scots' Confession,* 1560, III; cf. also XII.

> As the children of God are sensible that without the Spirit of God they are utterly devoid of truth, so they are not ignorant that the Word is the instrument by which the Lord dispenses to believers the illumination of His Spirit (I, ix, 3).

Moreover, the Spirit causes faith to stand firm by resting it on the gratuitous promise and using it to reconcile us to God by uniting us to Christ (III, ii, 29-30). Our assurance is from the inward work of the Holy Spirit, bearing witness by and with the Word in our heart (*Westminster Confession*, I, 5).[32] According to Beza the testimony of the Spirit of adoption lies in this — that each applies to himself the promise of salvation of which Paul speaks in Romans 8:15-16.[33]

Thus, in revealing God to us by His Word, the Spirit acts in a threefold way. He inspires the prophets and apostles in receiving and writing the Word. Again He accompanies the Word as it is preached, speaking by and with it, so that it becomes the Sword of the Spirit. Then the same Spirit penetrates into our hearts so that we believe the doctrine of the Scriptures as from the person of God speaking by the mouth of men (*Inst.*, I, vii, 4-5). The blessed circle is complete, from the apostles through the preachers into the hearts of the hearers. By this triple work of the Spirit with the Word we are drawn into the orbit of Christ and find ourselves no longer strangers but children in our Father's house, given a partnership in the covenant of grace.

B. *The Word is understood primarily as a means of grace.*

For the Reformation, the Bible is primarily the tool which God uses to give us His grace.

> The biblicist and the rationalist, the former more, the latter less, see in the Bible the book that shows us the way to God; but the Calvinist learns from the Bible first and foremost how God has found a way to us.[34]

32. W. Cunningham, *Theological Lectures*, p. 332, shows that the preposition *by* indicates the proofs or marks of God and His agency seen in the Word itself when men's eyes are opened by the Spirit to discern them; while the preposition *with* indicates the changes which are produced upon men's hearts and characters by the Spirit in using the Word, or its doctrines in effecting them. G. S. Hendry, *The Holy Spirit in Christian Theology*, p. 76, fails to recognize this usage of *with*.

33. *Th. Bezae Vezelii Opera*, i, (Geneva, 1582), p. 503, cited by B. B. Warfield, *Calvin and Calvinism*, p. 77.

34. D. W. Kolfhaus, *Vom christlichen Leben nach J. Calvin*, p. 86.

It is the history of God's dealings with His people. The Word of God in the Bible is an activity of God that creates and directs the personal relationship between Himself and us. "A Christian's life stands entirely in the exercise and experience of the things which one daily hears and reads from God's Word."[35] Believers are to read the Bible as if they heard the very words pronounced by God Himself, for therein God speaks to us and manifests His will for us.[36] Thus our knowledge of the truth of God is always an acknowledgement of what He has told us in His Word.

Christian faith is not a monologue but a dialogue. The Word of God demands our faith, and it is the ground, the substance and the life of our faith.[37] The Word and faith belong together as the sun and its rays, as the root and the fruit. Take away the Word and there will be no faith left. "By faith we repel all the attacks of the devil, and by the Word of God the enemy himself is slain." The Word is a mirror in which we behold God's gracious disposition toward us.[38] All the promises of God are Yea in Christ, and by the grace of the Spirit, ever and anon, the Amen of faith sounds from the believing heart (II Cor. 1:20). As God speaks through His word, the believer, by the grace of the Spirit, anchors in His promises. Accordingly the Christian opens the Word, praying, "Speak, Lord, Thy servant heareth!" and, "I believe, Lord, help Thou mine unbelief."

The Reformers knew that the personal God, who had made and redeemed them, "was speaking to them in this book, and was there making manifest familiarly His power and willingness to save." For them saving faith was simple trust, the trust of a child in his father's promises.

> The one essential thing was to hear and obey the personal God speaking to them as He had spoken all down through the ages to His people, promising His salvation now in direct words, now in pictures of His dealings with a favoured man or a chosen people. No detail of life was dead history; for it helped to fill the picture of communion between God and His people.[39]

By the operation of the Holy Spirit, believers are enabled to recognize that God Himself is speaking to them in and through

---

35. Luther, *Sermon on Rom.* 8:18.
36. *Inst.*, I, vii, 1; CR 54, 285, cited by W. Niesel, *The Theology of Calvin*, p. 36.
37. K. Barth, *Kirchliche Dogmatik*, I/2, 594.
38. Calvin, *Inst.*, III, ii, 6; *Commentary on Ephesians* 6:16-17.
39. T. M. Lindsay, *History of the Reformation*, I, 458f.

the words of Scripture. And "as all Scripture sets forth Christ,"[40] here God speaks, as a man speaks to his fellows, calling us to personal trust in the personal Saviour. By the grace of the Spirit, Scripture as the Word of God is efficacious to quicken the hearts of men and convert them to Christ by a living faith,

> the Law humbling the conceited natural heart and the Gospel, the message of divine grace in Christ Jesus as the power of God unto salvation to everyone that believeth engendering saving faith in Christ.[41]

As the Word is the instrument which the Spirit has forged through sundry centuries of God's gracious dealings with men, so it is the means which the Spirit effectually uses in calling us to Jesus Christ, the Good Shepherd of the sheep. As for Luther, "God's Word is an instrument and a tool through which the Holy Spirit works," so for Calvin, "Scripture is the school of the Holy Spirit," and it is no limitation of the Spirit to say that He uses the instrument of His own forging and tempering rather than the fluctuating opinions of men (*Inst.*, III, xx, 1, 3; I, ix, 2). Since it is God, rather than man, who is operative, "Christ does not need to be preached with a furious tempest of words. He cannot be preached save peacefully and calmly."[42] Since it is God who has the Scripture in His hand, the power of the Gospel is not in the lungs of a man but in the might of the Spirit.[43] Nor has Scripture been inspired once for all and then deserted by the Spirit, but it is continually carried forward, kept and rendered efficacious by this same Spirit who works with the Word as a Divine Person.[44]

The Spirit gives to the Christian soldier the sword of His own fashioning that he may proclaim the mystery of the Gospel (Eph. 6:17, 19). Faith comes by hearing and hearing by the Word which both comes forth from and presents Christ (Rom. 10:17). It pleases God by the preaching of this Gospel of the crucified, risen, reigning and returning Christ — the Gospel which men call foolishness — to save those who believe

---

40. Luther, *Preface to the Epistles of St. James and Jude.* Cf. on Rom. 3, "Since all the Scriptures show us Christ."

41. J. T. Mueller, "Luther's Doctrine of Inspiration," *Christianity Today*, 1, 8, 4.

42. Luther, *W. A.*, 57, 137, 20.

43. R. Prenter, *Spiritus Creator*, pp. 102, 255, 256.

44. P. Marcel, "L'Actualité de la Prédication," *La Revue Reformée*, March 1951, pp. 19-21.

(I Cor. 1). When the Apostle preached in Thessalonica and in Corinth, the Gospel came not in word only but in power and in the Holy Ghost, so that the faith of the believers stood not in the wisdom of men but in the power of God (I Thess. 1:5, 2:13; I Cor. 2:4-5; cf. Gal. 3:2). It is by the Spirit that Christ speaks (John 6:63), and the disciples receive this Spirit (Matt. 10:20; Luke 12:12, 21:15; John 14:26, 16:26), who takes of the things of Christ and shows them to us (John 16:14). From Calvin's comments on John 20:21 and from the Second Helvetic Confession (xviii, 8), Pastor Marcel concludes:

> By the Spirit this Word is thus connected with its Author, with Christ. Christ is and remains the Master of the preaching of His Word . . . . It is thus really a word proclaimed by the Christ, and therefore, by God Himself. It is truly a word *from God*, presented, borne, and made active by the Spirit . . . . It is entirely different from our merely human words. Written or spoken it is always God's own Word; He is ever present with it; He continually carries it onward by His all-powerful, ever-present might. When His Word is preached, it is God who addresses it to men; it is He who by it calls them . . . . The Word of God is never separated from God, from Christ, and from the Holy Spirit; it has no existence in itself; it is impossible to dissociate it from its Creator and from its Author.[45]

Or, as the noted Bible exegete John Albert Bengel expressed it,

> Scripture was divinely inspired, not merely while it was written God breathing through the writers; but also whilst it is being read, God breathing through the Scriptures.

One begins with the Word, but this does not lead Calvin to bibliolatry.

> The channel which conveys to us such a copious stream to satisfy our thirst must not deprive the fountain-head of the honor which belongs to it (*Inst., III, xxiv, 3*).

Christ has not made Himself unnecessary by giving us His Word. As the Spirit uses the Word in presenting Christ, the Yea and Amen of all the promises, it becomes the Gospel of salvation to everyone who believes. The Saviour is offered not merely as an ethical ideal, but as the gift of God's love. He is not primarily a set of laws, principles and demands; He is our peace, our forgiveness and our hope.

> The Spirit by this Word brings Christ into the heart as the gift of God, as the One who does not merely in a demanding manner prescribe our life, but who in mercy gives us life. . . .

45. *Ibid.*

> In this Word the risen Christ is present as God's gift to us
> and thereby directs the motion of faith (away) from all self-
> righteousness to Christ as our alien righteousness.[46]

Faith here is the living flesh of identification between the Word
and the Voice of Him whose Word it is, a trust in the living
Christ who now speaks. And justification by faith alone means
that all the efficacy of faith resides in Him who is its object.
With Abraham, this faith gives glory — all the glory of saving
the sinner — to God (Rom. 4:20).

John Witherspoon, the great evangelical divine of Scotland,
accepted the second invitation from the struggling little college
of Princeton on the colonial frontier. His entrance upon the
pulpit that first Sunday was like a king ascending his throne.
What would the great man have to say? Taking as his text,
"Paul may plant and Apollos may water, but only God gives
the increase," Dr. Witherspoon declared that the success of the
Gospel is wholly of God. Some years later he used the same
sermon at the organization of the first American General Assembly. God heard that humble avowal and so blessed the
Presbyterian family until, from those small beginnings, there
are now millions in the Presbyterian and Reformed Churches
in this land and their missionary testimony sounds to the ends
of the world.

C. *The Word is the basic means of grace.*

Not only is the Word to be considered primarily as a means
of grace; it is the primary means of grace. The preaching of
the Gospel is the instrument of faith, the formal cause by which
the goodness of God overflows upon us. The Holy Spirit makes
preaching effective by enlightening the mind in knowledge and
establishing the heart in conviction.[47]

Already for the pre-Reformers, Wycliffe's *Pastoral Office*
stresses the duty of the minister to preach. This is his highest
service, even as Christ occupied Himself most in that work. The
preaching of the Word is more precious than the administration
of any church sacrament. William Sawtre, the poor Lollard
chaplain of St. Osythe, was burned in 1401 for teaching, among
other things, that preaching was the priesthood's most important
duty. And despite the prohibition of the pope, John Huss in-

---

46. R. Prenter, *op. cit.,* pp. 124, 112.
47. Calvin, *Commentary on Ephesians,* 1:7, 13.

sisted that he must continue to preach, following Christ who did so in the homes and beside the sea.[48]

For Luther, preaching was the veritable Word of God, and as such, occupied the central position in the Church.[49] *Verbum est principium rerum.* In his commentary on Hebrews, he speaks of the Christian man as having a life hidden in the invisible God by feeding on Him who never appears except in the vehicle of the hearing of the Word.[50] According to Calvin, "True acquaintance with God is made more by the ears than by the eyes."[51] Indeed, the Church rests upon the Word as its foundation, with the sacraments as the supporting stays.

For the Reformers, God in His majesty and His holiness cannot come into contact with finite, sinful man by direct communication. He does not deal with us immediately or mystically, but sacramentally. All of God's revelation is through signs, visions, wrappings, veils, masks, mirrors, or disguises. Veiling His majesty He descends to our level and has fellowship with us here by words and deeds, by promises and fulfillments, by symbols and seals, by angels and theophanies, by the Word made flesh and now heard in the preaching of the Gospel. In the New Testament Church God makes Himself audible in the proclamation of His Word, and His acts become visible in the administration of the sacraments, as the Holy Spirit effectively uses these instruments. The sacrament is a visible Word, and the Word is an audible sacrament. Together they present God who speaks and acts, who makes a universal offer and seals it upon individuals and their households. "Though the sacraments are ineffective without the Word, nevertheless the bare word cannot have its full effect without the sacraments."[52] In the full worship service, the proclamation of the Gospel sealed with the sacraments, the risen Lord meets His people, His presence confirming His promises. While the evangelical finds in the Roman Catholic worship of the mass a false mediacy or an over-valuing of means, and in the Friends' failure to use the elements a false immediacy or an under-valuing of means, he proclaims a mediated immediacy of "the hidden God"

48. D. S. Schaff, *History of the Christian Church,* VI, p. 329 with citations, and pp. 353, 366, 368, 377.
49. T. H. L. Parker, *The Oracles of God,* p. 20.
50. *W. A.,* 57, 144, 10.
51. *Commentary on Exodus* 33:19.
52. R. S. Wallace, *Calvin's Doctrine of the Word and Sacrament,* p. 137.

who is masked in the medium but not thereby removed from the immediate encounter.[53]

Neither Luther nor Calvin think of the sacrament as primarily man's act. God or the risen Christ is the primary subject of the sacramental act as He is of the preached Word. For Luther, it is not the pastor who baptizes, but God Himself. For Calvin, a sacrament is a visible sign by which the Lord seals upon our consciences His promises of salvation. Robert Bruce of Scotland presents the living Christ as not less busy giving Himself to His believing people at the Supper than the pastor is in distributing the bread and the cup. The invisible presence of Christ in His Spirit,

> He makes effective and evident in the preaching of the Word, in the faithful administration of the Sacraments, in prayer offered in His Name, and through the newness of life whereby He enables the faithful to bear witness to Himself.[54]

Yet the Word became the chief means of grace with the sacrament confirming its blessed promises to each believing participant. The Word is the chief part of the sacrament, and "God has ordained His Word as the instrument by which Jesus Christ with all His grace may be dispensed to us."[55] Luther reminded the opposition that the old formulas spoke of hearing mass, and he twitted them with the charge that the service conducted in the chancel could no longer be heard by the congregation, only the "liftings" of the elements could be seen. Protestants erected high pulpits in the naves of the cathedrals that the preached Word might be heard. "The pulpit, instead of the altar, became the central point in the Lutheran, Calvinist, and Anglican Churches."[56] Luther reminds us that Christ wrote nothing and the Apostles only a little, but that they all spoke very much so that the Church is "a house of the mouth." In the sound of the spoken word, the Spirit makes the Gospel the living voice of the risen Christ. "In the proclamation we expect the gracious coming of the Spirit . . . because the Spirit is a person, the active God Himself."[57] For Calvin, the removal of the Word signifies the departure of Christ. The Word is the root of which faith is the fruit; the Word and faith are so close that one may be used metonymically for the other, and

---

53. So M. J. Heinecken, *Christ Frees and Unites*, p. 42.
54. *Edinburgh Conference Volume*, 1937, p. 231.
55. Calvin, *Opera Selecta* (ed. Barth, Niesel), I, 505, 524.
56. Parker, *op. cit.*, p. 21.
57. R. Prenter, *op. cit.*, pp. 114, 159, 171.

it must ever be held that there is a mutual relationship between the Word of God and our faith.[58] Since for the Reformers and for their evangelical successors[59] the Word is the primary thing, therefore, the Spirit is truly given with the faithful exposition of the Gospel and believing hearers are incorporated by Him into Christ and His saving blessings through preaching. The living Christ is present in preaching, confronting men and drawing them into covenant partnership with Himself as the Spirit accompanies the preached Gospel.

A brief survey of the New Testament vindicates their position. Each of the Gospels was written from the standpoint of Easter, the risen Christ, and from the standpoint of Pentecost, the coming of the Spirit. The Messiah is to anoint with the Spirit and as anointed by the Spirit the Messiah preaches the Gospel to the poor. Like John, Jesus came preaching; only His message was more clearly the good tidings (Mark 1:14-15; Luke 4:43, 8:1, 16:16). The seed of the Kingdom is the Word of God (Luke 8:10-11); and the Father is more ready to give the Spirit to make it bear fruit than parents are to give good gifts to their children (Luke 11:13). Out of His own preaching there was fashioned this gracious invitation: "Hither to Me, all ye that are weary and heavy-laden! And I will give you rest."

As the Father sent Him, so the Lord commissioned His disciples in His Name to preach to all nations repentance and remission of sins. He assured them that His sheep would hear His voice, and thus be gathered into His flock.

In accord with the repeated promises in the Gospels, the Spirit is given at Pentecost to the disciples so that they preach in the power of the Spirit (Acts 2:4, 11, 17, 18, 4:31). As they evangelize, the Spirit opens the hearts of the listeners (Acts 16:14), or falls on those who hear the Word (Acts 10:44). The Apostles proclaim the things of Christ with the Spirit sent down from heaven (I Peter 1:10-12), so that believers are born

58. *Inst.*, II, v, 1, 13; III, ii, 6; *Commentary on Hebrews* 11:11.
59. P. T. Forsyth, *The Church and the Sacraments*, p. 184; T. E. Peck, *Notes on Ecclesiology*, p. 48; Hermann von Bezzel, cited by K. Barth, *The Doctrine of the Word of God*, I/1, 79: "The Word has been the first and will remain the first . . . The Word was before sacrament and exists without sacrament, and will still also exist hereafter." According to R. Wallace, *op. cit.*, p. 73, Calvin "puts the sacraments in the strictly subordinate position to the word." For E. Schweizer, *Church Order in the New Testament* (p. 222), "Everything that can be said realistically about Christ's presence can be found in the New Testament much more clearly in relation to the Word than . . . in relation to the Lord's Supper."

again by this preached Word (1:23, 25). As Paul preached, the Gospel came to the Thessalonians in the Holy Spirit and worked in great effectiveness (I Thess. 1:5-10, 2:13). The Galatians and the Corinthians received the Spirit by the Word of the Cross (Gal. 3:2, 5, 14; I Cor. 1:17-2:5). For the Romans, faith comes by hearing and hearing by the Word of Christ (Rom. 8:17). To the Ephesians, the Word of truth is the Gospel of salvation, the preached Word is the sword of the Spirit (Eph. 1:13, 6:17). That sword is handed on to the succeeding ministers with this commission: *Preach the Word* (II Tim. 4:2).

Thus our Lord Jesus Christ accompanies with His Spirit the faithful proclamation of His Word. In this way, faith comes by hearing the Word of Christ, sinners are saved, sheep are called into the flock of the Good Shepherd. By this ministry of the Word, believers participate in the Lord Jesus Christ (Luke 24:46-47; Acts 16:31-32, 10:36-44, 11:15; Rom. 1:3; I Cor. 2:2, 3:11; I Tim. 1:15; Titus 1:3); in Him crucified (I Cor. 1:23, 2:2, 15:3; II Cor. 5:18-21; Gal. 3:1f.; I Peter 1:11-12, 2:24); risen (Rom. 10:9; I Thess. 1:10; I Cor. 15:4f.; II Tim. 2:8; Acts 4:33); interceding (John 17:20; Rom. 8:34; Heb. 7:25; I John 2:1); reigning (Acts 2:32-33, 5:31-32; I Cor. 12:3b); and coming in glory (I Cor. 1:6-9; I Thess. 1:10, 2:15f.; II Thess. 1:9-10; Titus 2:12-13). The Apostle describes his own ministry as proclaiming the Word of the Cross and gathers up the blessing of such a ministry of preaching thus: "For of Him are ye in Christ Jesus, who is made unto us wisdom from God, and righteousness and sanctification and redemption, as it is written: He that glories, in the *Lord* let him glory" (I Cor. 1:30).

3. Since the Spirit Mightily Used the Instrument of His Power, and the Evangelical Congregations Treated the Scriptures as the Source, the Norm and the Criterium of Preaching, the Reformers Formulated the Doctrine of the Authority, the Clarity, and the Sufficiency of That Word.[60]

A. *The authority of the Word*

As Romans, Galatians and the Psalms were understood, the people knew again the true meaning of authority, a more comforting authority than that of Rome. Faith became not merely intellectual assent but trust in the gracious Father founded on

60. J. T. Mueller, "Luther's Doctrine of Inspiration," *Christianity Today*, I, 8, 4; E. Doumergue, *Jean Calvin, La Pensée Réligieuse*, IV, X, 70-82.

the Word of promise fulfilled in Jesus Christ. The Reformation "put an end to the ecclesiasticizing of life and placed it once more under God's rule and thus gave all of it certainty and blessing."[61] The Scriptures became the sole authority, the master and the judge for the conservative Reformers. According to Luther, Holy Scripture and the Word of God ought to be regarded as an empress whom one should immediately follow, obeying what she commands, for "these words were spoken by the mouth of God."[62] The Prophets have not spoken out of their own minds, they have declared what they received from above. No authority is more certain than that of God's Word and we are to yield that reverence to His Word we owe to Him. The Reformers do not conceive of the Scriptures as primarily a human product more or less inspired by the Divine Spirit, but as a Divine product that has proceeded from the mouth of the Lord,[63] through the historical agencies of Prophets and Apostles.

They knew better than to try to prove and therefore to master the truth of the Bible. Nor did they look to the Church as the ground of its authority lest the truth of God be subordinated to the testimony of men.[64] Rather, they built up their doctrine of Holy Scripture upon its own self-witness as the Holy Spirit testified by and with it in their own hearts.[65] Their starting point was the response of faith to the challenge of the biblical message. In faith and obedience they received the testimony of the Word of God even in matters concerning its own nature and being.[66] For them, the ultimate validity of the Word lies in its true Author and Expositor. And "it is God who is its Author, and Christ who is its message, and the Divine Spirit who is its final interpreter to our hearts."[67]

As true disciples, the Reformers "handled the Scriptures of the Old Testament with the same reverence and submission with which both Christ and the Apostles treated them."[68] For them,

61. G. C. Berkouwer, *Recent Developments in Roman Catholic Thought*, p. 75; cf. p. 70.

62. Luther, *Vom Abendmahl Christi, Bekenntnis*, cited M. Reu, *op. cit.*, p. 54.

63. Calvin, *Commentary on I Timothy* 3:16.

64. Melanchthon, *CR*, iv, 350; Bullinger, *Decades*, V, 2; Calvin, *Inst.*, I, vii, 3; *Belgic Confession*, V.

65. Calvin, *Commentary on Ephesians*, 1:13.

66. G. W. Bromiley, in *The New Bible Commentary*, p. 17; and in *Christianity Today*, I, 6, 14-16.

67. R. Lennox, Inaugural Address, Presbyterian College in Montreal.

68. John Macleod, *Scottish Theology*, pp. 8, 16.

the New Testament was the divinely authoritative account of the witness borne by the Apostles to the revelation of the living Word. What our Lord spoke in His earthly ministry is witnessed by the record of the Gospels, and what the risen and glorified Lord gave His spokesmen through His Spirit "bears the stamp of an authority from which our Reformers felt that there can be no appeal."[69] Its message is given by inspiration of the Holy Spirit whose methods of working defy our psychological explanations. Like the Incarnation or the Trinity, Inspiration became for the Reformers a dogma which the Christian receives not because he sees or proves the truth thereof, but because God has testified it to be so. That is, this is not a scientific pronouncement, but a confession of faith.[70] Faith hears the authority of the Word in connection with Him whose Word it is, and confesses that the Word which Scripture speaks is the Word of God Himself. "We affirm the authority of the Scripture to be of God, and neither to depend on men nor angels."[71]

For the son of the Thuringian miner, the plain and simple stories of the Old Testament are the richest of mines, the ones that can never be worked out. Not in the thoughts of our minds nor in the feelings of our hearts, but here in the Scriptures we find the wisdom of God laid before us in such simple fashion that it quenches all our pride.

> Here you will find the swaddling clothes and the mangers in which Christ lies, and to which the angel points the shepherds. Plain and puny are the swaddling clothes, but dear is the treasure, *Christ,* that lies in them.[72]

For Luther, "Holy Scripture is the garment which our Lord Jesus has put on and in which He let Himself be seen and found." Of its several books, the Gospel and First Epistle of John, Romans, Galatians, Ephesians and First Peter are the true kernel and marrow, for in them "you find a masterly account of how faith in Christ conquers sin, death, and hell and gives life, righteousness, and salvation."[73]

Likewise for Tyndale, all the biblical writers preach the same Christ and bring the same Gospel. And yet "Paul's epistles, with the Gospel of John, and his first epistle, and the first

---

69. *Ibid.*
70. H. Bavinck, *Gereformeerde Dogmatiek*, I, 461.
71. *Scot's Confession,* 1560, xix.
72. Luther, *Introduction to the OT.*
73. Luther, *W.A.,* 52, 802, 1, and *Preface to NT.*

epistle of St. Peter, are the most pure gospel, and most plainly and richly describe the glory of the grace of Christ."[74]

God, moreover, "commanded His servants, the prophets and apostles to commit His revealed Word to writing," so that the Holy Scriptures are "the Word of God written."[75] When our proclamation is molded by the written Word, the Holy Spirit makes it to become the preached Word that brings men to Jesus Christ, the living Word. Or, as "Calvin would say, preaching *becomes* Revelation by God adding to it His Holy Spirit."[76]

Thus the Bible is not a mere dead past, delineated in writing, as the Romanists charge.[77] Rather, the presence of the risen Christ makes the Word to be not dead and static, but living and active (Heb. 4:12). It is not only that He, the living Lord, is being preached; but more than that, He is the One who is actively preaching. As the Westminster Catechism puts it, Christ executes the office of a prophet in revealing to us, by His Word and Spirit, the will of God for our salvation. He is the ultimate Subject, the Revealer, the Giver of knowledge who graciously makes Himself known to us in the preaching of His Word (I Cor. 8:3, 13:12; Gal. 4:9; II Tim. 2:19; Phil. 3:8).[78] His Spirit pierces our ears and opens our eyes to behold the revelation of God's love for us in the exposition of the scriptural witness to Christ. Accordingly, the facts of revelation and of spiritual experience may be gathered up in the statement that the Holy Scriptures contain, are, and become the Word of God.[79]

> Wherefore when this Word of God is now preached in the Church by preachers lawfully called, we believe that the very Word of God is preached, and received by the faithful; and that neither any other Word of God is to be feigned, nor to be expected from heaven: and that now the Word itself which is preached is to be regarded, not the minister that preaches; who, although he be evil and a sinner, nevertheless the Word of God abides true and good.[80]

Self-government is the prerogative of God alone, and for Calvin even God does not act apart from law (*ex lege*) but is a

---

74. Tyndale, *Prologue upon the Gospel of St. Matthew.*
75. *Belgic Confession,* III; *Westminster Confession,* I, ii.
76. T. H. L. Parker, *The Oracles of God,* p. 55, citing CR, LIX, 11.
77. K. Adam, *The Spirit of Catholicism,* p. 62; L. Pastor, *op. cit.,* VII.
78. R. Bultmann, "Gnosis," in TWNT, I, 709-710; W. C. Robinson, *The Certainties of the Gospel;* D. Ritschl, *A Theology of Proclamation.*
79. H. L. Ellison, "Inspiration" in *The Evangelical Quarterly,* 26:4:214.
80. *Second Helvetic Confession,* I, iv; so also Luther, *Wider Hans Worst.*

law unto Himself *(Inst.,* III, xxiii, 2). Accordingly, any effort on the part of the Church to set up her own judgments along-side of the Word of God is to make herself like God, to usurp His prerogative. Because the authority of Scripture is the authority of God over the creatures of His hand, therefore it stands unique and alone against every effort of man to substitute for this rule of his rightful Lord some form of human self-government. The Kingdom of God in the Lordship of Jesus Christ stands over against all forms of self-government, whether these be the authority of the papal church, or the historical consciousness, or the autonomy of the self-consciousness, or the religious experience of Neo-Protestantism. Every effort of the Church to set aside the Word or to place its own laws on an equality with the Word is to obscure the line between the Divine and the human. This is to abandon the Reformation which condemns "an unlimited tyranny under the name of the Church" *(Inst.,* I, vii, 1). "The Church is no longer the Church where it does not know a higher authority than its own, or an obedience other than that of self-government."[81]

This means that the Reformers did not take refuge in ethics as a categorical imperative in which man could direct his own conduct by his moral idealism. They did not assume with the later Edwardeans that man was able to direct his conduct by means of disinterested benevolence toward being in general. Though they highly esteemed Augustine, they did not agree that his short and simple precept, "Love and do what you will,"[82] took the place of the whole Word. With Augustine the actions of men properly have their root in love, in gratitude, in loyalty to Him who first loved us. Yet the Word is the lamp unto our pathway. For Calvin:

> The chief good consists in the practice of righteousness, in obedience to the commands of God; and the ultimate end of a happy life is to be beloved by Him *(Inst.,* II, i, 4).

The Reformed Reformation obeyed the second commandment and removed the pictures and statues which had been placed in the churches for worship purposes. Consequently, those of us who follow the Reformers dissent from the "new look" in ethics, in so far as it substitutes love for the Word of God.[83]

This doctrine of the Word finds its relevance in the recogni-

81. K. Barth, *Kirchliche Dogmatik,* I/2, 574-658.

82. Augustine, *Homily on First John* 4:4-12.

83. Joseph Fletcher, "The New Look in Ethics" in *Harvard Divinity Bulletin,* October 1959.

tion that it is trustworthy for faith and authoritative for obedience. On the truth of God's gracious acts in Christ we trust our souls, to the obedience of His precepts faith bows our stubborn wills. And this authoritative instruction is not abstract legality, but personal obedience to Him who loves us, who redeemed us from our sins with His own blood (Rev. 1:5). The risen Christ is Himself the Head and King of His body the Church, governing her through His Spirit and Word by the ministry of men.[84] By the work of the Spirit, Christ is present in the proclamation of the Word, and faith is the flash of identification between the Word of promise and the Voice of Him whose word it is. Faith, moreover, engenders love and love obedience. Therefore,

> *Trust and obey,*
> *For there is no other way*
> *To be happy in Jesus*
> *But to trust and obey.*

B. *The clarity of the Word*

Accordingly, the conservative Reformation holds that the Scriptures are sufficiently clear in presenting faith with the promises of salvation and the precepts and example for life. One of Zwingli's early sermons was *On the Clarity and the Certainty of the Word of God.* Since Calvin describes faith as more of the heart than of the head and declares that as the work of the Spirit it is more (heart) certainty than (intellectual) comprehension (*Inst.,* III, ii, 8, 14), it is by no means clear that he would have insisted on the implication for logical inferences of the disputed term "propositional."[85] But in the general sense of an expression in which a predicate is related to the subject by means of a copula, propositions are found in the most definitely revelational accounts in Holy Writ (e.g. Gen. 28:13; Exod. 3:6; Isa. 6:3, 7b; Acts 9:5; Rev. 1:17b-18; Mark 9:7, 14:62; Luke 20:22; John 10:11, 11:25).[86] Calvin's under-

---

84. *Second Book of Discipline of the Kirk of Scotland,* I, 12-13.

85. The neo-orthodox objectors to this term may, however, be reminded that Karl Barth recognizes that faith knowledge may be logical as well as factual in his *Dogmatics in Outline,* and in his *Kirchliche Dogmatik,* I/2:527, he states the doctrine that the Bible is the word of God in propositions (German: *thetisch klarzustellen*).

86. Among recent scholars Th. C. Vriezen, *An Outline of Old Testament Theology,* speaks of God's revelation "in the form of a word or statement" (p. 238), of "this revealing word" (p. 238), of the word as a means of revelation (pp. 105, 244, 251-253, 256). Of older statements cf. Warfield, "Revelation" in *International Standard Bible Encyclopedia.*

standing of Isaiah 59 definitely shows that he accepted communication by the Word as well as communion by the Spirit (*Inst.*, I, vii, 4). More generally, the conservative Reformers and we their successors do find an intellectual content indicated in such terms as: "My Word" and "My Words," *kerygma* and *torah,* promise and fulfillment, covenant and obedience, wisdom and understanding, revelation and acknowledgment of God's gracious knowing of us. Theirs was a Word and Spirit theology, in which the Spirit who inspired the Word so accompanies it as to make it a light that removes the ambiguities of human thought. "In Thy light we see light" (Ps. 36:9), for "the entrance of Thy Word giveth light" (Ps. 119:130). Or as it has been recently put:

> The message cannot be communicated except in personal relation to Christ the Truth, and that personal communion with Christ cannot take place apart from the communication of the message . . . . He communicates Himself to us as the Word addresses us.[87]

> Our commitment to the eternal and incarnate Word of God involves our subjection to the Scriptures as the real revelation of God's will. We may not accept the doctrine that revelation is encounter and communion but not communication. Neither may we say that revelation is communication, but not communion and encounter. Rather, these two must be seen as the two sides of the same coin.[88]

This historic Protestant view is to be distinguished from the Roman Catholic on the one hand and from the Neo-Protestant on the other. For the Council of Trent, Scripture is so uncertain that "Mother Church" must reveal its true sense to the reader. She does this from the Vulgate, including the Apocrypha, in the light of oral tradition. At the time of the Reformation, Noel Beda and the Sorbonne opposed the introduction of Greek and Hebrew into the University of Paris as unnecessary in view of the Church's official interpretation of the Bible. On the other hand, Luther, Melanchthon, Zwingli, Tyndale and Calvin eagerly availed themselves of the biblical tools placed at their disposal by Reuchlin, Erasmus, Colet, and other Renaissance scholars.

From the days of the Zwickau prophets and Castellio, the Ultra- or Neo-Protestants have insisted that the Word cannot give clear guidance, and hence that one must turn to inward mysti-

---

87. T. F. Torrance, *The School of Faith*, xxxii.
88. P. G. Schrotenboer, *Westminster Theological Journal*, xix, 2, 192.

cal revelations, to the religious consciousness, to Christian experience, to the human reason, or to some other form of subjectivism. The liberty of consciences has been used to assert for each individual the right to think whatever he pleases and to say whatever he thinks. Thus the authority of the Church to control the teachings of her ministers was often challenged and her creeds and confessions rejected as "tyrannical." But Luther remarked of subjectivists of his day that each one carried his pope "in his own belly." Like every form of self-government which rejects the authority of God's Word, this thinking forfeits the freedom that comes from His Word. Only God is self-governing. The pastor that tries to be autonomous ends by becoming enslaved to his own limited desires and ambitions. And for his congregation, "the tyranny of the pastoral will is often more arbitrary and intolerable than that of the [Roman] pope."[89]

The abstract *a priori* that the eternal truth cannot be put into human words is best answered, as other forms of Platonism are answered, by the Incarnation. God did become man, and as man He spoke His Good News in the human life, words, death and resurrection of Jesus of Nazareth. Likewise He has given us a trustworthy interpretation of the meaning thereof through His authorized Prophets and Apostles with which Holy Scriptures the Spirit guides the Church until the return of her Lord. The Creator who caused light to shine out of the darkness has shined into our hearts to give the light of the knowledge of the glory of God in the face of Jesus Christ (II Cor. 4:6). God accommodated Himself to our capacity, speaking to us sin-blinded sinners as a mother to a prattling babe.[90] Or to change the figure,

> The Word of God . . . is like a mirror in which faith may behold God . . . . Holy men of old did not know God otherwise than by viewing Him in His Son as in a mirror. When I say that, I mean that God has never revealed Himself to man otherwise than through His Son.

The countenance of God shines upon us in the preaching of Jesus Christ from the Word. As the Incarnate Christ is Himself the mirror of the Father, so the Word of Scripture is the mirror of Him. Thus the countenance of God shines upon us in the

---

89. A. Lecerf, *Reformed Dogmatics*, p. 352.
90. *Inst.*, I, xiii, i. Cf. *Commentary on I Cor.* 2:7; Doumergue, *op. cit.*, pp. 80-82; E. A. Dowey, *op. cit.*, pp. 134-140.

preaching of Jesus Christ from the Word — particularly of Him as crucified for us.[91] Luther said:

> I see standing before my eyes clear and mighty Scriptures, plain words that have taken my conscience captive . . . . the clearest, most certain, sweet words of God.

Thus did he and his associates pour out their lives translating the Bible into the language of the people in the home and in the market places.[92] Again,

> the Word of God is the touchstone, the rule and the plumbline that tells us what should be preached and whether it is in agreement with God's will and revelation.[93]

God is the author of faithful Bible preaching and has so connected His Spirit with it that His own voice is heard by His sheep in the declaration of its promises and the Father's gracious countenance is mirrored in the proclamation of Jesus Christ.

C. *The sufficiency of Scripture*

Finally, the Reformers insisted on the sufficiency or completeness of the Holy Scriptures as setting forth the Gospel and the way to glorify God. The scholastics generally, and the school of Occam and D'Ailli in particular, had taught that canonical Scripture could not err, though other authorities could. Yet when the matter came to concrete application they submitted themselves to the correction of the Catholic Church.[94]

For Luther, the Bible was authoritative not only in theory, but also in practice. He affirmed the *sola scriptura* against the Romanist view of Scripture plus church tradition, the humanist view of Scripture plus reason, and the enthusiast view of Scripture plus private revelation.[95] In the Leipsig Disputation Luther was driven to recognize that a believing Christian cannot be coerced beyond Holy Writ either by the decrees of Pope or Council. In *The Babylonian Captivity,* he says that it is permissible to hold as opinion what is asserted apart from Scripture or manifest revelation, but it is not necessary to believe

---

91. W. Niesel, *The Theology of Calvin,* pp. 27, 32, citing CR, 53, 560.
92. E. G. Schwiebert, *Luther and His Times,* pp. 661-663.
93. M. Reu, *op. cit.,* pp. 55, 57, 61.
94. R. Seeberg, *Textbook of History of Doctrines,* II, 192-193; B. A. Gerrish, "Biblical Authority and the Continental Reformation" in *SJT,* 10:4:339.
95. J. T. Mueller, "Luther's Doctrine of Inspiration" in *Christianity Today,* 1, 8, 3.

this.[96] In the same year, 1520, he hurled the canon law of the Catholic Church into the flames at Elster Gate, Wittenberg, thus denying to the Church and to the Pope a place beside the Word of God. At Worms he presented to Emperor and Diet a simple reply, namely,

> I do not accept the authority of popes and councils for they have contradicted each other. My conscience is captive to the Word of God.

Likewise at the Marburg Colloquy, he insisted on the *est,* because

> I am captive, I cannot escape, the text is too powerful for me and will not permit its meaning to be altered by arguments.[97]

In the *Archeteles* of 1522, Zwingli vigorously maintains the sufficiency of the authority of the Scriptures against the laws added by the Church. At Basel in 1524 Farel maintained the thesis that

> Christ has prescribed for us the absolute rule of living, to which He permits nothing to be added and nothing taken away.

In the disputation at Baden in 1526, Oecolampadius began with the declaration that he recognized no other rule of judgment than the Word of God. The theses of Berne declare that the Church of Christ makes no laws beyond (Latin *extra,* German *ohne*) the Word of God. The Tetrapolitan Confession of 1530 declares that nothing should be taught in the pulpit but what was either expressly contained in the Holy Scriptures or could be fairly deduced therefrom.

This *sola scriptura* affirms the rule of God alone over against any effort to subject His people either to the laws and traditions of others or to permit them to become a law unto themselves. Since Holy Scripture is the voice of God, the mouth of the Lord, therefore *sola scriptura* means theonomy in distinction both from the heteronomy of the papalists and the autonomy of the radicals. According to Luther,

> God wills that we should exclusively direct ourselves to hold fast upon the Word. He wills that we should select the core and not the shell and esteem the housefather more than the house. In Peter and Paul, He wills that we should not admire or adore the apostolic office but *Christ* who speaks in them, and *God's own Word which proceeds from their mouth.*[98]

96. *W. A.*, 6, 508, 19.
97. Cited by Reu, *op. cit.*, p. 50.
98. *W.A.*, 40, I, 173, 19-23.

To place words from any other source, such as the decrees of Church courts or the clichés of a popular preacher, on a level with the Word of God is to abandon the Reformation which maintains the line between the Divine Word and the human.

The Church is not to govern herself, nor is she God's confidential adviser to place her suggestions beside or in lieu of His Word. Self-government is the prerogative of God alone; its claim by His creatures can only be usurpation. For the Church to assert for herself the right of self-government is to commit the primal sin of man, making herself like God. Rome proclaims the equal authority of the Word and of tradition and then makes the Pope the living voice of tradition. When speaking *ex cathedra,* his word is infallible. Neo-Protestantism arrives at her self-government in another but equally fallacious manner. She recognizes the authority of the self-consciousness or of the historic consciousness or of the modern scientific dicta as the final directive in the Church. For the Reformers, as faith lives of the Word, so the obedience of the believer is to the Word of God as the only absolute or infallible guide. God's Word is sufficient, because the Word alone is the scepter of His reign. This is the voice of historic Protestantism.

The Bible is the one authority for Luther, and he applied the Word to ethics as to dogmatics. The basis of the one as of the other is the revelation of God in Christ Jesus and the outpouring of the Holy Spirit who makes the Word fruitful as God addresses it to us. For the conservative Reformers there is no setting up of an independent ethics. Luther sees good works as the work of the living Christ brought to fruition by His Spirit in His believing people.[99] Likewise in Patrick Hamilton's *Places,* good works do not make a good man, but a good man does good works.

In the *Institutes,* Calvin treats the Old Testament and the Ten Commandments only after his great chapter on Christ, the only hope of His people, the only way to the Father. The Ten Words reveal the will of the loving heavenly Father for the walk of Christ's people. Moreover, Calvin's exposition of the Christian life is embedded in his book on the application of the things of Christ to us by the inward work of the Holy Spirit. There it occurs between the treatment on faith on the one hand and justification on the other. Godly living is the fruit

99. Luther, "Sermon on Good Works," *Works of M. Luther,* I, 190, 203.

of the Holy Spirit through faith. It is the outworking in the believer of the power of Him to whom faith clings.

As the Reformation developed, however, there came to be divergences as to the completeness of Scripture for worship and Church praxis. These differences are best understood in the light of their distinct histories. During Luther's absence from Wittenberg, the Zwickau prophets took charge and carried the movement into radicalism. On his return from the Wartburg Castle, Luther made himself master of the situation by his vigorous proclamation of the Word, and he returned the worship and religious customs to the place they had when he left. Following thereon, he retained the mediaeval worship service, using the Word to prune away those items which were condemned by the Word. The result of this program, as well as the fact that he retained the Roman Catholic numbering of the commandments, has carried over into the Lutheran service some elements of the mediaeval liturgy and worship. The Lutherans do not, however, assert for the Church the right to introduce other elements into their worship except on biblical authority. And Luther testified against idolatry among Christians, calling upon everyone to see that his worship has been instituted by God and not invented by man.[100]

The sister branch of the conservative Reformation took the Word somewhat more exclusively as sufficient not only for faith and life but also for worship and Church government. This principle was developed by Zwingli, Lambert, Farel, Calvin, and Knox. Calvin's definition of religion includes the phrase "legitimate worship" (*Inst.*, I, ii, 2). Over against elements introduced into the worship of God by the will and reasonings of men through the ages (IV, xviii, 12), the Reformed Reformation sought here also the sole Kingship of Christ speaking through His Word, the scepter of His Kingdom. In place of the aesthetic cleverness of religious masterpieces developed during the middle ages and later to be elaborated by Jesuit genius, these Reformers sought a worship in which faith obeys the guidance of the Word. Since God has commanded us neither to add to nor to take from what He has commanded (Deut. 12:32), we are not to seek by new forms of worship to gain the favor of God, the true worship of whom consists in obedience alone. Nothing, therefore, was to have a place in God's

---

100. Luther, "Preface to the Prophets," 1545, in *Luther's Works*, ed. by Pelikan and Lehmann, p. 273.

worship except that for which a warrant could be found in His Word. What God has not expressly commanded, He means to prohibit (IV, x, 7). The purpose was to tread the courts of the Most High only in ways of His own ordering. Hymns were primarily the Psalms and paraphrases, and prayers pleaded the promises of God which were banners of encouragement to His believing people. The pulpit was given the focal center as a visible sign that the Word of God was ruling the Church and as a reminder to the preacher that he was not there to air the philosophies or the opinions of men, but to serve as *Dei verbi minister*.

Moreover, the Reformed Reformation, in the light of the two forms of the Ten Words found in Exodus and in Deuteronomy, so numbered them that the Second Commandment is wholly given to the prohibition of images and pictures as objects or as aids to worship. Crucifixes, statues, and pictures were removed from the churches that they might not deflect attention from the revelation of the Father's heart of mercy in the preaching of Jesus Christ and the sealing of His promises to those who participate in the Gospel sacraments. In these media, not in imaginary portraits of the face of Jesus, God wills that His gracious voice be heard and His saving acts be shown forth.

Luther's hymn, *Es wollt uns Gott genädig sein*, praises God for His Word, thus:

> *For Thou the sceptre, Lord, dost wield,*
> *Sin to Thyself subjecting;*
> *Thy Word, Thy people's pasture-field*
> *And fence their feet protecting.*
>
> *   *   *   *
>
> *Thy Fold, O God, shall bring to Thee*
> *The praise of holy living;*
> *Thy Word shall richly fruitful be,*
> *And earth shall yield thanksgiving.*[101]

101. Luther, *Hymns,* tr. by A. Russell.

CHAPTER SEVEN

THE ROOT AND THE FRUIT OF THE REFORMATION

The Evangelical Church

THE REFORMATION NOT ONLY HAD its material principle — in the *sola fide* — and its formal principle — in the *sola scriptura* — but it also had its sociological principle — in the priesthood of all believers as the body of Christ, the family of God. At the same time that it delivered believers from the thralldom of a papal heteronomy and made them free under God, it rescued them from a Latin ritual in which the chief concern had become prayers, masses, and indulgences for the dead, and it brought them into visible congregations with Word, sacraments, prayer and praise in living languages.

The Evangelical Church is the fellowship of believers gathered around the proclamation of the Good News and the confirmation thereof in the dominical sacraments. Here the faithful "are partakers of the Lord Christ and all His treasures and gifts," and everyone hears the Word of Christ exhorting him to live not for himself, but for his neighbor.[1] In place of praying to the martyrs and buying indulgences for one's ancestors, there reappeared the New Testament communion of the saints as distributing to the necessity of the saints who live among us (Rom. 12:3; Matt. 25:31f.). The focus of the fellowship changes from concern for the suffrage of the Church Triumphant and the sufferings of the Church Patient to the needs of the Church Militant. It moves from the Church in heaven — and in purgatory — to the Church here on earth. Instead of departed souls, whose interest, participation, and response are not evident, there appears the body of Christ into which the Holy Spirit gathers believers by an understanding of the Gospel, nurtures them in fellowship by the sacraments, and guides them in mutual helpfulness by its discipline.

---

1. *Heidelberg Catechism*, 55; Bucer, *Instruction in Christian Love*, p. 16.

151

1. THE FORMATION OF THE EVANGELICAL CHURCH

A. *The pastoral need for an Evangelical fellowship*

The Reformation was a piece of pastoral work, called forth by the needs of sheep wandering outside the fellowship of worshipping flocks or the comfort of Divine promises expressed in their own tongues.

Manipulations for the dead had taken the place of the communion of the living saints. When Monk Martin went to Rome on business for his order, he rushed "like a crazy saint" to every place where merit was offered. He climbed the *scala sancta,* offering a *Paternoster* on every step to get the soul of Grandfather Heine out of purgatory. But when he arrived at the top, this doubt arose: Who knows whether it is true after all? In France, Francis I showed considerable sympathy for the Reformed movement until Farel denounced prayers for the dead. Mechanical multiplication of private masses for the departed reached such proportions that Henry V of England provided in his will for the offering of 20,000 for his soul, and Henry VI directed that 10,000 be offered for his the first month after his death. At ordination every priest is given power to celebrate masses both for the living and for the dead. Ludwig Pastor in *The History of the Popes* admits:

> there is no doubt that Tetzel . . . did proclaim as Christian doctrine that nothing but an offering of money was required to gain the indulgence for the dead, without any question of contrition or confession . . .

> *As soon as money in the coffer rings,*
> *The soul from purgatory's fire springs.*[2]

Objection to the mechanical and mercenary character of these evils was widespread. In France, Guillaume Farel protested that the Lord's Supper, which once was the occasion for offerings to meet the daily needs of the flock, had become the mass, which dealt with the alleged concerns of the souls in purgatory — in order to fill the bellies of the priests and monks with money and estates left for that purpose. At Cambridge, little Thomas Bilney could find no peace in the uncertainties of the penitential system until Erasmus's New Testament translated *metanoien* as "change your attitude" rather than "do penance," and I Timothy 1:15 testified that even the chief of sinners found assurance in Christ. Thomas Wyttenbach of Basel taught the duty of being a conscientious pastor, and he proclaimed the

---

2. L. Pastor, *The History of the Popes,* VII, 349.

death of Christ as the only price for the remission of sins, and faith as the key which unlocks this treasury of merits. Accordingly at Einsiedeln, Ulrich Zwingli denounced Samson the indulgence-seller for fleecing his sheep and promising merit for pilgrimages instead of directing anxious souls to the intercessions of Christ. Oswald Myconius rejected John Tetzel's hawking of indulgences because his pious Franconian father had told him that the remission of sins and eternal life could not be purchased by money. Rather, "the blood of Christ is the only ransom for the sins of the world."

The Ninety-five Theses were the protest of a pastor against a wolf that was playing havoc with his flock. At Juterbog, not far from Wittenberg, Tetzel was selling papal letters "properly sealed" that granted pardon for all sins, according to Cardinal Borgia's cynical remark, "God desires not the death of a sinner, but that he live and pay." Luther preached against indulgences on July 27, 1516, on October 31, 1516, and again on February 24, 1517.[3] In the confessional, Father Martin instructed his parishioners that one might at the same time have the papal indulgence and the indignation of the Almighty. Christians who give to the living poor are better than those who buy indulgences for the departed. Thus he brought the communion of saints from heaven on to earth! Cast yourself, then, he urged, upon the mercy of God in Christ, rather than upon penances of the pope! When Jesus preached repentance, He called for an inner state of the soul, a life of penitence, not the performance of a sacrament.

At their meeting in October, 1518, Cardinal Cajetan required of Luther that he recant the fifty-eighth of the Ninety-five Theses. This thesis affirms that the merits of Christ work independently of the Pope.[4] The Thirty-second Thesis declares that those who are made sure of their salvation through letters of pardon will be eternally damned along with their teachers. On the other hand, Theses Thirty-six and Thirty-seven assure every contrite Christian plenary remission from punishment and guilt, together with a share in the benefits of Christ and the Church, even without letters of pardon. According to the indulgence-hawker, everyone who surrenders to the papal church can obtain salvation from all eternal and temporal penalties, if he act with shrewdness and a skillful priest. But Luther's theses

3. Luther's Works (Muhlenberg Press, 1915).
4. L. Pastor, *op. cit.*, VII, 373-374.

emancipate the believer from the domination of the papal ecclesiastical institution so that God Himself advances into the foreground, the Evangelical Fellowship appears, proclaiming the word of forgiveness in Christ; and the Holy Spirit, no longer subject to the machinations of men, graciously works faith in the sinner's soul. In place of papal pretensions in letters of indulgence, Luther re-established the Evangelical Congregation where believers commune with God through the proclamation of the Gospel and the sealing acts of the sacraments.

According to the papal teaching, God's clemency is confined to those who show themselves deserving of it by their good works, by making satisfactions for their sins, and by seeking the intercession of the saints. But when Calvin's conscience could find no peace from the terror of eternal hell in the penances and ceremonies of "The Holy Roman Church," then God suddenly subdued him to the obedience of His Word. Accordingly he confessed, "We must embrace the Divine mercy alone, and turning our eyes from ourselves, fix them solely on Christ" (*Inst.*, III, xix, 2).

B. *The reforming of the Evangelical Church*

As the Reformation arose out of pastoral situations met by evangelical churchmen, so congregations of believers, in which God freely justifies sinners through the redemption which is in Christ Jesus, grew out of the proclamation of the Word and the administration of the biblical sacraments. In place of pictures and statues, parades of hierarchal pomp, and the pageantry of the mass, the voice of God was heard in the exposition of His Word, His acts were seen in His sacraments, and through these means of His own ordering His loving heart was revealed in the face of Jesus Christ.

The Evangelical Church is the mother who by the Holy Spirit, through the ministry of the Word and sacraments, gives birth to the children of God. We are born of that free woman, Sarah (Gal. 4:21-31), to be the true heirs of the promise. Indeed, there is no way of entrance into life except to be conceived of her, carried in her womb, born of her, nourished at her breast, continually preserved under her care and government until she forms and fashions us into the image of Christ. Those who would have God as their Father must have the Church, by whose ministries He generates children, as their mother. In the Church God forgives sins so that apart from the body of Christ and the fellowship of His people there can be no hope of reconciliation with God.[5]

If at this place the Reformers use the language of Rome, their meaning is different. While the mediaeval cleric read the Bible in the light of the Church, the Reformers reversed the process and read the Church in the light of the Bible.[6] For Cardinal Sadoleto, whatever occurs in the worship and praxis of the Church is of the Holy Spirit; for Calvin only what is scriptural is of the Spirit. For Neo-Protestantism the church community through its life and work incites others to faith. For historic Protestantism, Christ in the power of the Holy Spirit conveys to men the benefits of His redemption by His own ordinances, especially the Word, the sacraments, prayer and praise.

For Luther, "Where the Word is, there is the Church."[7] What Calvin says of the Church he has already said of the preached Word. The teaching of the Word is our Mother by which God generates His children.[8] It pleases God by the foolishness of preaching Christ crucified to save those that believe (I Cor. 1:21; Rom. 10:17; I Peter 1:23; James 1:21). The preaching of the promises of God and their appropriation by the hearers in a general confession and supplication for pardon "absorbs the mediaeval doctrine of penance."[9] Thus in place of the house of the Pope, the face of the Kirk becomes visible among men in the Word and the sacraments, where God assembles His people and forgives their sins.

For the Reformers the visible Church consisted of all who confess Christ in baptism, including those who are Christians in name only and who eat and drink judgment to themselves at the Lord's Supper. But within this visible Church there is the invisible, which comes down from heaven and is made up of the elect. "To this Church belong all believers on the whole earth. It is invisible, not as if the believers were invisible, rather because it is hidden from human eyes who does believe: only God and the believers themselves know who the believers are."[10]

5. Luther, *W.A.*, 40, 1, 663; Calvin, *Inst.*, IV, i, 1, 4, 10; *Commentary on Isaiah* 33:24.

6. James Bullock, *The Kirk in Scotland*, pp. 30-31.

7. *W.A.*, 39 (II), 176.

8. Calvin, *Commentary on Galatians* 4:24, 26; Doumergue, *Jean Calvin: La Pensée Ecclésiastique*, p. 32-33.

9. H. A. Oberman, in *Harvard Divinity Bulletin*, Oct., 1961.

10. Zwingli, *Exposition of the Christian Faith*, addressed to Francis I, 1531; cf. *The Apology of the Augsburg Confession*, 7, 8; *Inst.*, IV, 1.

By this doctrine of the invisible Church the Reformers subtracted from the empirical Church of this world its claim of absolute prerogatives and rights over the lives of men.

To the mighty authorities assembled in the Diet of Worms Luther offered his conscience "thirled" by the Word of God. A goodly number of the princes of the empire and of the imperial cities heeded his *Liberty of a Christian Man* and closed their celebrated *Protest* of 1529 with this sentiment: "In matters which concern God's honor and salvation and the eternal life of our souls, everyone must stand and give account before God for himself." In the chapter on Christian Liberty, the *Institutes* take up the torch with the proclamation that God has exempted believers from the necessary obligation to all human authorities in matters of conscience.

Thus for Benedetto Croce, "Calvin actuated a great deliverance" and "became the progenitor of the spirit of modern liberty." "Without being a liberal, the great Reformer rekindled the fire on that hearth-stone which is the source of all liberties, inasmuch as religion has at its centre the conscience of human responsibility." The conscience that is never subject to man but always and ever to God Almighty is the palladium of personal liberty. "The man of conscience is necessarily led to claim all liberties" -- civil, political, academic and economic.[11] Thus did the Reformers' intolerance of papal domination in the things of God make them the great emancipators and educators of modern man.

The image of the autonomous and self-sufficient individual living in isolation comes, however, from the Enlightenment, not from the Reformation. Luther's whole emphasis on corporate communion with Christ and with fellow believers in the Lord's Supper is poles apart from the modern myth of the individual. While later centuries may have given occasion for the Campbellite contention that Protestantism disregards the consensus of the common sense of all the believers and rests upon the private judgment of the individual, it is contrary to what Calvin writes in the *Institutes* (IV, ix, 13):

> If a controversy arise respecting any doctrine, there is no better or more certain remedy than to assemble a council of true bishops, in which the controverted doctrine may be discussed. For such a decision, formed by the common consent of the pastors of the churches, after an invocation of the Spirit of God, will have far

11. Adeofo Omodeo, *Giovenni Calvino*, ed. by Benedetto Croce, pp. 82, 147, 151, 153.

greater weight than if every one of them separately were to maintain it in preaching to his people, or if it were the result of a private conference between a few individuals.

C. *The worship of the Evangelical Church*

For the Reformers the Church is the realm of God, for He alone governs, commands, acts and is glorified in it. The absolute relevance of God is evident in that the worship of the Church is stimulated by His Spirit, guided by His Word, directed to Him, the Creator and Redeemer, and offered in the name of the Mediator. Worship moves from the Godward pole to the Godward pole as a spiritual entity is envisioned coming down from above and eliciting a grateful response from believing hearts.

> At the climax of Protestant Worship it is God who speaks and acts and gives, as the very way the minister faces typifies. He is the representative not merely of the people, but even more of God . . . . In the sermon it is God's Word he brings . . . . As truly there as at the sacrament, he is Christ's hand offering hungry souls the bread of life. The service is God-centered. And Jesus Christ is in the midst.[12]

Since the overshadowing purpose of the evangelical fellowship is to introduce God to man and lead man to God, our Lord Jesus Christ is the sun about which the whole life of the Church revolves. In the man Christ Jesus the high and holy became the meek and lowly. Through Him we poor sinners find access to the throne of grace and receive mercy for every time of need. Through Him, the God of all grace allures us to Himself so that we worship with a tremendous sense of His glory and majesty. His mediation is our merit, His intercession our mouth in prayer. Or, as Ambrose puts it:

> He is our mouth, with which we address the Father; our eye, by which we behold the Father; our hand, by which we present ourselves to the Father. Without whose mediation, neither we, nor any of all the saints have the least intercourse with God.[13]

As truly as evangelical worship is offered in the Name of one Mediator, the man Christ Jesus, so also its prayers and hymns are directed to the Lord Jesus as God the Son who with the Father is the source of grace and peace. This may be conveniently seen in the appended prayer from Luther, in the Litany of the *Book of Common Prayer* of the Church of Eng-

---

12. A. J. Gossip, *In the Secret of the Most High*, p. 123.
13. Ambrose, cited in *Inst.*, III, xx, 21.

land,[14] and in Calvin's hymn, "I Greet Thee, Who My Sure Redeemer Art."

God has graciously come to us in Jesus Christ. He has established union and communion with us by taking our nature and giving us His Spirit (*Inst.*, IV, xvii, 8). He has made Himself our God and us His people. He calls us and keeps us in covenant fellowship with Himself by His Spirit and His Word (Isa. 59:21), confirmed by His sacraments. "It is the Spirit who leads the Church by means of the Word and sacraments in the communion of the exalted Lord."[15] According to Luther's *Babylonian Captivity*, "The Church is born through faith in the Word of Promise. For the Word of God is incomparably above the Church." In the *Theses of Ilanz* (1526) and *Theses of Berne* (1528), Christ's Church is born and lives of the Word of God, and hears not alien voices. The Word is both the instrument in God's hand for creating the Church and the reforming censor of what is practiced in the Church.

Martin Bucer began his work in Strasburg with the declaration that the Kingdom of Christ and the true Church are surely where the Word of Christ is heard with pleasure and observed with diligence (Isa. 55:11).[16]

For Luther, the Word of God is equivalent to the grace of God. The Word (with the sacraments) brings to us the consolation of God and leads to the miracle of meeting God in person. Thus, Christ's Kingdom is a hearing kingdom rather than a seeing kingdom. For not the eyes but the ears lead us to Christ as we hear the Word read, preached, prayed, sung, and as we personally respond. As the nationality of an army is known by its banner, so the certain mark of the Christian

14. May Christ our dear God and the Bishop of our souls, which He has bought with His own precious blood, sustain His little flock by the might of His own Word, that it may increase and grow in grace and knowledge and faith in Him. May He comfort and strengthen it, that it may be firm and steadfast against all the crafts and assaults of Satan and this wicked world, and may He hear its hearty groaning and anxious waiting and longing for the joyful day of His glorious, blessed coming and appearing. May there be an end of this murderous pricking and biting of the heel, of horrible poisonous serpents. And may there come finally the revelation of the glorious liberty and blessedness of the children of God, for which they wait and hope in patience. To which all those who love the appearing of Christ our life will say from the heart, Amen, Amen. *W.A.*, 54, 474-475.

15. G. C. Berkouwer, *The Conflict with Rome*, p. 219.

16. *Instruction in Love*, 1523, p. 16.

congregation is the preaching of the pure Gospel. God is so present with His Word that it does not return unto Him void (Isa. 55:10). As it is proclaimed, the sheep hear the voice of the Good Shepherd and follow Him (John 10:27; cf. II Thess. 2:3). "The Christian congregation should never assemble unless God's Word is preached and prayer made no matter how brief the time may be . . . . Where God's Word is not preached, it is better that one neither sing, nor read, nor come together." After half an hour of such reading and expounding the Scripture, however, it is appropriate to praise God with a psalm and pray to Him in a service lasting a total of an hour or more. There is to be preaching at both the Sunday services, using the Gospel in the morning and the Epistle in the evening. In the daily services the Old Testament may be appropriately used in the morning and the New in the evening. The pope looks to externals, to law and order, but the Church is only made by God's Holy Word, by preaching, by prayers and faith."[17]

In Zurich, Zwingli dropped the assigned postils or pericopes and began the custom of preaching through a book at a time, starting with Matthew and following with Acts, using the Psalms for feast days. Calvin's similar custom brought forth commentaries on most of the books of the Bible. For Calvin, the Word is so definitely the sign of the presence of Him whose Word it is, that the removal of the Word signifies the departure of the Lord (*Inst.,* II, v, 13). And when the Church recedes from the truth of God as her rule for worship, she ceases to be the wife of Christ and becomes an adulteress.[18] In the Psalms and canticles, the Word furnishes the staple of praise. Prayer is primarily pleading the promises of God.

The Reformers likewise used the Lord's Prayer, the Ten Commandments and the Apostles' Creed both in catechetical work and in Divine worship. The Creed was accepted as a summation of the faith. Zwingli provided for its use responsively at the celebration of the Lord's Supper in Berne in 1528.[19] It had a place in the service as used by Luther, by Calvin, and by Knox. The Church of England, however, gave the people a larger part in worship than did the Reformed churches of

17. Luther, *The Right and Power of a Christian Congregation to Judge All Teachings and Call Teachers,* 1523; *Concerning the Ordering of Divine Worship; On Councils and Churches,* 1539.

18. Calvin, *Tracts,* I, 103.

19. Zwingli, *Eine Auswahl aus seinen Schriften,* 611, 711.

Scotland or the churches on the Continent. In the English churches the congregation joined in many prayers, repeated the Creed and the Lord's Prayer, as well as chanted the Magnificat and the Psalms. In view of the predominant place given the Word when the Reformation was in power, it is appropriate to ask our evangelical congregations whether the Word has an equally significant place in our worship today? Or have we changed as men have changed the adage of Scotland's great city? The old adage ran, "Let Glasgow flourish by the preaching of the Word"; the new became, "Let Glasgow flourish."

According to the Reformers, the sacraments are used by the Holy Spirit to confirm the Word. The Church rests upon the foundation of the Word, with the sacraments as supporting stays. By the Word God addresses His promises to all, by the sacraments He seals them upon each of His people. The Word is the audible sacrament even as the sacrament is the visible Word. By their means God is graciously present, speaking and acting for the salvation of His people. And at the same time, every communicant is actively proclaiming the Lord's death each time he gathers around the holy Table and eats the broken bread.

While some of Zwingli's statements present Christ as only the object of men's meditation and devotion, Luther and Calvin stress the trans-subjective presence of the living Christ. The interest of these great Reformers is primarily in religious faith rather than scientific definition. Luther is concerned to maintain the presence of Christ in the sacrament that Christ may bring us into His fellowship and that of His Church and certainly convey to us His inestimable blessings. That Christ describes Himself as the bread of life means for Calvin primarily that we feed upon Him. There is more here that the heart appropriates than the mind can understand, and more that the mind understands than the tongue or pen can express. For both Luther and Calvin there is a double participation; that is, of the visible bread and of the invisible Christ. Christ is not less busy conveying Himself and the blessings of His redemption afresh to the believing communicant than the minister is in giving the bread and the cup to the communicant.

The unity of symbol and essence is expressed by the Lutheran thus: the communicant receives Christ by, with, from and under the bread. In some difference therefrom, the Reformed holds that the bread in the hand and in the mouth of the believing participant is the seal that Christ is truly feeding the soul by the life which the Spirit brings from the Head to His members. In such sentiments as the following Luther and Calvin seem to concur:

> God's promises never deceive; of their truth I receive a pledge at my baptism; if God is for me who shall be against me? . . . . On this promise, received by faith, depends our salvation.[20]

> The sacraments, when we partake of them in a sincere manner, are not the works of men, but of God. In baptism or the Lord's Supper, we do nothing but present ourselves to God, in order to receive His grace. Baptism, viewed in regard to us, is a passive work: we bring nothing to it but faith; and all that belongs to it is laid up in Christ.[21]

D. *The priesthood of all believers*

In his *Appeal to the Christian Nobility of the German Nation* (1520), Luther called upon believers to set aside the prerogatives of a special priest caste or spiritual order. The reunion conferences of 1540-41 were wrecked on the difference between Rome's mediating priest who alone can approach the altar and the Protestant priesthood of all believers. The acts of the Edwardian Reformation stripped all vestiges of this mediating priesthood from the English clergy and provided that they were to be simply ministers of the Word.[22] Farel denounced the papal mass for keeping the people of God outside the chancel, where they received only the bread and that but once a year, while the clergy filled the chancel, were served also the cup, and that with great frequency.[23] In Zurich, Zwingli had the faithful communicate first, seated, and then the ministers.[24] Likewise under Bullinger, a sitting position is preferred, since the Lord sat at table with His disciples.[25] The Geneva Book of Common Order, prepared by John Knox for the Protestant exiles from the persecutions of Mary Tudor and "approved by the famous and learned man John Calvin" provides that:

> The exhortation being ended, the Minister cometh down from the pulpit, and sitteth at the Table, every man and woman taking their place as occasion best serveth.

20. Luther, *The Babylonian Captivity of the Church.*
21. Calvin, *Commentary on Galatians,* V, 3.
22. So G. R. Elton, in *The New Cambridge Modern History,* II, 242.
23. G. Farel, *Summary of What a Christian Ought to Believe.*
24. E. G. Rupp, *The Swiss Reformers,* Volume 2 of *New Cambridge Modern History,* p. 101.
25. J. T. McNeill, *History and Character of Calvinism,* pp. 86, 87.

This was also the procedure in the "model" churches of London supervised for Edward VI by John a Lasco.[25a]

Thus the children of the heavenly Father gather as the family of God at the Table of the Lord[26] and enjoy the freedom of His whole house. By the baptism of Christ the laymen are of the same estate as the clergy; that is, the clergy-laity distinction does not accord with the New Testament (I Peter 2:9, 5:3), or with the Reformation. Whether or not a believer has an office in the Church, he is a king and a priest before God. The one undivided Christian people is the royal priesthood to offer up spiritual sacrifice unto God.

All of God's people are ordained by the Word and the sacraments to the priesthood of believers; that is, to the service of others. "Every Christian is a king for himself, a priest for others." "When Christ said, 'As the Father has sent me, so send I you,' He consecrated us all priests in order that one may proclaim to the other the forgiveness of sins." Each Christian is to seek to be "a Christ to the other man," showing as far as he can that love, service, forgiveness and prayer which Christ has shown him. "Every believer has Christ wholly, yet no one has Christ wholly. This is the communion of saints whereby all have this in common."[27] This means leaving one's gift at the altar and going to be reconciled to the brother, even as the event which issued in Luther's own death was a journey to reconcile the brother Counts of Mansfeld. In this participation in Christ and in each other, the people of God are to bear "the holy cross"; that is, endure the wrongs and resist the solicitations to evil for the sake of Christ.[28]

E. *The ministry of the Evangelical Church*

Every Christian baptized and having God's Word is taught of God and anointed by Him to the priesthood (John 6:45),

25a. F. A. Borwood, in *Reformation Studies*, p. 191.

26. Cf. James Bullock, *The Kirk in Scotland*, pp. 89, 94.

27. Luther, *W.A.*, 16, 407, 34; *Commentary on Galatians* 4:7; *On the Liberty of a Christian Man*; *W.A.*, xiv., 714.

28. Cf. Luther as cited by Saarnivaara, *The Lutheran Quarterly*, V:2:149, thus: "The holy Christian Church . . . must endure all hardship and persecution, all kinds of temptation and evil . . . from the Devil, the world, and the flesh: it must be inwardly sad, timid, terrified; outwardly poor, despised, weak, thus it becomes like its head, Christ. The reason is necessarily the fact that it holds fast to Christ and the word of God and therefore suffers for Christ's sake, according to Matthew 5, Blessed are they that are persecuted for my sake."

and it is his duty to confess, preach and spread the Word (II Cor. 4:13; Ps. 51:13). Where there are many Christians, the individual is not to thrust himself forward, but is to permit himself to be called and drawn forth to preach and teach by the commission of the rest. This right of the whole congregation to judge all teachings and call a fellow Christian of gifts to conduct the rites of Divine worship was exercised in St. Andrew's Castle in the call of John Knox, and in the home of La Ferriere in Paris by that of La Riviere. If a single Christian find himself where there are no other Christians he is bound in brotherly love to preach to the heathen. The Church is the building of God, but in the construction thereof He uses people as His workmen (I Cor. 3:5-9; Eph. 4:11f.). The Christian community has the right to withdraw from the authority of a bishop who opposes God and His Word and to select teachers and preachers of the Word.

It belongs to the Holy Spirit to call men for the ministry of the Word (Acts 13:2), and for the people to agree and confirm the call. Thus the service of ordination properly invokes the Holy Spirit in hymn and prayer that He may endow with His gifts the candidate thus consecrated.[29] There is need for an inner or secret call from God, the certain testimony of one's heart, the approbation of the congregation and the ordination by those who are already ministers of the Word (*Inst.,* IV, 111, 11-16).

In distinction from Roman bishops who do almost everything but preach, Luther insists that "the man to whom has been committed the office of preaching has committed to him the highest office in the Christian Church." The testimony of our Lord and of His Apostles shows that preaching is a higher function than baptizing (John 4:2; I Cor. 1:17; cf. Acts 10:48). Accordingly, let the preacher preach and, if need be, leave baptizing and other "minor offices" to others as Christ and Paul did.[30] Likewise for Calvin the minister of the Word is the first office for usefulness in the Church since God employs ministers as His delegates, using them as instruments in the performance of His work. The authority which they exercise is, however, "not unlimited but subject to the Word of God." Their authority and dignity is thus not in the strict sense given

---

29. Luther, *The Right and Power of a Christian Congregation;* E. G. Schweibert, *Luther and His Times,* pp. 619-625; Calvin, *Tracts,* I, 52.

30. Luther, *The Rights and Power of a Christian Congregation* in *Works of M. Luther* (Holman edition), IV, 84.

to themselves, "but to the ministry over which they are appointed, or to speak more correctly to the Word, the ministration of which the Lord has committed to them." "They should bring forward nothing of themselves, but should speak from the mouth of the Lord," fixing "the boundary line for the Church's wisdom at the point where He stops speaking." We are not to enter the pulpit to introduce our own dreams, inventions, or speculations. We are not to by-pass the Scriptures so as to arrive at some idea of our own about God. "The only way to edify the Church is for the ministers themselves to study to preserve to Jesus Christ His rightful authority, which can no longer be secure than while He is left in possession of what He received from the Father, that is, to be the sole Master in the Church."[31] That the Scriptures furnish the authoritative and final direction for the Church with respect to doctrine, discipline and worship was the first premise of the Reformation argument in German-speaking Switzerland.[32] Following in the footsteps of the Reformers many ministers used after their names the letters D.V.M. There are sundry degrees given by different colleges and universities, but never one higher than these letters indicate, *Dei verbi minister.*

As Luther found the office of teaching and preaching ordained for the Church, so Calvin's study of the Holy Scripture yielded four permanent offices in the Christian Church; namely, pastor or preacher, doctor or teacher, ruling elder or governor, and deacon. Speaking of preachers, elders and deacons, the Second Book of Discipline of the Church of Scotland adds, "and all these may be called by one general word: ministers of the kirk." The installation of these several offices kept the cleavage between the pastor and the people, the teaching and the hearing Church from developing so rapidly. The priesthood of the people is safeguarded by giving them the right to elect, or at least the right of consent and of approbation, in the choice of their ministers, and by the giving of persons engaged in secular callings duties and responsibilities as elders and deacons in the Church. The elders share with the ministers of the Word in discipline and in worship. They have a significant part in the administration of the Lord's Supper. Despite these emphases, eternal vigilance is the price of maintaining the priesthood of all believers against a creeping clericalism that is not

31. *Inst.*, IV, viii, 2, 4, 1, 13; cf. T. H. L. Parker, *Portrait of Calvin.*
32. John T. McNeill, *op. cit.*, p. 73.

limited to the Church of Rome. As the several offices are honored in a congregation and the pastor and people walk together in the Word of the Lord, that congregation is able to meet the challenge of the domination of the state, or the world. Any minister who stands alone without the support of the priesthood of his believing brethren is inviting a fall.

2. THE CHARACTERISTICS OF THE EVANGELICAL CHURCH

A. *The continuity of the Church*

It is being currently suggested that *reformatio* is characteristic of the conservative, while *restitutio* describes the radical Reformation.[33] The classical Reformers and their disciples labored both for the reformation of the existing church and for her renovation or renewal (*instauratio*) according to the pattern of the primitive Church. Some interpreters of the Scottish Reformation see chiefly continuity in this movement, while others magnify the element of restoration in the Protestant settlement.[34] Much later, the Oxford Tractarians claimed continuity only for the English Reformation. In his letter to Francis I, Calvin refused the dilemma that the evangelicals must either affirm with the Anabaptists that the Church had been extinct for a long time, or else admit the Romanist contention that they had departed from the Church. Rejecting both horns, Calvin declared that the Church may exist without any visible form, and that no mark of it was conspicuous in the external splendour which some foolishly admired, but it is distinguished by the pure preaching of the Word and the legitimate administration of the sacraments.

> The Church of Christ has lived, and will continue to live, as long as Christ shall reign at the right hand of the Father, by whose hand she is sustained, by whose protection she is defended, by whose power she is preserved in safety.

The Gallic Confession condemns participation in "papal assemblies," where the Word of God is banished and the sacraments corrupted with superstitions and idolatries, and declares that God has raised up men in an extraordinary manner to restore the Church which was in ruins and desolate. Yet, like Luther, Melanchthon and Calvin, it still recognizes enough of the Church in the mediaeval institution to make Roman Catholic

---

33. F. H. Littell, *The Anabaptist View of the Church.*
34. Contrast J. Bullock, *op. cit.,* p. 132, with J. H. S. Burleigh, *A Church History of Scotland,* p. 177

baptism valid. "In the name of our common faith, of our common baptism, of Christ the author of salvation and of life," Zwingli pleaded with the Coadjutor of the Bishop of Constance not to regard the Zurichers as schismatics for so trivial a matter as the observance of a fast.[35] In Scotland, with the acceptance of baptism as marking the continuity of the Church, there was a general rejection of apostolic succession through the bishops of the old Church, largely because of their incompetency and immorality.

> Ye say to the Apostils that ye succeid,
> But ye shaw nocht that into word nor deid.

In addition to his letter to Francis I, Calvin opposed certain Anabaptists in his *Psychopannychia* and in the definitive edition of the *Institutes* (III, iii, 14). Guido de Bres opposed their teaching in his work, *La racine, source, et fondamente des Anabaptistes,* as also in the *Belgic Confession.* Thus the conservative Reformers tried to steer a line between the papal protagonists who treated their own organization as the essential form of the Church, and the Anabaptists, who set out to begin an entirely new work to take the place of a Church which, according to them, had not existed for a millennium.

The left-wing of the Reformation rejected *reformatio* and stressed *restitutio.* Their interpretation of history involves a fall, often with Constantine, and a setting up again of the Church with their own movement.[37] Some of this was earlier found in Montanism, in Joachim de Fiori, in the Spiritual Franciscans, and in the Petrobusians. More recently, it flowered in the restoration movement led by the Campbells and in the Latter Day Saints.[38]

In the twelfth century, Peter the Venerable answered the attack on infant baptism by showing that for five hundred years Europe had had no Christians not baptized in infancy, and hence according to the sects no Christians at all. But if no Christians, no Church; if no Church, then no acting Christ. Then all the fathers of these centuries must have perished,

---

35. M. D'Aubigne, *History of the Reformation,* VIII, xi, citing *Zwingli Opera,* iii, 11.

36. G. Donaldson, *The Scottish Reformation,* pp. 102-110, citing Sir David Lindsay.

37. F. H. Littell, *op. cit.,* and "Christian Primitivism" in *Encounter,* 1959:31.

38. A. T. DeGroot, *The Restoration Principle;* H. Nibley, "The Passing of the Church" in *Church History,* June 1961.

for being baptized in infancy they were not baptized at all.[39]
The logic of the Anabaptist position thus required them to
teach the fall and decease of the Church and the subsequent
necessity of its restoration. M. Servetus entitled his book,
Christianismi Restitutio. Representative Anabaptists looked upon their movement with its believers' baptism and spiritual
congregations as the restoring of the deceased Church. A recent
American study distinguishes the Anabaptist from the main
stream of the Reformation also on the decisive doctrines of
justification, original sin, free will, man's commitment, and
good works. In these aspects, it finds Anabaptism closer to
Roman Catholicism.[40]

For the conservative Reformers, Christ is always actively continuing His ministry at the right hand of God, and since His
is the one essential ministry there has never failed to be a
Church on the earth. As Luther finely put it, "It is not we who
sustain the Church, nor was it our forefathers, nor will it be
our descendants." The Church was preserved in the centuries
past by the Christ who was the same yesterday, it is preserved
by the Christ who is the same now, and in the ages to come it
will be preserved by the identical Lord who is our help in
trouble, "for vain is the help of man."[41] According to Calvin,
"it is impossible for the devil with all the assistance of the
world ever to destroy the Church; it is founded on the eternal
throne of Christ" (*Inst.*, II, xv, 3; II, vi, 2). Christ armed with
eternal power is the bulwark ever supporting the Church.

In the first edition of the *Institutes*, predestination occurs in
the section on the Church. As the body of Christ, the Church
manifests the eternal election of God, and this election occurs
in Him who is the constant and unchangeable truth of the
Father.[42] In the definitive edition of the same work, Calvin
argues that the adoption of the chosen people from the beginning depends on the grace of the Mediator and the perpetuity
thereof rests on the Messianic reign of Christ at the right
hand of the Father in fulfillment of the promise of an everlasting throne to David. Christ is always exhibited, even to the
Old Testament fathers, as the object of faith, and the happiness

39. D. Schaff, *History of the Christian Church*, V, 485.
40. H. J. Hillerbrandt, "Anabaptists and the Reformation" in *Church History*, XXXIX, 4:404-418.
41. Luther, *W.A.*, 54, 470.
42. *Inst.*, (1536), II, 4; cf. E. Buess, in *Theologische Zeitschrift*, May-June, 1956; J. S. Whale, *The Protestant Tradition*, p. 146f.

of the Church has always rested on Him. Accordingly the Evangelical Church is continuous with the worship of and witness to Him in all the ages: the Old Testament, the apostolic, the patristic and the mediaeval.

Being very conscious of their continuity with the past, the Reformers sought to retain in their worship what was genuinely scriptural from the preceding centuries,[43] such as, the Creed, the Lord's Prayer, the Gloria, the *agnus Dei,* the *sursum corda,* confession and absolution, the *anamnesis,* the *sanctus.* Indeed, when the early Reformation martyrs Henry Voes and John Esch of Antwerp were burned, they repeated the Apostles' Creed and sang the *Te Deum.* The Prayer Book provided for the Protestant Church of Edward VI "is the most conservative of all liturgies of the Reformation; its authors wished to build upon, and not to destroy, the past."[44]

On the Continent and in England much of the Church Year was retained, and ministerial succession of a rough kind was carried on, in some places by bishops, in others by priests and professors. Of the six Johns who wrote the Scots' Confession and Book of Discipline, five had been ordained priests in the Roman Church, the other in the Anglican;[45] and it is estimated that over fifty percent of the staff of the Reformed Kirk of Scotland had been in orders in the pre-Reformed Church.[46] Luther and Knox were ordained priests, Peter Magni of Sweden bishop, and Thomas Cranmer of Canterbury archbishop according to the canons of the mediaeval Church. Calvin directed that those chosen as ministers be ordained with prayer and the imposition of the hands of those who were already ministers of the Word (*Inst.,* IV, iii, 16). Moreover, the French Confession of 1559 condemns the visionaries (Fantastiques) who seek to destroy the ministry and the preaching of the Word and the sacraments.

At the time of the Reformation, however, this continuity was not tied to an "historic episcopate in apostolic succession." Under Edward VI, ministers from the Reformed churches on the Continent, and in the early years under Elizabeth ministers ordained according to the form and rite of the Kirk of Scotland were licensed to minister in the Church of England without

---

43. P. E. Hughes, in *Christianity Today,* 3:16:62.
44. *The Cambridge Modern History,* II, 484.
45. J. H. S. Burleigh, *A History of the Church of Scotland,* pp. 164, 169.
46. G. Donaldson, *The Scottish Reformation,* p. 85.

further ordination.[47] An apostle was an eyewitness of the fact of Christ's resurrection (Acts 1:21f.; I Cor. 15:8, 9:1-2) and therefore the office of an Apostle cannot be continuous, nor does a foundation (Eph. 2:20) repeat itself.[48] Rather, the Christian Canon of Scripture fixed the apostolic doctrine and every faithful preacher of the authentic New Testament gospel is continuing the genuine apostolic succession.

The Reformers confessed the body of Christ in those congregations of Roman Catholics which testified to Him, at the same time as they denied "the papal cancer." The Church existed before the papacy and can exist without it. It is distinguished by the pure preaching of God's Word and the proper administration of the Gospel sacraments. The unbeliever sees only the outward activities of the Church. The believer hears the Gospel, receives Christ, entrusts himself to the grace of God. Thus faith sees through the outer community, in which there are many wolves, to the inner community created by the Gospel.

Christ is the Head, the Lord of the human fellowship of God's people, which He builds up and which is His present earthly form of manifestation. The Church continues, as the Risen One, the living Lord Jesus Christ, carries on His work as Prophet, Priest and King in and through her. Since His work is the one essential ministry in the Church, one may say that ecclesiology is Christology; but it should be kept in mind that Christ is the Head and the Body at the same time, while the Church is only the Body. Moreover, He who is Head is also the Lord and the Judge of the Church, her Bridegroom and her Life.

Protestantism takes seriously the promise of Christ's continued presence with His Church by His indwelling Spirit. For Zwingli, "God reveals Himself through His Spirit, and nothing is learned of Him without the Spirit."[49] In the work of the Holy Spirit, He calls men into the fellowship of His Church, builds them up there in love, guides and disciplines them until He receives them into glory. Yet this presence of Christ is "a real *presence*, not a fusion of identity."[50] For if the union between Christ and the Church were a fusion or a

47. So, for example, Mr. John Morrison was licensed by Archbishop Edmund Grindal in 1582, D. Neal, *The History of the Puritans*, p. 310.

48. P. E. Hughes, "Is There an Apostolic Succession?" in *Christianity Today*, V, 2, 55f.; O. Cullmann, *Christus und die Zeit*, p. 152.

49. J. T. McNeill, *op. cit.*, p. 74.

50. G. Hendry, *The Holy Spirit in Christian Theology*, p. 67.

confusion, the mission of the Holy Spirit would be redundant.

Thus, the evangelical differs from the Roman Catholic presentation of the Church as the object of faith without recourse to a Jesus outside, behind or prior to the Church, but only to a God in, with and under the Church. For them, the Church has been changed from a place of worship to an object of worship. For us, the Church is not identical with Christ; she is His servant, not His confidential adviser. She is to proclaim His Word, not to place her word on a level with or above His. It belongs to His Majesty to rule His Church by His Spirit and Word through the ministry of men, not to be replaced by majority decisions of synods or councils or traditions embodied in and emanating from popes. The Church is to magnify the Lord and not to permit the praise of God to disappear "in the gurgling gullet of modern religious self-confession."[51] The witness of the Spirit in the Church is not, "Thou, Pope John XXIII, art the Rock," but rather, "Jesus is Lord" (I Cor. 12:3). The Church of the Reformation is only a means and never an aim, only an instrument and never an end. The aim and end for which the Church must serve is Jesus Christ Himself.[52]

> In the Protestant understanding the Spirit does truly indwell the Church; only He makes His indwelling presence known, not by inflating the Church with a sense of its own privilege and power, but by directing its attention to its living and exalted Lord and by exposing it to His grace. This is the reason why the *locus* of the Holy Spirit in the Church is defined more specifically as "the means of grace" (the Word, sacraments, and prayer) — i.e., precisely those functions of the Church in which it looks away from itself to Christ.[53]

There are occasions when the evangelical says with Bucer: "We are believers in Christ, not in the Church." In the Westminster Shorter Catechism, the entire matter of the Church is treated under the means of grace. Thus for Protestantism, the Church and her ministry are not means of grace alongside of, or in addition to, the Word and the sacraments. The Church's power is nothing other than a power of administering the Word and the sacraments, and spiritual effects are engendered by these means only through the effective operation of the Spirit. God is the efficient cause of salvation and the Holy Spirit alone

---

51. K. Barth, *Kirchliche Dogmatik*, I/2, 256.

52. G. Casalis, *Die Kirche der Reformation Hort der Freiheit, Antwort*, pp. 450-451.

53. G. S. Hendry, *op. cit.*, p. 66.

makes the preaching of the Word and the administration of the sacraments to be the means of grace.

In the interest of the continuity of the Church, the Evangelical Church likewise opposes the enthusiasts who separate the Old Testament believers from the New Testament faith, those who assume that the dispensation of the Spirit has superseded that of the historical revelation of Christ, and those who find in the Gospel only a stimulus to their own spirituality. Against them Luther and Melanchthon said that the devil is a knave who can mislead even fine and pious and learned preachers. When the fanatics of Zwickau attacked the sufficiency of the Word, objecting to attaching oneself so strictly to the Bible, Luther replied to Stubner, "Nothing that you have said rests on the Holy Scriptures. It is all fable."

For such Anabaptists as Pilgram Marpeck,[54] the Old Testament covenant involved only material rewards without forgiveness or true righteousness. They dismissed the Old Testament as a "Yesterday" that was annulled to make way for the "Today" of the new covenant in Christ, which for the first time brought genuine redemption and the gift of the Holy Spirit. On the other hand, Luther's *Introduction to the Old Testament* shows that this part of the Bible was also a book of faith about such believers as Abraham and David. Bucer accepted the patriarchs, who held to the promises as men of faith; while for Zwingli and his successor Bullinger, "Abraham participated in the one eternal covenant and rejoiced." God has only one people; our faith is a unit with that of Abraham; the New is the further unfolding of the Old Covenant. Calvin shows that all those whom God has adopted into the society of His people are in the very same covenant, for even the Old Testament saint was offered the hope of immortality, founded on the mere mercy of God and confirmed by the mediation of Christ (*Inst.,* II, x, 1-4).

Indeed, the enthusiasts so emphasized the sovereign freedom of the Spirit as to sever the connection between the mission of the Spirit and the historical Christ. Their emphasis fell upon the subjective experience of the Spirit in the individual rather than upon the Spirit's mission of enabling the believer to appropriate the redemption wrought by Christ in His incarnate life. "The real attitude of enthusiasm (and this was openly

54. J. C. Wenger, on "Pilgram Marpeck" in *Mennonite Quarterly Review,* xii: 3, 4.

avowed in its more extravagant forms such as Montanism and Joachimism) is that the dispensation of the Spirit superseded the historical revelation of Christ."[55] One effect of the maintenance of the *filioque* clause in Western Christendom has been to establish an indissoluble connection between the mission of the Spirit and the work of the incarnate Christ. God's objective revelation of Himself is the work of Christ; God's subjective revelation that of the Spirit. The Spirit speaks not of Himself; He takes of the things of Christ and shows them unto us, thus glorifying Him (John 16:13-24). In severing this connection, enthusiasm left itself with no objective criterion and exposed itself to the danger of unregulated spirituality. Instead of the saving knowledge of God revealed in Jesus Christ, it offered sundry varieties of religious experience. For, "where the Holy Spirit is sundered from Christ, sooner or later He is always transmuted into quite a different spirit, the spirit of the religious man, and finally the human spirit in general."[56] As Luther pointed out, the Holy Spirit is called a witness, because He witnesses to Christ and to no other.[57] The Apostles declare, "We preach not ourselves, but Christ Jesus the Lord" (II Cor. 4:5).

Likewise, the evangelical faith distinguishes itself from that Neo-Protestant pre-occupation with its own religious inwardness. Generally Neo-Protestantism begins with a protest against the objectivism of an allegedly dead orthodoxy. It claims to represent the interest of the subjectivisation of objective revelation, but in reality it places over against the knowledge and life of faith in Christ an autonomous knowledge and faith which it professes to receive from the Holy Ghost. The true Holy Spirit comes from God, from the ascended Christ, and brings in His hand to shed abroad in our hearts the love of God revealed in the death of Christ for sinners.[58] Consequently, it is not enough for a preacher to be a religious genius who fancies that by the recital of his own or some others' current experiences he can awaken the dormant possibilities of religion in the heart of the hearer. Nor is it sufficient to have a philosopher of religion presenting himself as an example of faith or as a possessor of human understanding, or even using the crucifixion of Jesus or the stoning of Stephen as a stimulus to bring an

55. G. S. Hendry, *op. cit.*, p. 68.
56. K. Barth, *Kirchliche Dogmatik*, I/2, 251.
57. *W.A.*, Ti., 6, 6654.
58. Rom. 5:5f. Cf. K. Barth, *Kirchliche Dogmatik*, I/2, 249, 252.

existential decision to a student. While these may give the appearance of devotion to Christ they do not locate the glory of salvation in His atoning work for us. Rather "the historical revelation of Christ is treated as the stimulus to a subjective spiritual experience in the individual, not as itself the content of that experience. The spiritualist individual experiences his conversion and the resultant spiritual glow rather than Jesus Christ and Him crucified," so that "when he bears his testimony, it is to speak of his new found peace and happiness rather than to confess that Jesus is Lord."[59]

Representatives of this school frequently declare that it is **not the birth in Bethlehem** but the re-birth in their hearts which counts, not the Cross on Golgotha but their own dedication to live for eternity rather than time, not His bodily resurrection but their own faith in immortality. But true preaching from the Holy Spirit who came at Pentecost leads the hearer back through all his experiences to the source of all true and proper experiences; that is, to Jesus Christ. It calls him to no other faith than faith in the Christ who was born in Bethlehem, who died for our sins on Calvary, who rose from the dead on the third day.

B. *The apostolicity of the Church*

The conservative Reformers sought "a real reformation, not an unwarranted revolution,"[60] "a cleansing of the outward Church of the papacy, the canon law, the sacramental system, saint worship, indulgences and many other abuses and a restoration of the pure doctrine of the New Testament."[61] They were concerned to set aside the papal heteronomy, not in the interest of the autonomy of the Renaissance — or of the Enlightenment — but of the theonomy of apostolic truth. Their stand for liberty was not for a conscience freed from all authority, but for freedom from the exactions of prelates, that believers might obey the voice of God in His Word. They claimed no new miracles, for they regarded miracles as witnesses to new revelations. They were busy rediscovering the revelation of God in Christ attested by the miracles of Scripture. "Our agreement with antiquity is far closer than yours," Calvin replies to Sadoleto. While Luther writes, "For we are the Church, or in the

59. G. S. Hendry, *op. cit.*, pp. 68-69.
60. G. C. Berkouwer, *Modern Uncertainty and Christian Faith*, p. 37.
61. Schweibert, *op. cit.*, pp. 8, 746.

Church which the papists would let go to destruction in order that they may remain."[62]

The Church is built upon the foundation of the Apostles and Prophets, that is, upon their proclamation of Jesus Christ as the chief cornerstone (Eph. 2:20). The Apostles had companied with Jesus throughout His ministry and were eyewitnesses of His resurrection. By the apostolic *kerygma,* God brought those who had not seen Jesus into a like precious faith with the Apostles. As they directly represent Christ and speak with the authority He confers, so there is no way to Him which detours around the apostolic witness to Christ. The recognition of the Apostles means the acceptance of Him whose Apostles they were. As indicated, in view of the nature of their function as eyewitnesses, the Apostles can have no successors, nor does a foundation repeat itself in the superstructure. With the completion of the New Testament canon the norm of their authority was established in the apostolic Scriptures. The Church which heeds their apostolic writings and holds on her heart their content — Jesus Christ and His grace — is the apostolic Church.

In the great Church Epistle, Ephesians, the communion of the body with and her subjection to her Head replaces Rome's rigidity of identity, by which a member, the Bishop of Rome, becomes as infallible as Christ the Head — something which Peter himself was not (Matt. 16:23; Gal. 2:14). Her Lord sustains her in apostolicity as she listens to His voice through the exposition of the apostolic Scriptures.

The Reformers magnified the apostolicity of the Evangelical Church by insisting that the flock is where the voice of the Good Shepherd is heard, where Mary sits at Jesus' feet and hears His Word. When the Church follows the true doctrine of the apostolic Word she is the pillar and ground of the truth (I Tim. 3:16), when she departs from the Word of God she ceases to be the spouse of Christ and becomes an adulteress. "As Paul declares, Eph. 5:24, II Cor. 11:2-3, her chastity consists in not being led away from the simplicity of Christ."[63] At the Zurich Disputation of 1523, Zwingli maintained that "the Spirit of God out of the Holy Scripture itself is the Judge."

62. Luther, *On the Councils and the Churches,* in *Works of M. Luther* (Holman edition), V, 136.
63. Calvin, *Tracts; Commentary on I Timothy* 3:15.

The Reformers reached for the apostolic elements in the liturgies, the hymns, the creeds, the councils, the writings of the Church of all ages. The Apostles' Creed was given a conspicuous place in the morning worship, in the administration of the sacraments, in catechetical instruction and in creedal formulation. Charles V softened his attitude toward Luther when he found that the Saxon Reformer accepted the twelve articles of the Creed. The Apostles' Creed provides the outline for the greatest of the systematic Protestant formulations, Calvin's *Institutes,* even as Augustine and Luther, together with Ambrose, Chrysostom, Hilary, Gregory Nazianzen, Bernard of Clairvaux, provide much of the substance of the *Institutes.*

The Reformers found the truly apostolic ministry in those who followed the example of the Apostles in their lives and teaching. Developing the lines of Luther's *The Liberty of a Christian Man,* Martin Bucer's *Instruction in Love* sets up a practical test of apostolicity. A church is apostolic when her ministers have the mind of Christ (Phil. 2:5), and of His Apostles; that is, when they live not unto themselves but in service of the brethren and in deeds of love for their neighbors. Likewise, the Second Book of Discipline of the Kirk of Scotland describes all the office-bearers as ministers, since all are ordained for serving. These ministers are to fulfill the purpose of their creation and of their ordination in the Church by concern for others, and particularly by ministering the comprehensive promises which meet men's spiritual needs. Since the removal of the Word signifies the departure of the Lord (*Inst.,* II, v, 13), the apostolic Church is to be found only where ministers present from the apostolic Scriptures Christ clothed with His Gospel.

The Reformers made careful provision for continuing the apostolic teaching in the ongoing Church. In Saxony there were visitations, instructions, and consistorial courts; in Geneva the Venerable Company met regularly for mutual self-scrutiny; in England there were "prophecyings" designed to teach the rectors to preach the Gospel. Theological training was developed at Wittenberg where Melanchthon won the accolade, "the Preceptor of Germany," then at Leipsig and Tübingen, in Marburg, where Patrick Hamilton the first Scottish Martyr wrote his *Loci,* in Zurich, where the Munster became the Carolinum for Biblical study, in Heidelberg, whence came the Palatinate Catechism, and in Geneva, where Calvin and Beza established the Academy or University. Theses, pamphlets, commentaries, systematic theologies, apologetics supplemented catechisms and confessions. The Bible, with the liturgy of hymns, prayers and sermons in the language of the people, rooted and grounded them in the apostolic faith, instructed, exhorted and disciplined them in Christian discipleship. The claim of the Evangelical Church to identity with the apostolic Church is thus founded on its aim to reform and ever more completely to reform the Church according to the apostolic Word, to proclaim the Apostles' message, that Christ may be seen in the garb of Scripture, to offer forgiveness according to the Divine promises sealed with the sacraments, and to call men to the obedience of Christian faith.

C. *The catholicity of the Church*

As the Son of Man and the Saviour of the World, Christ has commissioned His Church to disciple all nations. This command is accompanied with the assurance of His continued presence (Matt. 28:18-20), and is supplemented by His promise that where two or three are gathered in His Name there He is (Matt. 18:20). From this it was an easy step for Ignatius of Antioch to reason that wherever the bishop appears there let the congregation be; "even as, wherever Jesus Christ is, there is the Catholic Church" (*To Smyrnaeans*, VIII). The Good Shepherd makes His presence known as He calls His sheep by the voice of His Word and seals them with the sacraments of His promise. Accordingly, Christ's Holy Catholic Church exists wherever believing people meet to hear God's Word and receive His sacraments, and our task is not to create the Ecumenical Church but to recognize the Body of Christ wherever it manifests itself and to promote its free course in all the earth. "The particular Church is the local representative of the Church Catholic, mystically comprehending the whole, of which it is the local manifestation and expression."[64]

Expansion was a primary concern of the primitive Church. At Pentecost, the proclamation of the mighty acts of God in Christ reached representatives from three-fifths of the Roman Empire. Paul carried the Gospel to Rome and the West. Justin Martyr boasted that there was not a single race among whom prayers and thanks were not offered through the Name of the crucified Jesus (*Dialogue* cxvii). Augustine described the Church as "Catholic because it is scattered throughout the world" and

64. R. Davidson, *The Nature of the Church*, p. 56.

is "the Christianity published to all nations."[65] In his *Commonitorium,* Vincent de Lerins set forth universality, antiquity, and consent as the marks of catholic truth. Our study in continuity and apostolicity has shown that the Evangelical Church reaches back through the worship of the centuries, even as the Protestant Confessions carry on the faith of the ancient creeds and of the first six ecumenical councils.

The Council of Trent followed Boniface the Eighth's bull *Unam Sanctam* in limiting the Catholic Church to those who yielded obedience to the Pope and in specifically excluding as heretics the Protestant Churches where the Word and the sacraments were faithfully used. Subsequently the Roman body further narrowed and limited its concept of the Catholic Church by condemning Jansenism and by requiring the acceptance of the dogmas of the Infallibility of the Pope, the Immaculate Conception, and the Assumption of the Virgin Mary. The new Marian dogmas made it increasingly difficult for even the High Church Anglicans to look toward reunion with Rome. The infallibility dogma excluded Ignaz Doellinger and his associated Roman Catholic scholars, who knew their church history. After the crushing of the Jansenists, the Ancient Catholic Church of the Low Countries and of Switzerland carried the Augustinian banner. As the real antithesis to Augustinian Catholicism is not *sola gratia* evangelicalism but Pelagian heresy, so the counter distinction to Protestantism is not Catholicism but Papalism.

In the face of the decision of Trent, Thomas Cranmer, Archbishop of Canterbury, invited Melanchthon, Bullinger, Calvin and other leaders of those excluded by the Romanist Council to meet and set up a truly catholic rule of doctrine. In reply Calvin offered to cross ten seas for such a good purpose:

> I ought to grudge no labour or trouble, seeing that its object is an agreement among the learned to be drawn up by the weight of their authority, according to the Scripture, in order to unite Churches far apart.

At the earlier reunion conferences Calvin had voluntarily signed the Augsburg Confession in the sense meant by Melanchthon, its author, and had labored with Bucer to bring the Lutherans and the Zwinglians together on the Lord's Supper. When he had been himself exiled from Geneva, Calvin insisted that his friends there continue to stand by the Church, decadent

65. Augustine, *Epistles,* LII and LIII.

though they declared it to be, as long as it preached the essence of the Gospel.

The charge that world missions was neglected by the Reformers, made by Gustaf Warneck in his *History of Protestant Missions* and repeated recently by Professor F. H. Littell in *Protestantism and the Great Commission,* needs re-examination. Few men in all Christian history have reached more people with the Gospel in the active years alloted them than did Luther, Zwingli, Bugenhagen, Calvin, and Bullinger. They did this through their preaching, their teaching, their students, their writings, their hospitality, their liturgies, their prayers, their Church organizations. Luther welcomed printing as "God's latest and best work to spread the true religion throughout the world." His disciples won Scandinavia as well as Saxony; Gustavus Vasa sent missionaries among the Laps and there were Lutheran missions in the Balkans. Both branches of the conservative Reformation reached Poland, Bohemia, Hungary and Transylvania with the Gospel. Reformed ministers, trained in Switzerland, poured into the Netherlands, Britain, France and the Rhineland, establishing churches frequently at the cost of their own lives. In the face of such records one must dissent from the allegation that "Anabaptist missioners were, practically, the only missionaries of the time."[66] Indeed, current Protestant studies are recognizing the evangelical, biblical, and Christocentric teaching of many of the early Spanish missionaries to Mexico as exemplified in the wholesome book on *Christian Doctrine* by their good Bishop Zumarrago.[67] The faithful exposition of Scripture and the catechetical work of these early missionaries gathered congregations which belong to that Catholic Church of which Christ is the Head. And though Zumarrago's volume was banned by the Inquisition, Christ has never placed his evangelical testimony on a list of prohibited books.

In his commentary on the Great Commission, Calvin finds the successors to the Apostles in those who devote their services to Christ in the preaching of the Gospel. For "the Lord commands the minister of the Gospel to go to a distance to spread the doctrine of salvation into every part of the world," in order "to reduce the world under His sway," and "to bring all

66. F. H. Littell, "Protestantism and the Great Commission" in *Southwestern Journal of Theology,* II:i, p. 32.

67. G. Baez-Camargo, "Evangelical Faith and Latin American Culture," in *The Ecumenical Era,* p. 126f.

nations to the obedience of the faith." In his exposition of the Lord's Prayer, Calvin writes:

> Now since the divine word resembles a sceptre, we are commanded to pray that he will subdue the hearts and minds of all men to a voluntary obedience to it . . . . God therefore erects his kingdom on the humiliation of the whole world . . . . It ought to be the object of our daily wishes, that God would collect churches for himself from all the countries of the earth, that he would enlarge their numbers, enrich them with all gifts, and establish a legitimate order among them . . . . There will be nothing absurd, then, in understanding this [the third petition] as an explanation, that God's kingdom will then prevail in the world, and all shall submit to his will (*Inst.,* III, xx, 42-43) .

The prayer which Calvin used in one of his sermons on Jeremiah closes:

> May we strive to bring into the way of thy salvation those who seem to be now lost, so that thy mercy may extend far and wide. Thus may thy salvation obtained through Christ, thine only-begotten Son, be known and embraced among the nations.[68]

Calvin sent two ministers and a group of high-minded Christians to establish the faith in Brazil. Here they were betrayed and their work stopped. It was impossible for Protestant missionaries to work in foreign lands ruled by princes of the Counter Reformation. The Preface to the Scots' Confession of 1560 begins: "Long have we thirsted, dear Brethren, to have notified to the Warld (*orbi terrarum*) the Sum of the Doctrine quhilk we profess"; and in the Calvinistic Liturgy prepared for the Palatinate the sermon is followed by a prayer "for all men in the whole world" and for the persecuted.[69]

The revival of modern missionary interest stems from the Evangelical Church, and in the last century and a half has reached well-nigh every people and clime. The Protestant claim to catholicity rests not only on this ecumenical outreach, but also upon its recognition of every worshipping group which expounds God's Word in the Name of the Lord Jesus Christ and observes the Gospel sacraments — whether these congregations call themselves Evangelical, Anglo-Catholic, Roman Catholic, Orthodox, or Monophysite. Where Christ the Head is, there is His body, the Catholic Church.

When National Socialism threatened to supplant the revelation of God in Christ with an alleged one of race, blood, and

---

68. C. Manschreck, *Prayers of the Reformers*, p. 143.
69. Cited by J. T. McNeill, *History and Character of Calvinism*, p. 272.

soil, the Confessing Church declared at Barmen that the one Word we have to hear in life and in death and obey is Jesus Christ our Lord. This evangelical testimony was heeded in Germany and by the Reformed in the Netherlands and the Lutherans in Norway. In their own way, an Orthodox metropolitan of Athens and a cardinal archbishop of Munich responded to it as God's Word. For the first time since the Reformation Protestants and Roman Catholics in France and Germany witnessed together in their testimony for the Law of God and the lives of their Jewish neighbors which were being snuffed out by a recrudescence of paganism. Somewhat less well known was the testimony against Shinto Shrine worship raised by the Presbyterian (US) Secretary of Foreign Missions in Korea and responded to by representatives of many branches of the one Church of God. There is only one Christ, therefore there can be and is only one Church; there is one Head and one body; one Shepherd and one flock. It is disclosed as the Gospel is preached and the sacraments celebrated.

D. *The unity of the Church*

The Church's unity, as her continuity, holiness and catholicity, is ultimately in Christ. It is "not in anything that men have done or can ever do for themselves, but in what God has done for men in Christ." "That Christ is, as apostles and catholic fathers unanimously insist, the Head of the church; and that Christ is, in Luther's phrase, 'the King and Lord of Scripture' . . . make the unity of the Church something more than a slogan."[70] These truths place our unity before the judgment of something given, something that has happened once for all. By the action of God there is "one body and one Spirit, even as ye all are called in one hope of your calling, one Lord, one faith, one baptism, one God and Father of us all."

In his *Reply to Sadoleto*, Calvin acknowledged that he had been taught that he was redeemed by the death of God's Son from the liability to eternal death by the Roman Catholic Church. When an effort was made to restore the Klu Klux Klan in the 1920s, President Ethelbert Warfield of Wilson College declared to the men of the Gettysburg Presbyterian Church:

> When I am asked to join a body organized against the Negro, the Roman Catholic and the Jew, I cannot forget that I was nursed in infancy by an old Kentucky mammy, that the Chris-

70. J. Pelikan, *op. cit.*, p. 178.

tian faith was preserved through the middle ages by the mediaeval catholic Church, and that my Saviour was, according to His flesh, a Jew.

All the congregations of the believing, worshipping, witnessing people are the one Church of God in Christ Jesus. This Church is one because it has one Head. There can no more be two Churches than there are two Christs. As He is the sole Head and only requisite for the existence of the Church, nothing more than Christ's presence can be made a condition for recognizing those gathered in His Name as participating in His body, the Church.

The vital Headship of Christ makes the Church; her mission is to testify to His living Kingship. Over against all rulers, ecclesiastical and secular, who have sought to dominate her life, evangelical ministers have set forth the sole Kingship of Christ over the Church. His vital Headship invites the effective recognition of the juridical Kingship of Christ. He is Head over all things to His Church, and He who was publicly crucified as a malefactor is to come as the visible King of kings and Lord of lords. Until He does, the evangelical is to attest His sole reign in the Church and to find in Him her true unity. A holy unity exists among us, when consenting in pure doctrine we are united to Christ alone.

> The Church of Jesus Christ is the holy congregation of the faithful believers who through real faith are united and incorporated into Jesus Christ of whom they are members. And inasmuch as Jesus Christ is true Son of God, all his members are through him children of God (Eph. 4:4-16; 5:23-27, 32). Jesus is the head; the true Christians are his body (Eph. 1:22-23; Col. 1:18). He is the bridegroom; the faithful believers are his bride (S. of Sol. 1:1-5) whom he has cleansed by his blood, giving health to her body. Jesus has freed his people from their sins (Matt. 1:21; Heb. 9:11-28).
>
> This Church does not consist in diversity of degrees, laws, ordinances and orders given by the will of man, but in the true union of faith in our Lord Jesus, in hearing and believing his holy voice (John 10:27).[71]

The Bible is the great unifying factor of Christendom.[72] When Calvin found the soldiers routed and scattered, he raised the standard of God's Word to recall them to their posts, not

71. So G. Farel, *Summary of What a Christian Ought To Believe*, pp. 15-25, ch. 16.
72. So H. Sasse, "A Binding Dogma: The Inspiration of Holy Scripture," in *Christianity Today*, 3:16:62.

a foreign ensign, but "that noble banner of Thine which we must follow, if we would be classed among Thy people." "O Lord, always, both by word and deed, have I protested how eager I was for unity. Mine, however, was a unity which should begin with Thee and end in Thee. For as oft as Thou didst recommend to us peace and concord, Thou, at the same time, didst show that Thou wert the only bond for preserving it." "It may not be purchased with the denial of Thy truth. For Thy Anointed Himself has declared, that though heaven and earth should be confounded, yet Thy Word must endure forever (Matt. 24:35).''[73] The "Reply to Sadoleto" concludes,

> The Lord grant, Sadoleto, that you and all your party may at length perceive, that the only true bond of ecclesiastical unity would exist if Christ the Lord, who has reconciled us to God the Father, were to gather us out of our present dispersion into the fellowship of His body, that so, through His one Word and Spirit, we might join together with one heart and one soul.

The unity is in Christ, and the marks of that unity are the means He has ordained as signs of His presence, chiefly, the Word and the sacraments. Historically, organizational unification was the mark of unity neither for the Lutherans of Germany and Scandinavia, nor for the Reformed of Switzerland. Each Lutheran principality and kingdom had a different organization; they were not all in a great compact visible body. Calvin was exiled because he would not permit Berne to dictate the worship and practice of the Church in Geneva. Accordingly, the position of the Reformers is to be distinguished from that of all those who make a form of government, a continuity of structure, or an organizational unification the mark of the unity of the Church. This applies whether the visible embodiment be in the interest of such a sect as the Kingdom of God in Münster, or of Bellarmine's definition that the Church involves "obedience or subjection to the rightful shepherd, the Roman pope,"[74] or of apostolic succession, or of a merger program which identifies organizational unification with unity in Christ.

Wherever a sect sets itself up as the Church of God and ex-

---

73. Calvin, "Reply to Sadoleto," *Tracts,* I, 56, 59.
74. R. Bellarmine, *Disputationes de Controversiis,* Tom. II, Controv. 1, Lib. III, Cap. 2, Mirbt. 502. Vatican Council, Session IV; 1st decision in re. Church. The bulls *Unam Sanctam* by Boniface VIII and *Pater aeternus* by Leo X, approved by the Fifth Lateran Council, make subjection to the Roman pontiff necessary for salvation.

cludes from the Church all other groups in which the marks of the Church are found there a multiplicity of churches is inevitable. This sect may be an Anabaptist group, a Puritan-Separatist congregation, a reunion movement which makes itself alone the Church of Christ, a historical body that lifts itself above its fellows because of its special doctrine of the sacraments or of the ministry. It may be a Neo-Protestant movement, singing, "Some Great Cause, God's New Messiah." For clearly there may be a multiplicity of great causes each professing a New Messiah and each New Messiah having his own Church. Each such separatist theory is distinct from the Reformation for which Jesus of Nazareth is God's true Messiah attested by both the Old and the New Testaments, the one Shepherd of the flock of God calling men, women and children to Himself wherever His Word is faithfully proclaimed and its promises sealed by the proper administration of the sacraments.

While Roman Catholic apologists have talked much of the variations of Protestantism, nevertheless the Evangelical Church with her unity in Jesus Christ and her priesthood of all believers has more spiritual unity than the papal Church. Beneath her monolithic façade there are many rifts in the Roman structure. For one thing there is the tremendous cleft between the clergy and the laity, clarified by the chancel which separates the layman who may not drink from the cup of which the priest drinks at the mass, and made evident in the anti-clerical movements in many "Catholic" countries. Then there is the distinction between the secular and the regular clergy, which has had heavy repercussions in the history of Latin American Catholicism. In the same countries, as elsewhere, there has been a cleft between the rule of the popes and that of the kings.

Since the Reformation, the French Church has been racked by the suppression of the Jansenists, of the Quietists, and of the Jesuits under the attack of other Roman Catholic factors. Chinese Romanism was shaken to its foundations by the conflicts over the rites issue between the Jesuits of the Portuguese padroada and the Franciscans and Dominicans of France and Spain.

Not only has Rome been divided by distinctions in the body, but she has set up at least two competitors to Christ's sole Headship and Kingship over His body the Church, namely, the Pope in Rome and the Virgin in heaven. The Pope is, for the Roman Church, not only the rock and foundation, but the center, the principle, the concrete personality in whom the

Church allegedly finds her unity in time and space. Thus as the living Peter, the current Pope dominates the juristic, hierarchal structure of the Church, regulating and ruling the whole as identical with Christ the Bishop of all believers. For Rome, the voice of the infallible pope becomes the voice of Christ by His Spirit. But this is the old issue between Sadoleto and Calvin. The cardinal insisted that all the Roman Church did was by the power of the Holy Spirit. For Calvin, Christ alone, the heavenly King, rules His people by the scepter of His Word so that the Holy Spirit is only known to be present where the Church cultivates unity in the teachings of the Word. Here, of course, Calvin is a good disciple of Luther, for whom, "Christ binds the Holy Ghost to His mouth and sets Him His goal and measure that He go not beyond His own Word."[75] There is greater real unity where there is one King, than where two are professed. For no man can serve two masters.

Not content with dividing the allegiance of the Church between an earthly and a heavenly head, Rome also divides the heavenly place of Christ with His mother, whose body has, according to the dogma of the Assumption of the Virgin, been taken up into heaven. Of course, this dogma of the Assumption of the Virgin rests only on ecclesiastical pronouncement, while the Ascension of Christ is a matter of Biblical revelation. Rome has developed an analogy between the Virgin Mary and the Church. As the Virgin brought forth God incarnate, so the Church through her priests creates God in the sacrament. More and more, the Virgin is lifted to the position of co-redemptrix so that as Christ merits man's redemption by the grace of condignity, the Virgin merits it at least by the grace of congruity. Mariolatry turns the eyes of faith away from the graciousness of God's mercy in Christ to an effeminate pity. The Virgin becomes a symbol of humanity's pity for itself. The French positivist, A. Comte, made the Virgin a symbol for his non-theistic "religion" of humanism. Human co-operation comes in by the Virgin's intercessions (with those of other saints) and by the Church's earthly sacrifice, the mass, and challenges the sole efficacy of God's grace and the all-sufficiency of Christ's sacrifice and intercession. The unity of the Church is in Jesus Christ, her Head, her Lord, her King, her Saviour; that unity is not to be split between Christ, the Pope, the Virgin, the priests and the saints. And this unity is to be recovered as the

75. *W.A.*, 21, 468, 35.

several branches of the one Church gather around the one Shepherd and Bishop of our souls, hearing only His Word, heeding only His voice, yielding only to the scepter of His gracious reign. She is not identical with her King but stands beneath Him, not placing her word on a level with His but yielding obedience to His Word. As His body, she finds her unity in Him, her one head. As a man is recognized by his face, so the Church is seen where Christ appears clothed with His Gospel.[76]

E. *The holiness of the Church*

The one, catholic and apostolic Church is holy in Jesus Christ her Head and Representative. As He is her sanctification as well as her righteousness (I Cor. 1:30), so in Him she stands before God holy and without blame (Eph. 1:4). Since this holiness is in Christ as He stands for the Church and as she stands in Him before God, it is invisible before men. Before the world the Church travels in disguise, with her real nature known to God. The Body of Christ in the world has been cleansed by the washing of water with the word (Eph. 5:26), and is in process of being made holy. The Lord is daily smoothing out the wrinkles of the Church and wiping away its spots. Its holiness is not yet perfect. It makes daily progress but has not yet reached its goal.[77] At His coming, her Saviour will present the Church to Himself holy, without spot or wrinkle or any such thing.

Believers are those whose trust is not one whit in themselves, but wholly in Jesus Christ, and it is this faith alone which makes a man a Christian. Our cry is ever, Look, Father, look on His anointed face, and look not on our misusings of Thy grace. Faith boasts not of the believer but glories in Him on whom faith rests. The true people of God worship by His Spirit, glory in Christ Jesus and have no confidence in the flesh (Phil. 3:3). That is, "the Church is a society of sinners, who claim no virtue but humbly rest their broken and burdened lives upon the grace which God has eternally revealed in Christ Jesus."[78]

Ever and anon, when a disciple falls, as did David or Peter, the Lord returns him by true penitence to Christ his righteous-

---

76. Calvin, *Tracts*, I, 36-37, 102-103; *Inst.*, III, ii, 6.
77. Cf. Calvin, *Inst.*, IV, i, 17, citing Eph. 5:25-27; *Geneva Catechism*, A. 96.
78. C. C. Morrison, "The Church is a Society of Sinners," cited by R. Brown, *The Spirit of Protestantism*, p. 99.

ness. In His Cross, God showed Himself just and able to justify all those who entrust themselves to Him, even as He taught Peter to forgive seventy times seven times and as He restored to David the joy of His salvation. Believers are not those who boast of their impeccability or of their constancy. All their trust is in the faithfulness of God, in the sufficiency of Christ's atonement, in the efficacy of His intercession, in the grace of the Holy Spirit to call, to restore, to keep those who are His.

The holiness of the evangelical fellowship is that of a humble, a contrite, a praying, a penitent people. It is the holiness of those who confess themselves sinners at the same time as faith affirms that they are holy when seen in Christ their Head and Surety. It is a holiness in which we need daily forgiveness and restoration from many lapses. It is a holiness in which we are taught ever anew that there is no merit or worthiness or strength to hold out in ourselves, but that all our merit and worthiness and preservation are in the Lord our Righteousness.

> Every believer is a saint in so far as he belongs to the communion of saints, the new reality which is holy in its foundation; and every saint is an ordinary believer, in so far as he belongs to those who need forgiveness of sins.[79]

In distinction from those Anabaptists who insisted that believers' baptism regenerated people to a pure and angelic life, the conservative Reformers insisted that the Lord requires from the saints as long as they live a daily confession of sins, to which He affixes a gracious promise of pardon (*Inst.*, IV, 1, 22, 23). Accordingly, in the Lutheran, the Anglican and the Reformed churches a general confession of sins is a part of the regular order of worship. At the time of the Reformation, the Prayer Book of the Church of England provided that the minister invite the people to join him in making this confession. In other branches of the Evangelical Church this custom is being more and more followed.

As truly as it is God who justifies (Rom. 8:33; Isa. 43:25, 44:22), so also the God of peace makes holy, sanctifies (I Thess. 5:23; II Thess. 2:13; John 17:17). He does both "in the Name of the Lord Jesus Christ, and in the Spirit of our God" (I Cor. 6:11; I Cor. 1:2, 1:30; I Peter 1:2). The Spirit uses the Gospel, which is the power of God unto salvation, to bring

---

79. P. Tillich, *Systematic Theology*, I, 122.

His people to trust more and more in Christ as their one Saviour and yield themselves ever more completely to Him as their only absolute Master and Lord. The Holiness or sainthood is a status conferred by God, and at the same time a call to live in a grateful obedience becoming this graciously given standing. Saints occur in the New Testament in the plural and the verb sanctify in the same number. Thus the Church is called to be the communion of the saints, in which all believers, as members of Christ, have fellowship with Him and all His benefits; and "everyone who has received gifts ought to employ them readily and cheerfully for the common profit and salvation of all."[80]

Since, in everyday life, the fruits of the Spirit are mixed with the weaknesses and sins of believers, the further exercise of the keys is necessary. In *The Lord's Supper and the Order of Service* and *On the Councils and the Churches,* Luther showed from Matthew 18:15-18 that the people of God have the keys whereby the Holy Spirit, acquired by Christ's death, restores holiness to fallen sinners, and whereby those who do not desire to be converted and sanctified are to be cast out of this holy people. The *Instructions for the Landeskirche* specifically defined the sins which exclude members from the Christian congregation.[81] Yet Luther had to deal with large territories, Calvin with a small compact city. Consequently, "Calvin's reform was more radical, more consistent and more effective than Luther's."[82] Thus, he and his disciple, John Knox, carried discipline into the life of the Church as her third mark more strenuously than did the great Saxon Reformer. Calvin sought by the use of ruling elders, deacons, catechisings, and enforced church attendance to change a *Volkskirche* into a congregation of true believers. Granted that the work was imperfectly done, the stamp of his impress upon the private morals and the public life of Geneva was evident half a century after Calvin's death.[83] As Calvin followed Augustine in finding the invisible Church in the electing purpose of God, and Cyprian in stressing the need of the Church's doctrine and discipline, so he was the

80. *Heidelberg Catechism*, A. 55.
81. B. L. Woolf, *Reformation Writings of M. Luther*, II, 230; U. Saarnivaara, "The Church of Christ According to Luther," *The Lutheran Quarterly*, V:2:148; Schweibert, *op. cit.*, p. 618.
82. W. A. Mueller, *Church and State in Luther and Calvin*, p. 74.
83. V. Andreae, cited by Schaff, *History of the Christian Church*, VII, 518.

precursor of John Wesley in striving for a godly temple of the Holy Ghost.[84]

In the exercise of discipline over both doctrine and conduct the Church has ever to remember that the infinite wisdom of God needed the Cross of Christ to put together His rich grace and His holy justice. As the mother of the faithful the Church is to exercise the power of the keys with Christian love and pedagogic tact (Gal. 6:1-2), and the believer is to receive the same in humility and filial love. Only in the path of Him who was meek and lowly in heart can discipline be exercised unto holy living. Both the Church on the one hand and the individual Christian on the other must confess from the heart the distress of the Church and the misery of the Christian man.[85] As Augustine so often recognized, the primary mark of Christian holiness is humility. It is all too easy to err in one's judgment as to who are and who are not Christians. The Calvinistic distinction between the elect and the non-elect invites the judgment of charity. As faith is the child of election, so belief in Christ brings one the assurance of election, an assurance strengthened by faithful attendance upon the means of grace and by godly living. But one can never be sure that some other living person is non-elect. If today he seem to have no faith, God may give it him tomorrow, so that one must exercise toward him the judgment of charity.

Many label Calvin an extremist in discipline, and then forget that the Reformer was zealous for the restoration of the excommunicate after due repentance and saw a number of them actually restored in Geneva. One wonders whether his disciples — and his critics — are equally concerned to restore such a one in the spirit of gentleness, considering themselves lest they also be tempted (Gal. 6:1; II Cor. 2:6-10). Are there weaker brothers, or groups, that have been put out of our churches and no interest shown in their restoration?

84. J. S. Whale, *The Protestant Tradition,* pp. 151, 152.
85. A. Lecerf, *Reformed Dogmatics,* pp. 353-355.

Deal kindly with the erring,
  Oh! do not forget,
However darkly stained by sin,
  He is thy brother yet.

Heir of the selfsame heritage,
  Child of the selfsame God,
He hath but stumbled in the path
  Thou hast in weakness trod.

Deal kindly with the erring:
  Thou yet may'st lead him back,
With holy words and tones of love,
  From misery's erring track.

Forget not thou hast sinned,
  And sinful yet must be:
Deal kindly with the erring one,
  As God hast dealt with thee.

Now,

To Him who loves us, who redeemed us from our sins with His blood, who made us to be a kingdom of priests to His God and Father,

To Him be the glory and the victory (the doxology and the dominion) forever, and ever, Amen (Rev. 1. 5b-6).